ETIQUETTE FOR OUTLAWS

ETIQUETTE FOR OUTLAWS

Rob Cohen and David Wollock

HarperEntertainment
An Imprint of HarperCollinsPublishers

For my wife, Christine, without whom nothing
would be possible (or so she tells me).
—*Rob Cohen*

For my uncle Lou, who is probably wondering
why I dedicated this book to him.
—*David Wollock*

HarperCollins books may be purchased for educational, business, or sales promotional use. For information please write: Special Markets Department, HarperCollins Publishers Inc., 10 East 53rd Street, New York, NY 10022.

FIRST EDITION

Designed by Jeannette Jacobs

Library of Congress Cataloging-in-Publication Data has been applied for.

ISBN 0-380-80152-3

01 02 03 04 05 RRD 10 9 8 7 6 5

First a Word from Our Lawyer

As an attorney practicing in California, I have seen firsthand the tragic consequences of much of the behavior described in this book. No sensible person would condone these activities, and certainly the authors do not intend by their analysis of etiquette to condone or glorify any of the behavior described herein. The reader is advised not to rely on the information presented as gospel. Indeed, in a world where moral flexibility often seems a prerequisite to survival, prudence dictates that readers consider this book a fiction of sorts. With that in mind, I am compelled to issue the following warning:

Caution: *Many of the lifestyles, sins, and indulgences described in this book are accompanied by significant risks, including but not limited to risk of physical injury, disease, damage to reputation, and loss of income.* Etiquette for Outlaws *is not a tour book to navigate your "Innocence Abroad" travels through the seedy underbelly of crime, perversion, or intemperance. The information presented in this book is intended to entertain you and enlighten you, to provoke some conversation and laughs. It will not protect you from yourself or others. Hence, if you are inspired to explore some of the outlaw pastimes chronicled herein, you do so at your own risk. Do not come crying to us if you find yourself facedown in an alley somewhere, penniless, addicted, diseased, maligned, or locked up in a city jail (in which case, see the information in "Jail" in Part VI). Do not come in bleeding on our nice carpet if your dominatrix impales you with a stiletto heel. Do not send us your hospital bills if some tough guy bounces you around a bar because you pointed out that according to* Etiquette for Outlaws, *real men don't drink daiquiris. Do not sue us for loss of consortium if your spouse leaves you for suggesting a threesome with the baby-sitter or a gang bang with your beer buddies. Do not come around asking us for money because you blew all your dough on whores, drugs, gambling or some other nonsense. In short, do not blame us for anything. If there is one overarching, sacred rule of etiquette for outlaws, it is to take responsibility for your actions, because, damn it, we won't.*

—R. J. Comer
Attorney at Law

Gentle Reader:
You, sir, are an anarchist, and Miss Manners is frightened to have anything to do with you.

—Miss Manners

Contents

Acknowledgments

ROB THANKS:

Betsy Amster, Angela Cheng, April Benavides, Josh Behar, Kate Romero, R. J. Comer, Debra Rosenthal, Gregory Buttler, Ali Ohta, Bret Witter, Coats, Pleasant Gehman, Shawna Kenney, Michelle Roche, Scott Rader, Billy T. Fox, Jason Leopold, Loni Sandoval, Leah Camplan, Ran Michels, Barbara Lewis, Janel Sobeck, Joe Sehee, Mark Varouxakis, Paul Stephan, Roger da Silva, Robert O'Neil, Steve Westerholm, David R. Aldridge, Barry Gregg, Daniel & Jeanie, Brian McNelis, Damian Hall, Susan Mainzer, Wendy Weisberg, Barry Gregg, Brian, Tracee Smith, Lynn Garrett, Nora @ Patio Music, Rick Mahr @ Backyard Wrestling, Bill Reveles, David L. Ulin, Karen Filipi, Mike Tuinstra, Sam Wick, Lyndsey Parker, Violet Brown, Robert Green & EZFLix.com, my mom, dad and the rest of my family for asking me every single week if the book was done yet... and Albie, who would have loved this shit.

DAVID THANKS:

Rob, Betsy, Angela, April, OG, EZ-B, The Glaub, Kitten, my amazing sister Qlara, Michael, Marv, Mom, Nora, Pooch, Trudy, Ciema, Ru, Kristen, Germ, Jen Levine, Vib, Judith, Weber, Chris Howe, Violet Brown, Loni, Barbara, Leah, Janel, A-Love, Meshak, Susan Mainzer, Lori Halliday, Michele Botwin, Ben Darby, Doc, The Rat, R.J., Shireen, Matt... and anyone else who put up with my bullshit over the past four years.

MUCH OBLIGED TO THE FOLLOWING OUTLAWS FOR THEIR HELP AND INSPIRATION:

George Shohet, R.J., David Glaubiger, Brian Kriezel, Loray Bartels, Stephen "The Human Tripod" Rock, Chris Barrish, Natalie Nichols, Cil, Corey Levitan, K-Max, Freeze Luv, Toni Tuna, Joseph Runyon, Fran,

Marcia Kriezel, Kevin Gerstein, David Perry, Pleasure Chest, Peri Booth, Mare, Jen G, Tasha (flight attendant with nice cans), Danielle Oberosler and Dean Berton @ Melrose Tattoo, Rick @ Thirteen B.C., Slick, Chanda Rankin, Dick Numier, Tony White, LAX Range, Tony Harris, James Dawes, EZ Flix, Evolution, Jack, Michelle from Navy Street, Kelly Siehn, Chris Howe, Marcelino Velazquez, Crete, Jill Basinger, Laurel Stearns, Frankie, Dan Force, Deverill Weekes, Sana Fey, Sebastian Dungan, Bill & Co. @ Thee Parlor, Bartels in Marina Del Rey, Marc Pakin, Mary Ridgway, Dreamer, Bruce Burton, Patricia, Sean Daniels, the homeless guy we ate brunch with, Loray Bartels, Skip and everyone @ Dublin's, Cleopatra Records, Jumbo's Clown Room, the S/M stripper from Cheetah's, Penn, Krasher, Glenn Alai, Suzie, Sandra Oh, Lisa Bernabe & Sunset Strip Tattoo, Inc., Gen, Mike Tuinstra, Pete Sanchez, Mack Daddy D, Ramon Hernandez, Mitch & Body Grahics Tattoo, Graham Chaffee & Purple Panther Tattoo Studio, Martin G. Godin, Ken Phillips, Ice-T, Annabella, Dave Navarro, Jackie Martling, Peter Fonda, Shawna Kenny, Damian Hall, Mack 10, Gen, Ron Newt, James Stone, Pat Boone, Mr. Marcus, Ron Slanina, Debra Summers, Tricia @ Bar Sinister, Ann @ Prehistoric Pets, George @ Bordner's, Velvet Underground, Mistress Simone, Mistress Catherine, NRA, PETA, LA Gun Club, George W. T. Flint, David Brown, Renée Geddis, Larry Gaines, Paul Stephan, Brett Himmel, Paul Ramaker, Carrie del Torto, Bob Bell, Suzanne Tobler, Frankie Villarreal, Scooter, Devin, Aleister Buttler, Gregory Einstein, Colin Malone, Danielle Farrar, Bill Pierce, Tom Pinkus & VitalStream, Ratboy, Kerry & Wax Poetic, TC Smith, and those whom we can't name without "the man" finding them out. Finally, thanks to accountants Ray Simm and Steve Coker for advising us that visits to nudie bars are tax deductible.

Photo credits:

All good photos by Kate Romero. All others by Rob & David, except for some stock art, and pix of Ice-T (Deverill Weekes), Slick (courtesy of Slick), James Stone (Benjamin Hoffman), tattoos (courtesy of Thee Parlor, Purple Panther, Sunset Strip Tattoo), Mr. Marcus (Scott Preston), Shawna Kenny (Carlos Batts), Genitorturers (courtesy Gen), and Summer Knight (courtesy of Summer Knight).

Introduction

There is only one rule for the formal table and that is that everything must be geometrically spaced...the places at equal distances...all utensils balanced...salad fork placed directly to the left of the plate.

—Emily Post

Never mind the salad fork, this is *Etiquette for Outlaws*.

While most etiquette or manners guides concern themselves with where you place the silverware or whether or not you should wear a tux before 5:00 P.M., *Etiquette for Outlaws* lays down the other, less talked about rules of various subcultures, sins and indulgences: where to place your first tattoo, or what to wear when you're attending a Fetish Ball. It's a rule book for rule breakers, a guide for the misguided. Emily Post never bothered to address topics like, say, the do's and don'ts of farting. As if her shit don't stink. Light a match, baby!

Consider us friends, if you will, older brothers of sorts, bestowing upon you the benefit of our mischief.

In the following pages, we lay out the conventions and unspoken codes of conduct for drinking, smoking, boffing, moshing, gambling, ho-ing, stripping and other "ings," based on extensive hands-on research and interviews with cops, shrinks, doctors, jailers, nymphos, lawyers, lounge lizards, music scenesters, thugs, piercers, smut shop owners and carnivores.

In addition, various celebrities and recognized authorities have graciously agreed to relay personal pointers, peeves and anecdotes about their respective indulgences in a wide range of colorful sidebars found in each section. While not every sidebar specifically addresses rules of etiquette—some are simply tangential musings—they all serve to illuminate the basic philosophies and principles behind each subculture discussed.

We can't emphasize enough that this is not a "how-to," *Preppie Handbook*-style guide for outlaws and sinners. It is not designed to transform you into a badass or a sex machine. Some of the rules outlined in the following pages will no doubt apply to you. Others will only apply to "them"—gang-bangers, porn stars, rock stars—providing an insider's peek into some very exclusive groups and clubs. Think of yourself as an honorary member, but don't expect to try all of it at home.

Finally, we want to add that you need not read this book cover to cover. It's designed to help *everyone*, from the naive beginner to the hard-core sinner, and some of the parts, particularly "Traditional Vices (The Basics)" covered up front, may seem tame, even pedestrian, to some. Feel free to skip around.

That said, pick a sin, locate it in the index at the back of the book, and dive into all the manners Miss Manners simply missed.

EFO will show her and all the other etiquette experts exactly where to put the salad fork.

ETIQUETTE FOR OUTLAWS

PART I

Traditional Vices

(The Basics)

Vices are sometimes only virtues carried to excess.

—*Charles Dickens*

What progress, my friends! With what rapidity I advance along the thorny road of vice!

—*Marquis de Sade*

Drinking, smoking, screwing, going to titty bars and betting on the ponies are God-given rights, as American as apple pie, as right as rain, as normal as McDonald's fries washed down with a chocolate milkshake . . . and if you haven't tried any of 'em yet, then you're probably too young to be reading this book.

Herein are the foundations of outlaw behavior; indeed, some might argue, the foundations of modern society. They're the things that make growing up fun and growing old bearable. Try one, try them all, but practice them correctly and safely. Follow our advice, and you're in for a helluva good time: you can run with the hunted, bypass the amateurs, and watch the bar doors swing wide open. Ignore our advice, and those doors are bound to smack you in the ass on your way out.

Booze

A GOOD STIFF DRINK

A man who exposes himself when he is intoxicated has not the art of getting drunk.

—Samuel Johnson

Vodka martini ... shaken, not stirred.

—James Bond

That alcohol consumption is viewed as both a sin and a sacrament is indeed ironic. Even more ironic is that while drinking wine at communion is the spiritual equivalent of drinking Christ's blood, during Prohibition blood was spilled by the cask to make sure that hooch was available. The utter failure of Prohibition (and the ultimate death by drunkenness of one of its chief crime fighters, Elliot Ness) further proves what lengths we as a society will go to for a good stiff drink.

Our first section is devoted to booze because it's the Everyman of vices. Who hasn't been in a bar? Who doesn't need a shot and a beer at the end of a long day of work? Who hasn't stood by supportively as a friend who's had one too many pukes their guts out?

But there's more to drinking than just sipping Manhattans at your local watering hole or knocking back beers in front of the tube. Any real drinker will tell you (or perhaps slur gracefully) that there's an art to inebriation: a preferred way to imbibe and survive. In this section you'll find out the etiquette of bar, alley and sofa. Drink up!

BAR BEHAVIOR

When it comes to boozing, most of the the rules pertain to drinking in public, in that internationally recognized, centuries old bastion of sin known as the bar. It's a good place to start.

THE JOKE MAN DRINKETH

Remember: the only way to avoid an alcohol-related accident is to get so fucked up you can't find your car.
—from Jackie Martling's F. Jackie CD

Jackie Martling, the stand-up comedian who knows every joke there ever was, and head writer for the Howard Stern television and radio shows, stole a few minutes to give us a few tips on getting tipsy.

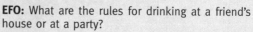

EFO: What are the rules for drinking at a friend's house or at a party?

JACKIE: There are no rules. If you want to follow rules, don't drink. Booze was created to help us break rules. If you can't innately not do horrible things, stay home and read, don't go out and drink.

EFO: If you puke at a bar, restaurant, or party, do you offer to clean up, make restitution, or head for the closest door?

JACKIE: I don't puke. One skiing trip in 1965 I threw up my many screwdrivers all over the back-seat of my pal Butch's father's station wagon at the end of the night. We were too bombed to clean it up. The next day I spent two hours trying to scrape up all of the smelly frozen orange Popsicle that had found its way to every nook and cranny under and around the seat, and on the way home, when the heat came on, the car reeked so bad we all almost puked again. After that I learned my lesson, and have only barfed maybe eight or ten times since then. Where? I forget.

EFO: What makes a good drunk?

JACKIE: A good drunk is someone who everybody knows drinks too much, but yet they're still glad to see them when they walk into a party or a bar.

Cocktail Mix

Jackie was kind enough to jot down his own list of do's and don'ts for heavy drinkers.

I love to drink. With people. I'm not a guy who sits alone and drinks, because it's not the taste I'm in it for. I like to drink when I'm anywhere socially, because I like how it loosens me up, as well as everyone else, and how it makes everyone better looking. Jackie Gleason once said, "I drink to get rid of warts and pimples . . . on other people."

There are a few very basic rules that must be followed. My mother, Dot, was brilliant, and long ago she told me, "Beer then whiskey, very risky; whiskey then beer, never fear." It's absolutely true . . . do yourself a favor and never move to hard liquor after beer. After drinking beer, you'll suck real drinks down too fast, and you'll get way more wasted than you ever intended, not to mention probably wind up sick as a dog.

Conversely, after a few booze drinks, you can always slow down and move to beer. It's often very smart. Most times when Nancy (my wife, singer/songwriter Nancy Sirianni) and I go out to dinner, I'll have a few Bloody Marys before settling in with countless Budweisers. My sometimes pal Stuttering John will often have a few martinis and then move to beer.

Also to avoid getting sick, I never mix booze drinks. If I'm drinking Scotch and Diet Coke (yes, Scotch and Diet Coke, a great drink I was turned on to by my college chum James Wolanin), I don't suddenly have a gin and tonic, or a glass of vodka. And always avoid sugar in your imbibing. If you want a surefire headache, reach for lots of those sweet rum punch concoctions, or sour drinks, or Southern Comfort. If you're having a few, fine, but when you're in for the long haul, no sugar.

Beers, beers, beers. You can't go wrong.

Getting Noticed

First things first: you need some service. Just because you pony up to the bar doesn't mean that you won't stand there for twenty minutes before getting your drink. Bartenders are busy people with a shooting gallery of customers vying for their attention. Getting to the top of their mental queue is, at this point in time, your life's ambition. But how do you get there?

Hell, the best way is to be built like a brick shithouse and ooze sex appeal. For the rest of us, there are several ways to get the attention of a bartender, waiter or waitress across a smoky, dimly lit drinking establishment.

Eye contact is the easiest. Simply find their eyes and tilt your head, and they will put you in the line for service. If you must, a wave in their direction is fine.

Flashing a twenty-dollar bill or more is also an acceptable way to get attention. Act like Bobby De Niro and pull out (at least) a crisp folded $20 and let Andrew Jackson work his magic. To a bartender, the quick sale is the best way to keep up their profit margin. People who flash money tend to know what they want and won't take up time fumbling with credit cards. People with cash also tend to be bigger tippers. Money talks.

Giving a shout out to the bartender is both the best and worst way to get their attention: "Hey, Skip, bourbon rocks!" To make this work, introduce yourself to the bartender, then simply remember their name. A more devious proposition is to learn the bartender's name from someone else working at the restaurant (or by simply reading their name tag). If the bartender doesn't know who you are, however, you can come across as a presumptuous jerkoff. But odds are they won't remember whether or not they've ever met you, and they'll play along. If the bar's crowded and you need a drink (hey, who doesn't), take the chance.

Never call them "barkeep" or "Sam," whistle at them, yell obscenities in their direction, or pelt them with peanuts.

These same rules apply to waiters and waitresses who orbit the bar. Try to make eye contact, be polite, et cetera. If you remain drinkless after a goodly amount of time (10 minutes seems right), it's all right to head to the bar and get the drinks yourself. Sure, you might end up stepping on your designated server's toes by passing them by, but after ten long, parched minutes, it's time to take matters into your own hands! You can make amends later by ordering from them and tipping accordingly.

POOL TABLE ETIQUETTE

The Right Way to Stick It

Getting loaded and shooting pool are about as American as things get. "I'm drunk, time to hit something." Many bars have their own idiosyncratic rules for the billiards table, but we've listed a few of the more universal ones.

1. To get a game on an occupied table, look for a sign-up board, or put a quarter down on the side, behind the line of other quarters.

2. In many bars and pool halls, betting on games is not permitted. Feel out the venue before you try to lay a wager.

3. The person with the big stick has the right of way. If someone's taking a shot, get out of their way. If you interfere, you may be subjected to stinkeye, a verbal lashing, or even a poke.

4. All pool tables open to challenge.

5. Winner owns the table, and determines if the next game is singles or doubles.

Exception: when you're in a restaurant, you are at the waiter's mercy. In this case, it's fine to either track them down or ask another one to fetch you a drink.

Know What You Want

Pouring drinks is a volume business: the more drinks poured, the more tips in the jar. Hence, your bartender or waitperson isn't in the mood to chat with wishy-washy customers. Here are a few suggestions for ordering successfully and getting the best possible drinks.

Know what you want (and what your party wants if you are ordering for more than yourself) before you flag down a bartender or server, particularly if the bar is crowded. Call your brand if you have one (Jim Beam on the rocks). If you need additional info such as what kinds of beers they carry, feel free to ask, but have a backup plan if your choice isn't on their menu (a default drink that everyone serves, like Miller Genuine Draft).

Always make sure you know how to prepare any drink you order. Maybe you've heard that a boilermaker is tasty, but if neither you nor the bartender knows how to make one, you look like a dork.

If you're going to run a tab, pull out your credit card and hand it over to the bartender or waitperson. Most places won't let you run a tab without plastic.

Money Talk

As with many of the services covered in this book, money is always the preferred language of love. Generally fifty cents to a buck per drink is the proper tip. If you're drinking at an upper-class bar (where the drinks cost more), tip bigger.

That initial BIG TIP (usually the first one) is a good way to befriend . . . well, anyone . . . but especially the person pouring the drinks. Bartenders are in it for the money. But as with many money issues, there's a catch. Some bartenders are wary of big tippers, who tend to feel that they own the bar. If you don't have that attitude, you're fine. If you do, it's two to one whether or not the bartender will care since, hell, you're tipping nicely.

Finally, if you're at a party with an open bar, make sure to tip. It's a weird thing that people get even cheaper when the drinks are on the house. The smart drinker recognizes the chance to have the "well" booze (the cheap shit) substituted with "call" (your name brand) by merely tipping the server. We think you'll appreciate the difference.

6. Challenger forks over the quarters and racks.

7. Winner breaks.

8. Straight eight-ball is the typical game, subject to negotiation between winner and challenger. Winner ultimately calls it.

9. Shooters must keep one leg on the floor at all times.

10. No slop. Call all shots, including trick shots (such as a massé shot, where the cue is held perpendicular to the ball and slammed into the table).

11. Opponents generally shake hands after the game.

Give 'Em Room

Whether you're sitting at or standing by the bar, there are a few rules that you should follow. If you're sitting and someone is trying to order over your shoulder, give 'em room. Sure, we know this can be annoying, but the bar's there so people can pony up to it. If you don't like it, try a different piece of real estate. If you're a leaner, try to keep a low, side profile to accommodate people ordering. Finally, steer clear of the wait stations, where the waiters/waitresses pick up their orders—it's always bad form to interfere with someone doing their job.

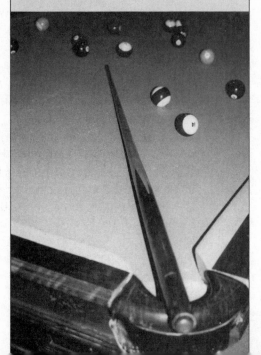

Buying Someone a Drink

As long as there have been bars, men have bought women drinks. Offering to do so is the pick-up line of pick-up lines (next to "What's your sign, baby?"). More recently, it's become acceptable for woman to buy men drinks without everyone in the bar thinking they're easy (although we can still hope). Here are some rules, so you don't look like a chump.

Some men will just walk up to a woman and ask if they can buy her a drink or signal to the bartender to get her another. The approach is forward and direct. While acceptable, it can make the woman feel trapped and uncomfortable—particularly if the guy is a real creep (and you know who you are).

We suggest sending the drink through the bartender or waitress. Have them ask her: "The man over there wants to buy you a drink. What would you like?" That way, you're not trapping her; you're not in her face. She can then say, "Thank you, no," if a) she has zero interest, b) she's with her boyfriend, or c) she's just about to leave. You also ensure that you get her the drink she wants.

If the bartender is super-busy, just ask him or her to send the woman what she's already drinking.

If the woman accepts the drink, common courtesy dictates that she at least give a wave or the classic "nod of acknowledgment" and thank you across the bar. It's nice if she comes by and says "Hi," but you shouldn't push it. A $5 greyhound does not buy you a conversation. In fact, she doesn't owe you anything—especially if you're a real creep.

If a woman is bold enough to send a man a drink, he should always be flattered and appreciative, and then try to score one for the team.

Spilled Milk

If you spill a drink on someone, offer amends, or, if he outweighs you by a considerable amount, offer to pick up the dry cleaning bill. If you spill someone else's drink, offer to replace it.

If a waitress or bartender buses your beverage before you're done, ask for a replacement on the house. It's your right. Exception: If the bar is closing, bouncers, bartenders and servers alike might snatch that glass or bottle right from your hand. Sure, it's not polite, but respect the fact that public drinking establishments have strict, city- or state-mandated cutoff times. It's not their fault you've been nursing your beverage.

Getting Loaded and Other "Norms"

Remember that you're at a bar either to drink or to tip. The place is there to make money, and you're taking up space. Either order something every half-hour or so, or make sure to tip big.

Be polite to the staff and other patrons. Have some respect for the drunk next to you, or the blond soon-to-be object of your affection across the bar.

Finally, know when to say "when" and pack it up. Norm may have been funny on *Cheers*, but by and large, those drunk beer-guzzling slobs genetically fused to their seats are frowned upon by professional drinkers and bartenders alike. Once the rising decibel range of your slurred speech has made you the center of attention, just cool it. Recognize that you've had a few too many, and start to slow down. Monitor what you're drinking and keep an eye on the quality of the company you're trying to score with. Maybe switch to club soda or Coke.

If you don't pay attention, you could end up stinking drunk. At this phase, nobody likes you: you're loud, you're sloppy, your breath reeks, and no one wants to see your tattoos. Be prepared for the following: a) refusal of service (from anyone), b) getting asked by the bouncer to leave, and c) the ire of friends. If any of these are the case, it's time to recognize that you've had too much, try to sober up, and look for a ride home. The bartender will happily call you a cab.

Finally, there is a fine, state-determined line as to when someone becomes legally intoxicated, and we're not here to give you legal advice. We'll just offer that only an idiot-soon-to-be-criminal drives while under the influence of anything. Feel free to kill yourself in any number of ways, just don't take anyone else with you. Assuming you have a ride home or will stay put 'til sober, getting loaded is fine as long you're mindful of this basic drunken protocol.

Heads Up!

Bear in mind that bartenders are under legal obligation to cut off the already intoxicated, and are held criminally libel if you go out and kill someone. Respect that. The following are red flags to bartenders: slurred speech, droopy face, and asking them if they know any good hookers. The automatically ejectionable offense at a bar is to put your head down on the table. Since they don't know if you're tired or drunk, they assume the latter.

VOMITING

The only things worse than public intoxication are getting into a drunken bar brawl and losing (see "Fighting" in Part IV) or puking on yourself or others. Please do your best to refrain from both.

If you just gotta hurl, best to do it out of public view. The alley or the bathroom toilet are both respectable places to blow chunks. Sinks are not. If people are outside the door, turn on the sink faucet or shower to drown out those unpleasant heaving noises.

If you're with a friend who's praying to the Porcelain God, try to hold their hair up out of the bowl water, and out of the path of the spew.

If possible, brush and rinse thoroughly after every vomit, or pop a Mentos. Don't forget to wipe down and flush, particularly if you're at a friend's house. If your puke zone is a bar or restaurant, apologize, tip, and get the hell out. And by all means, DO NOT try to give the person you were hitting on a good-bye smooch.

Upchucking out the window of a moving vehicle after a night of imbibing is also quite common. Make sure all windows behind you are closed, and be considerate of the car behind you. Asking the driver to pull over first is an excellent way to prevent yourself from drenching the side of the vehicle. If, however, you do leave splatter, offer to pay for a car wash the next day.

CHOOSING YOUR POISON

Yes, it is a free country and you can order anything you want, but the truth is all real drinkers have a simple drink they order consistently.

The Shot and a Beer The hall of fame, tough-guy ensemble drink. Feel free to order

whatever beer and shot you wish. Great for kicking off any alcohol-drenched evening, a shot and a beer is the perfect catalyst drink for unwinding in a hurry. Bartenders also like it, because it's a guaranteed two-sales-in-one.

Straight Up Running a close second are the straight drinks: bourbon, scotch, whisky, vodka, tequila, gin, etc. Order it by brand or ask for the well, then specify "neat" (nothing), "up"

(first shaken in ice, then strained into a glass), or "on the rocks."

Mixers Adding a mixer is the next level of drinking: gin and tonic, Jack and Coke, etc. While not as respected as straight alcohol (you are diluting your passions, after all), order one particular mixed drink consistently and you're fine in our book. But there are exceptions . . .

The Fuzzy Navel and Other No-No's Like asking a stripper if you can get change for a five (see "Strip Clubs" later in Part I), order  certain drinks and you're guaranteed to look like a novice at a bar (if not get carded). The following are for nondrinkers, those under age, and frat boys: "Sex on the Beach," "Fuzzy Navels," "daiquiris" or other blended drinks (unless you're on vacay), "Zombies," "Blow Jobs" (unless you really mean it), "Snakebites," "Monkey Brains," "Piña Coladas," "Terminators" (or anything with Jägermeister or Goldschläger), a "Windex," or a "Kir Royale" (it's for pansies).

Champagne While champagne is foofy, it adds an air of festivity or celebration to any occasion. Ordering cham-  pagne is cool if you're in a large group; a guy and gal ordering champagne is also cool. Two guys sipping flutes of bubbly is too limp-wristed for our outlaw taste.

Martinis As martini lounges open up all over the place, the shaken and stirred drinks of Prohibition are making a comeback. The most important thing to remember is that the classic martini is made with gin. If you prefer the vodka variety, make sure to call it. If you consider yourself a tough guy, the cocktail probably isn't for you; indeed, we'd suggest avoiding anything in stemware. There is, nonetheless, a certain style associated with such cocktails, especially since most of them are solid booze. They're good, they're tasty, and they'll get you loaded in a hurry.

DRINKING AT HOME

What you do at your own home is your own damn business. Some suggest that if you drink at home, it should be after 5:00 P.M. unless there's a good game on the tube. We agree, except on holidays or weekends.

Never help yourself to the last beer in your buddy's fridge. It's not only rude, but cruel.

DRINKING AT A PARTY

Proper party drinking etiquette is totally dependent on the party, how well you know the hosts, and how many drinks it takes you before you make a complete ass of yourself.

Here are some quick rules of thumb: It's generally not cool to get plowed at a party hosted by your parents, your partner's parents, your boss, or anyone you might want to talk to again. It's perfectly acceptable to get shit-hammered drunk (as long as you have a sober ride home) at your ex's, soon-to-become ex's, or any party advertised as a "kegger" or where they're serving shots of Jägermeister (hey, what do they expect?). Only the alcohol that's in an obvious "drinking zone" is acceptable to consume without the express permission of the owner.

Going after someone's 21-year-old single-malt scotch hidden behind the bar is bad form. Just use your best judgment.

At weddings or funerals, it's okay to get drunk if you know the betrothed/deceased well. If they are casual or business acquaintances, best just to have a few and call it a night.

THE HANGOVER

Don't whine. You did it to yourself—take it like a man. The best etiquette is to not bitch too much and try to act like it doesn't suck to be you. Nurse with aspirin, water, and sleep. Raw eggs and bitters with lemon and club soda are reputed to help. If you really have to get going, the hair of the dog that bit you should get you through the next few hours. We suggest a Bloody Mary. Have a small one and you might be good to go.

THE APOLOGY

Hey, we all get stupid drunk sooner or later, saying things we mean only at the time. Try to make amends either by apologizing or by offering to clean, fix, or replace anything of value that you may have damaged, whether it's at a bar, restaurant, or private home.

Cigarettes

MORE THAN JUST BLOWING SMOKE

Thou weed, who art so lovely fair and smell'st so
sweet.

—Shakespeare

Smoke 'em if you got 'em.

—every World War II flick

Smoking is far more than just a habit or an addiction.

Cigarettes have always suggested either sophistication or dangerous rebellion, whether the smoker is a heavy-lidded Bogie, exhaling slow, thick trails of smoke and tossing out a pithy comment; a brooding, squinting James Dean, jacket collar up and butt dangling from his mouth; or a Marlene Dietrich, wielding a long cigarette holder in one hand, a martini in the other, propped for an incisive verbal assault.

Simply put, smoking is classic outlaw behavior—right up there with premarital sex and hitting the sauce. This section brings to light the proper protocol for smokers new and old.

LIGHTING UP

When you gotta light up, you gotta light up. If you're in one of THOSE states, find a designated smoking area. Since smokers' public turf is increasingly being encroached upon, if someone asks you to refrain in a place where smoking is explicitly permitted, tell 'em to stick it.

As far as private property is concerned, if you are in someone's house, car, bed, or any private, confined space with others, ask if it's kosher to light up. If you're at a table having a meal, ask if it's okay, even if you're in the company of smokers.

If you're at YOUR home, unless you have kids, do whatever the hell makes you happy.

Smoking in an elevator is illegal and always way uncool.

THE RIGHT PUFF

Far more important than what you puff is how you go about it. We've highlighted some do's and don'ts, ranging from Bogie to bogus.

To this day, exhalted exhaler Bogart is the pinnacle of smoking coolness.

Letting the butt hang off your lip should be reserved for plumbers from New Jersey.

The "Power Puff" is always the sign of a serious smoker.

Dainty, pursed lips do not a cool smoker make.

A cigarette can be a nice accent for the contemplative starlet.

But reserve the cigarette holder for Halloween parties and old age.

Lighting up for two is always a suave move.

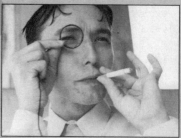

The "German Spy" look (or "two-finger pinch") won't win big points with the babes.

OFFERING A LIGHT

It's always appropriate to offer to light a lady's cigarette for her. Furthermore, if someone asks you for a light and you have one, it's expected that you oblige; either strike the flame for them, or just hand them your matches or lighter.

FIRE

Actually lighting up your smoke can take many forms—a simple match, Bic light, or stove top. While how you do it is a question of your own personal style, there are two rules you need to keep in mind. First, if you're using matches, make sure you've thrown them away in a proper receptacle: ashtray, toilet, we'll even accept the floor of a bar. Please make sure not to throw them on the carpet or near flammable material.

Second, if you're using a lighter, adjust the flame appropriately unless you want to look 14 years old. Six-inch flames may have looked cool to you in the movies, but trust us, you'll look really stupid wincing in pain with fried eyebrows and singed hair. Worse: imagine torching someone who simply needed a light. Fire good, flamethrower bad.

WAITING TO EXHALE

Unless you hate someone, it's always considered bad form to knowingly blow smoke in their face. More and more studies indicate that secondhand smoke is in some ways worse than the actual puff. As a rule, try to blow smoke away from people (specifically, nonsmokers and children). If you're in a crowded space, particularly around non-smokers, exhale upward. Of course, if the folks around you are really irritating and you just want them to go the hell away, blowing smoke in their general direction can be a good tactic.

ASHES TO ASHES

The sign of the amateur smoker, or someone with Obsessive-Compulsive Disorder, is constant ash-flicking—tap, tap, tap. A simple periodic tap is just fine. The exception to this rule is if you're in bed, when you might want to ash quickly to avoid setting the sheets on fire.

NO BUTTS ABOUT IT

The world is not your ashtray. While city streets and bar floors are generally acceptable places to squash and leave a butt, friends' driveways, park lawns, and the beach are not. Cigarette butts do not biodegrade easily, and leaving them around is just plain rude. Hey—would you want to dig your toes or lay your head into a sandy mountain of butts left by strangers on the beach? No. Would you want the planter on your patio filled with butts? No. Pack it in, pack it out.

Never toss a burning cigarette out of a moving car. Not only is it littering; it's also a hazard to other motorists. Motorcyclists seem to get nailed quite a bit. If the motorcyclist happens to be a cop, that butt could get you a fat moving violation on top of a fine for littering.

When in a bar, use an ashtray—they're usually accessible, and show much better form than an empty beer bottle. Besides, in the darkness of a bar, someone might mistake that empty for their drink, and your butt won't do much for the taste.

THE RIGHT SMOKE

Like drinkers, smokers all have their brand of preference. While cigarette brands don't make the man (or woman)—it's more about how you smoke than what you smoke—certain labels have a higher "hip" factor than others. Of course, if someone's jonesing for a nicotine fix, virtually any kind of cigarette, in any condition, will do.

THE "HIPPEST" SMOKES The hippest brand of smokes around is Camel, perhaps because their marketing consistently taps into that romanticized, thrill-seeking bad boy image that many smokers find appealing. Marlboro occupies the next tier of cool. Many also stick by imports like Dunhill's or Silk Cuts from England and Exports from Canada, which, like other imported delicacies, have a worldly air that suggests refined taste. (For many of us, it's that Philip Marlowe/Joel Cairo dilemma.) Brands like American Spirit, which boast pure tobacco without nasty additives or chemicals, are quickly gaining ground due to better taste. Novelty brands like Death cigarettes and Harley-Davidson are basically on the cheap or lame side.

ROLLING YOUR OWN Once very "in," rolling your own with a bag of Drum and papers is now kind of dated, often denoting hippie throwback, though they can also be the mark of an independent smoker who cares enough about his smoke to do it his/her way. Or you're just a pothead.

BUMMING A ROUND

Bumming a smoke off a stranger is *always* acceptable—it's like honor among thieves, crossing race, creed, and economic lines. The smoker with a full pack should empathize with the smokeless

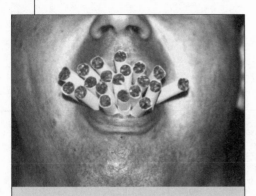

THE MINTY FRESH SMOKE Menthol cigarettes will often evince looks of utter disgust from many smoking diehards. The concept is bizarre: you get that minty breath freshener rush when you inhale, as if you were smoking a cough drop. Years ago, the tobacco industry embarked on a niche-targeted marketing campaign for these nasty little suckers aimed straight at the African American community, which has subsequently embraced menthols as the smoke of choice. At the top of the menthol heap is Newport. Still, many smokers can't stand menthols. If you happen to be one of those who like menthols, and someone burns one off you, please forewarn them. On the other hand, if you're feeling stingy, packing menthols is a good way to ward off mooches.

CLOVES For many younger folks, spice-enhanced "clove" cigarettes are like training wheels, and their sweet, herbaceous aroma is common at teen-heavy rock concerts. While older smokers will indulge in a clove now and again, there remains a sophomoric stigma attached to them.

EXTRA LONG If you're under 5'2", steer clear of extra-long 100's—it's like wearing Daddy's oversized clothes.

HARD VS. SOFT Hard-pack vs. soft-pack is a matter of personal taste, though many consider the soft-pack a bit too dainty. Hard-packs also provide better protection from squishing.

smoker. How many you give away, or how many you ask for, is purely subjective—a matter of personal boundaries. Friends generally have carte blanche to ask for as many as they like, but our studies suggest that two is a reasonable cutoff point with strangers. After that, you can tell 'em to bug off and buy their own damn pack—after all, cigarettes don't grow on trees.

If you bum a cigarette for later, you can stick it behind your ear. Just make sure it's not lit.

If you oblige a request for a cigarette, also offer a light. If you don't have matches or a lighter, light it off your own.

If someone asks for a hit of your cigarette, don't "hot-box" (taking a long drag so that the butt gets unpleasantly hot) just before passing it along. The person requesting the hit should be mindful of this, too: just take a regular-size drag, enjoy, return the smoke to its owner and move on.

THE BEST SMOKE

For smokers, the best cigarettes are the first smoke of the day (breakfast of champions: coffee and a smoke) and the traditional post-coital smoke. If your lover does not smoke, you might want to ask him or her before you light up in the bed. If your lover does smoke (or at least on special occasions), feel free to light one up for him or her. Also, make sure there's a light and an ashtray within arm's reach. Running naked through the house looking for a place to land your butt is a hassle. Puff 'til you're ready to go again.

SMOKE AND MIRRORS

Tricks are, generally, for kids. But if they are executed properly, the results can be impressive.

If you want to flip a cigarette into your mouth (à la Godard's *Breathless*), just make sure you're a natural, as missing makes you look like a dork.

If blowing smoke rings comes naturally, more power to you. If it appears belabored, refrain.

French inhaling entails taking a drag, exhaling though your mouth, and simultaneously pulling the smoke back up into your nostrils. A small percentage of women can look sexy when they do this. The majority of the population just looks silly. Really silly. Like something out of a John Waters movie. If this sounds like you, don't do it or we'll make fun of you.

Likewise, we're not big fans of the dragon-style exhale through the nostrils, though some feel it's the mark of the diehard of diehards— that individual who finds smoking as natural as breathing.

ROLLING A PACK IN THE SLEEVE

Avoid, unless you're playing Kenickie in a revival of *Grease*.

EQUIPMENT

When it comes to lighters, Zippos are the hands-down coolest, although adding lighter fluid can be a pain. Childproofed lighters blow, period. "Unsafe," outlaw-friendly lighters can be obtained in Canada, but that's a bit of a trek.

Don't Bogart That Joint

The following tips were provided by our buddy Willie G., who currently pays his rent via the distribution of organic sticky green. Understandably, Willie keeps a low profile. We'd tell you more about him, but then we'd have to kill you. (Authors' note: Marijuana is illegal. We don't condone or approve of its consumption, unless of course for preapproved medical purposes. Just say no!)

Buying Tips

1. When calling in an order, ask for the good stuff: the "chron" or "chronic," "bombay," "indo," "sticky green," "frosty leaves," "fluffy puffs," the "kill," the "Kevork," the "Hussein." Skip the "dirt" (dirt hurts) and the "backyard boogie."

2. The smaller the amount, the less it counts. When purchasing herb, expect dimes and doves ($10 and $20 bags) to be short, and don't bitch about it. The people with the least amount of dough tend to whine the most.

3. Likewise, don't expect to sample wares when you're buying such a small amount.

4. Don't request that the dealer break out the scale unless you're buying an eighth of an ounce or more.

5. Connoisseurs know their herb by sight and smell, but at an eighth or above, you can ask to sample the goods. Tread lightly, though: a good dealer should tell you the quality beforehand, and second-guessing him can be insulting.

6. No clients accepted without a referral from another established customer—you need an application to get in the door. Never send a dealer a customer or give out a phone number without prior consultation, since most dealers are paranoid as fuck (in part from fear of the law, in part from smoking all that weed!).

7. Don't refer to marijuana and other illegal terminology when on the phone with your dealer, or when you're with your dealer in front of strangers.

8. Don't argue with the basic premise of supply and demand. Weed is illegal—it's generally a seller's market, and you pay a premium for it. Don't whine if the price is a few dollars more than last time. Good shit doesn't last, and each deal—price and quality—can vary from day to day. Unless you're dealing in ounces, keep negotiations to a minimum.

9. Don't expect freebies from dealers just because they're your friends.

Smoking Tips

1. No peer pressure.

2. No showing without sharing! If you don't want to smoke it with the group, don't flash it.

3. If you ain't buying and you ain't supplying, don't worry about how many times the host hits his own weed!

4. Don't baby-sit the blunt, puff puff give! In other words: Don't Bogart that joint, pass it around!

5. Don't suck that blunt like a dick—take small hits of the "choke."

6. Don't leave smoke in the chamber, and clean your plate (the whole bowl, baby!).

7. Don't fire up in a friend's car without permission.

8. Fuck a roach. Toss 'em. They're more trouble than they're worth. Don't save 'em in the ashtray, as they can get your car confiscated and your license suspended.

Cigarette cases add a touch of class, though they can tread into pretentious territory. Those little cigarette purses are either for retro-trendies or bluehairs.

If your name's not Richard Petty, cigarette promo gear (hats, T-shirts, tote bags emblazoned with brand logos) are a definite no-no. Obsessing over "Camel Bucks" is for 15-year-olds and white trash.

If you're dating a nonsmoker, carry breath mints or gum. Ashtray breath is a drag.

Unless you're at a costume ball or you're Bette Davis, cigarette holders are for old people, not outlaws.

Cigars

SMOKE SIGNALS

Sometimes a cigar is just a cigar.

—Sigmund Freud

Much to the chagrin of longtime fans, cigar smoking has become more than just a relaxing pastime. These days, it has become a trendy hobby for upstart X'ers and rap stars alike.

Unfortunately, since many of these new smokers did not learn about cigars from their boomer parents (stogies skipped a generation), it's been up to shop owners and smokers alike to educate neophites. Many of these shop owners are not amused, nor are older smokers who've watched the prices of their favorite smokes skyrocket. Here's how to avoid looking like an amateur.

BUYING A CIGAR

If you're looking for advice on what to buy, dropping at least $20 at your local smoke shop is the best way to endear yourself to a tobacconist.

It's bad etiquette to ask for a Cuban or a "special" (wink-wink) cigar. It is illegal to buy or sell Cuban cigars in the United States. While many smoke shops do in fact have access to them, they're not going to sell them to the likes of you unless they know and trust you—so just get the idea out of your head. If you've been to the same shop for more than a year, try asking—but don't be surprised if they get irked. If they hook you up, odds are the cigars are phonies anyway.

Never ask for a "sweet" cigar. It's sort of like people who drink coffee with three creams and eight sugars. If you ask for a sweet smoke, don't plan on returning to that store once you have grown up. No exceptions. Same thing applies to cognac-soaked stogies; they're for pansies.

Never buy a cigar that already has a hole cut in it, or anything from the drugstore. They're crap. However, some people will buy 'em, split 'em, discard the tobacco and use the leaf to roll monster joints, or "blunts." When it comes to rolling blunts, Phillies are the brand of choice. Cops know this, too.

It's always bad form to quote cigar magazine rating guides, as it makes you look pretentious.

Never roll a cigar under your nose or ear. If you don't know what you're doing, you're blemishing the fine leaf with either snot or earwax. Or you might break the wrapper. Instead, ask the tobacconist to recommend a few for you to try, or ask a savvy smoker buddy to help you out.

Good cigars make wonderful gifts. Bad or cheap cigars don't. If you're unsure about a purchase, ask the tobacconist for help.

You don't have to tip a shopkeeper for helping you and giving you information—just make sure to buy an equitable amount of cigars. Otherwise, don't waste their time—they have to deal with hundreds of you each week.

TORCHING UP

While you can smoke in a smoke shop, don't smoke in the humidor. Your smoke can distort the taste of other cigars. If the shop is one giant humidor, smoke away, and then find a better shop.

In a private home, always check with the host before lighting up. While this is a pain, it's better than lighting up a good smoke and then having to put it out. If you're smoking indoors, keep at least one window open for circulation.

Feel free to smoke in your car (you should smell ours!). If someone else is in the car, it's polite to ask, but remember: It's YOUR GODDAMN CAR, so if you really want to smoke, go ahead. If you're in someone else's car, ask first and remember: It's THEIR GODDAMN CAR!

If you're at a cigar-friendly club, you may wish to smoke at the bar or in the back; you'll enjoy greater space and run less of a risk of people giving you shit for the smoke.

ORAL FIXATIONS

The amount of the cigar you put in your mouth (or any other part of your body) is up to you. Some tend to keep the end relatively dry, while others tend to chomp and soak the end. High schoolers playing

2 Great Tastes That Taste Great Together

Like caviar and vodka, chateaubriand and vintage burgundy, and milk and cookies, cigars have a well-defined list of complementary beverages. Here's a quick guide to popular smokes and the drinks that go with them.

Cigar	Libation
Cuban Bolivar	Vintage Port or Cognac
Holo De Monterrey Excalibur #1	Single-Malt Scotch—we recommend Lagavulin
Macanudo Hyde Park	A nice California Pinot Noir
Bering Imperials	Domestic Keg Beer
White Owl or Swisher Sweet	Pink Zinfandel Franzia Wine-In-A-Box
Philly Blunts	Olde English 40-ouncer

poker while Mom and Dad are away tend to put at least half of the stogie into their mouth—avoid this.

ASHES TO ASHES

Unlike cigarette ashes, a long ash is the sign of a well-constructed cigar, and you don't have to compulsively dump your ash after each drag. Dump your ashes when they look like they're going to fall off—at about an inch or so. If you're driving, you might want to dump your ashes more often so they don't end up in your lap when you hit a pothole.

Don't grind your stogie out like it's a cigarette, as this leaves a fetid smell. Just rest it on the ashtray and let it go out naturally, particularly if you plan to relight and resume smoking it later. Don't relight the next day—a cigar is not good the next day. If you think it is, you're lame.

BUMMING

Because of the cost involved, bumming a cigar is not like bumming a cigarette. If you're planning to smoke around a friend, it's a good thing to carry an extra just in case. You don't have to give them your best cigar, but you won't win any friends or converts with a Night Owl.

If someone wants a puff off your cigar, go ahead and let them. If you don't want them to do it, slobber over the end; they won't ask again. Conversely, if you're bumming a drag, make sure to keep the drool to yourself.

If you have enough "means" to own your own humidor, treat it like a good bottle of booze. Hide it if you don't want guests going after your private stash. If you leave it out, don't be shocked if you see someone puffing away at one of your good smokes. Same thing if you're a guest at someone's house. However, it never hurts to ask before helping yourself to cigars, since you may be burning something that's really expensive.

Talking about cigars is much like talking about golf or cars. If the people around you aren't interested, by all means shut the hell up—you're being a bore. Lots of people say you can taste everything from chocolate to cedar in cigar smoke; we think they're pretentious. On the other hand, you might find these flavors yourself. If that's the case, please just keep it to yourself unless you're around others of your ilk who care.

THE CLOUDY AFTERMATH

If you're a real smoker, the room doesn't "stink," it's "aromatic." What you do in your home or car is strictly up to you. But others may not share your nose for cigar scent. You can get the stink out with a special chlorophyll-enhanced "cigar candle" available at many cigar retailers. Nu-Car and other sprays work, or leave an order of McDonald's fries in the car overnight.

Cigar breath is also a matter of personal preference, but your breath, as always, could affect both your business and personal relationships if you're dealing with a nonsmoker. Breath mints and Listerine do little to alleviate cigar smoker's breath. We haven't cared enough to try Breath Assure tablets, so we've got nothing to say about it. You can brush your teeth and tongue and gargle, but your sig-o will still know you've been smoking. Bear in mind that in any good relationship, he or she should love you for who you are, which includes your stogie habit, or other arrangements (like breaking up) should be made.

The "smoking jacket" was created so smokers wouldn't stink up their clothes. But unless you're deeply into lounge music or are in your late eighties, they're kind of dated. Eventually, the smoking jacket evolved into a tuxedo; you can smoke in them. Leather jackets or tweed coats are also great to smoke in. For some reason, cigars blend well with the natural smells of the material.

Check your bottom lip in the mirror for leftover brown to avoid any misunderstandings.

Pipes

PUT *THIS* IN YOUR PIPE

This is not a pipe.

—René Magritte

Pipes are for pussies.

If you can name anyone cool who smoked a pipe (excluding Einstein), then you've got us. They're expensive, awkward, get that gnawed pen-cap look and make you look like an aristocratic pansy. Sherlock smoked a pipe; Clint gnawed a cigar. We rest our case.

LEGAL FICTION

Head Shop Rights and Wrongs

While the sale of drugs is generally illegal, the sale of drug paraphernalia (bongs, pipes, etc.) is legal under the right circumstances. The rules governing the sale of these items are drawn up by the state and are enforced at the head shop. Basically, the laws state that you can buy drug paraphernalia as long as you don't refer to it as such. For example, you can't buy a "bong," but you can buy a "water pipe." If you ask for a bong, the merchant will simply refuse service and point you to the door (you can come back again the next day, however, if you change your lingo). Since the laws are severe on merchants breaking this legal fiction, the proper etiquette is to abide by this silliness and refer to any item by its "nice" name.

BAD

GOOD

POT PIPE

PIPE FOR "FINE TOBACCO"

BONG

WATER PIPE

STRAIGHT SHOOTER/ CRACK PIPE

GLASS

PAY WITH THIRD-PARTY OUTTA-STATE CHECK

PAY WITH CASH

Other head shop etiquette: show up sober (like a bar, they can't serve the already intoxicated), and don't try to score from the employees . . . no matter how stoned they look!

Gambling

PLAYING YOUR CARDS RIGHT

There's a sucker born every minute.

—P. T. Barnum

For many, gambling's just a hobby. It's going to Vegas on vacation, having some buds over for a weekly poker game, or playing the office football pool. You win a few, you lose a few. It's the game that's fun; winning is a nice bonus.

Gambling is also a long shot at the American Dream. "Maybe this week I'll win the lotto!" "I'm just a pull of the lever away from quitting my job!" "If my horse comes in, I'll buy you that house!" Most of the time, the fantasy is the best payoff you can expect. And is that so wrong?

For others, gambling's not just a game. It's a way of life and a source of income. These people are there to pay *today's* bills.

Both kinds of gamblers—the professional and the amateur—deserve respect in the arena. Pros shouldn't treat ams like assholes, and ams shouldn't be, well, assholes. Whether you're there for fun or there to win, it's best to know the proper way to play.

The next few pages give you an overview of rights and wrongs for the various types of betting, from aces to the races.

CASINO BASICS

Casinos are mined with rules, superstition and mythology that can't be learned just by watching *Casino* or reruns of *Vegas!* While most faux pas won't get you the boot, it's best to know how to behave before you make your moves.

Losing and Winning

Expect to lose. It'll save you a lot of disappointment. Bet. Lose. Move on.

To avoid leaving a casino penniless, the proper protocol is to have a predetermined amount of money that you can afford to lose, and that you're psychologically ready to lose. When you've hit your mark, go home or check out a show. If you continue to spiral down the road to ruin, feel free not to take anyone with you. It is always existentially appropriate to waste one's own life, but losing the farm for you and your entire family is bad form. Also refrain from any yelling, screaming, and chair-throwing. Tantrums won't bring your money back; they just make you look like a jerk.

Though most folks lose, what keeps gamblers coming back for more is the chance for success, the big payoff, the new duds, the expensive prostitutes . . . well, maybe that's just us.

If you happen to be that lucky winning slob, feel free to celebrate your victories. Yell and cheer. The casino likes to see people make a big deal out of winning so the other losers burn more dough. Just be sure you don't piss off your fellow gamblers, or karmically mess up your own winning streak.

Do not celebrate every five-dollar victory. The biggest put-down in Vegas is, "Sounds like someone won five bucks." Hold off, and celebrate the bigger scores. There is a huge difference between being happy about a few coins tinkling into the tray and screaming your head off. It's annoying, particularly to any serious players in the vicinity who are down on their luck.

If you hit a big jackpot on a slot, make sure to tip the people who bring you the money (if it doesn't all come out of the machine, ya know), the waitperson who's been keeping your drinks flowing, etc. You hit, you tip. Feel free *not* to tip the IRS guy (stationed at many casinos). Fuck him!

Cheating

The difference between having a system and cheating is this: *Having a system doesn't work, while cheating works until you get caught.* Cheating includes counting cards, marking cards, or being in cahoots with the dealers.

The next time you go to Vegas, Atlantic City, or any other bastion of betting, look up at the black half domes in the casino's ceiling. Each contains several video cameras with direct feeds into security booths. Big Bro is watching you! Even if you're Rain Man, you're going to get nailed if you're not playing by the rules. Casinos have a lot at stake, and they do everything they can to keep the odds in their favor.

What happens to cheaters? Mix the cops with the gaming control board, add a few Mafia connections and . . . well, you do the math. We don't recommend it.

We also do not recommend accusing the dealers of cheating for reasons we've outlined above, as well as the ire of your fellow players, who'll think you're a jerk . . . and they'll be right.

Free Drinks

As long as you're gambling, drinks are usually on the house. Bear in mind the reason for this: the casino wants you to be loaded and unaware of time (no clocks or windows in a casino), so you'll play worse and lose more money. They also don't want you to get out of the money seat. The gambler's etiquette is to take these free drinks only to the point that you're happy, and not to the point that the cards look blurry. It's always bad to lose money because you're too loaded to play smart. It's all about the Benjamins, baby!

Some casinos will also bring you food and smokes while you gamble away your retirement funds. Feel free to ask casually.

To ensure that your drinks, food, et cetera, get to you in a timely manner, tip the waitress and be nice to her (that "please" and "thank you" shit).

Getting Comped

Back in the day, it was fairly easy for the consistent gambler to land free rooms, meals and shows. The aim was to get you and your dough into the casino as often as possible for as long as possible.

Well, times have changed. Loss leaders like comped accommodations are not nearly as popular as they used to be. Don't expect it, don't demand it. While you can always ask (either at the desk or in the casino), the casino doesn't owe you anything, even if you've dropped or plan to drop thousands of dollars at the tables. It's always bad form—and embarrassing—to demand free shit from anyone. It's even worse to be publicly denied.

Getting a Marker

Don't be shy about asking for a "marker," which is essentially a credit (or IOU) with a casino. It's generally reserved for big-time gamblers, but if you're a home owner or have decent credit, the casinos will let you lose money you don't have on you. They're nice guys, after all. You'll have to fill out a credit application and sign some papers. That's all. If you are turned down for a marker, it's best not to lose anymore or to make a scene about being denied. You can bet that if you've got the money to lose, they'll happily take it.

Win, lose or draw, you don't have to pay the marker until you check out of the hotel. If you forget to pay the marker, no worries. You usually have a few months to pay your debt before they go after your bank account or send a tough guy to break both your legs. Even better, the casino cannot charge you any interest on the marker. Once you pay up, you're usually square with the casino to owe them more money at a later date. The last thing a casino wants is for you to be bashful about coming back. You can bet on that!

LET THE GAMES BEGIN

Now that you know the general stuff, it's time to gamble. While we won't teach you the games, here's the inside skinny on how to behave inside the arena.

The One-Armed Bandit

We'll start with the easiest game of all. Just insert coin, pull lever or push button. To the amateur, there may not seem to be much etiquette involved in trying your luck at the slots—it's like a video game, right? Wrong. To the serious player, it's a living.

Ahoy, matey, them there are "territorial waters" that surround all slot machines, and you are expected to abide by them. When picking a slot machine or video poker machine, always ask the person sitting next to it if it's available. Many serious players consider the machines to the right and left of the one they're playing to be within their territorial waters, and/or they might be playing several machines at once. The cool thing is that this rule also applies to you! Once you sit down, feel free to play your machine as well as the ones to the right and left. As long as you're popping silver in the machines, the house has your back. Still, asserting your territorial privileges is always easier during off-peak gambling hours.

Never ask someone to move so you can play their machine, even if they're just taking up a seat while their friend gambles.

Penn Jillette on Casino Etiquette

Penn and Teller are a pair of Las Vegas–based magicians, well known for their bizarre, often gory tricks (shooting and hanging each other, severing limbs), and well loathed by magicians worldwide for their practice of revealing the secrets to their illusions (a no-no in the magic community). A self-described "nut" and an avowed sober atheist, Penn, the talking half of the duo, runs down casino do's and don'ts.

EFO: We caught an episode of your TV show, *Sin City*, where you guys got thrown out for doing a card trick inside a casino.

PENN: Yeah, it was totally fake. We staged the whole thing. Even fooled my mother.

EFO: What will get you kicked out of a casino for real?

PENN: Lots of things! Using a camera. Winning too much money.

EFO: Bringing your own deck of cards, even if it's to do a card trick?

PENN: Yeah. The thing you have to remember about a casino is, they're not operating from any sort of natural law, or morality. It's their rules, and their rules dictate that they have to win. If you look at any of the mathematical papers, you know the laws of very big numbers. Although your chances of winning or losing are up in the air, the casinos [don't leave it up to chance]. They can tell you, with much greater precision than a percentage point, exactly how much money they are going to make. If you flip a coin one time, you can't tell whether it's going to be heads or tails, but if you flip a coin 10,000 times, there's a pretty good chance you'll get heads fairly close to 5,000 times. And that's what casinos are doing. So people who do real card counting, which is, of course, very, very very rare, and doesn't work that well and is very elaborate, will be thrown out. Their faces will be made, and they won't be allowed to come in again. I've also found that running is a very, very bad idea in a casino. If you just stand on one end of a casino, and take off along the carpet, as fast as you can, all sorts of people who just looked like regular citizens, all of a sudden, you find out, jeez . . . they're working here! And they'll grab you, and they will just stop you for just plain running. That's something that's going to make them really nervous. A friend of mine was running to get a pack of smokes before a show, and was afraid he was going to miss the opening number, which had a lot of pussy in it, so he went across the casino at full speed, and was stopped by six people within about 50 yards.

EFO: What about just being wasted?

PENN: That's nothing but good! They like people as fucked up as possible! Sure! I mean, I know that if you talk to the real casino cats, they'll talk to you about people who believe that a slot machine is going to get hot, and who will just not move from it, and they'll piss and shit in their pants.

EFO: Are you a gambling man?

PENN: No, no I'm too good at math.

If you need to leave to go to the bathroom or something, feel free to call the slot foreman over to watch your machine while you go. Tip him.

Always watch your change bucket. There are tons of crooks, con artists and recently impoverished gamblers waiting for you to turn your back.

Same basic rules apply to video poker and video blackjack.

TABLE GAMES

Whereas the slots and video poker are generally monetary masturbation, the table games are full-on orgies where you'll either climax or find utter rejection.

One sweeping rule at the tables is this: Don't try to endear yourself to the dealer with wit. They're generally not interested. Avoid smartass or cutesy questions like, "Are you being nice to us today?" (Are you giving out good hands?), as they are utterly cliché, and make you look more like a card guppy than a shark.

Blackjack

Check out the minimum bet before you sit down at any blackjack table. If you don't know how to play, find a table that's not busy and ask the dealer to teach you. Since blackjack is a relatively simple game, they will usually explain the game to you, no problem. Make sure to tip.

Seats at the table are for players. If you're there with a friend who's playing, you can ask the dealer if it's okay to sit down next to them, but don't take it personally if the dealer says no.

You always get the chips at the table. Wait until the previous hand is done and ask for change. Put the money to be changed to the left of the betting circle. Do not put the money within the betting circle, or it could be confused with a bet. If you want to trade in your smaller chips for bigger ones (25 blue for 1 green, for example), check the dealer's rack to see if they need the smaller chips. They usually do, in which case it's cool to ask them to "color up."

Cards will be dealt to you either faceup or facedown, depending on the house rules. If the cards are dealt facedown, you can pick them up and check your hand. Use only one hand to hold them, as two hands makes it easier to mark the cards. And don't try to hide them or manhandle them in any way: keep cards over and above the table, and never bring them too close to your body, lest there's something up your sleeve.

Most blackjack games are played with the cards faceup. In this case, leave the cards alone; no touchy, hands off. In a faceup game of blackjack, the dealer does all card handling. Touch them and they'll give you a warning. Touch 'em a few times, and they'll sic the pit boss on your sorry ass.

When you "double down"—doubling your original bet *after* you see your cards—put your second bet to the side of your first bet, but not on top of it. If you accidentally stack the two, they might think you're trying to "cap your bet" or "take a shot" (unfairly adding to a bet after the cards have been dealt). Know where to place your money so there are no misunderstandings. Ask the dealer if you're unclear.

Tip the dealer when you're winning. Many dealers would rather you make a bet for them instead of handing them a toke (tip). To make a bet for a dealer, put a chip in front of your chip (make a bet in front of your bet). Never bet less than a dollar for a tip (50¢ is unacceptable). Dealers don't expect a tip when you're losing, but don't let that stop you: the tip is the sacramental offering to Lady Luck—it's good gambling karma.

Poker

Arguably the gambling professional's preferred game. If you're good, you can earn a living at it. Far more complex than blackjack, it has its very own set of etiquette.

First off, don't sit at a table unless you know how to play; unlike the blackjack dealer, the poker dealer will not teach you, and the other players will be severely annoyed at you. Most hotels have a gambling channel that will show you how to play, and there are plenty of good books. Try playing with your friends before you go pro.

Play with all of your chips on the table. It's considered bad form to take your winnings off the table before you leave the scene of the crime. Basically, when you have your chips on the table, it's a sign to the others that they can still win their money back (i.e., take more of your money). Since you're playing against other players (rather than the house), this is an important rule of etiquette. Money on the table means there's hope for the losers.

As in blackjack, keep cards over the table. But you are allowed to protect your hand from prying eyes. When the hand is over, either leave the cards on the table for the dealer to pick up, or move them in the dealer's general direction. Never throw your cards at the dealer.

While this might look cool in old western flicks, it's really bad form and can garner a warning from the pit boss.

People sit at a poker table to take other people's money. All interaction with your proposed victims should be informed by this premise. You're not there to make friends. With that in mind, don't talk to people when everyone has a hand, never talk about a hand, and never try to peek at anyone else's hand.

Every time you win a pot, tip the dealer. Tip proportionally to your winnings.

Craps

Craps etiquette is usually confined to knowing when the dice are in play and when it's safe for you to put your money down (or pick up your winnings). If you want change, drop money on the table outside the betting area; the dealer won't take money out of your hand. Simply drop the money on the table and say, "Change." Make your bet early, and pick up any winnings before the dice are thrown. If not, your bet continues with the next throw whether you meant it or not.

If you're the one rolling the dice, make sure that both dice hit the back wall of the craps table. It ensures the randomness of the roll and prevents "sliding" (simply sliding the dice down the table without them turning over). If you don't, the dealer will yell at you; if you do it several times, the pit boss will get on your case.

To tip the dealer, you can make a bet for them. Or you can throw the dealer a chip.

SPORTS BOOK

The smart man bets not with his heart, but with logic. It's fine to root root root for your home team, but don't put money on 'em if they suck.

When you bet on sporting events at a casino, you mark your ticket, then you and your fellow betters check out the game on one of many TVs. The important thing to remember is that you're not in a sports bar. Low-profile displays of excitement and anxiety are acceptable, but no over-the-top hooting, hollering and cheering for your team or player. Also refrain from telling those around you who you bet on—it's bad luck.

DON'T JUDGE A BOOKIE BY HIS COVER

While betting on sporting events at a casino is legal, making bets through a private bookmaker, or bookie, is not, even in a city where gambling is permitted. The rationale is one of economics: private betting is difficult for the government to tax.

Nevertheless, bookmaking continues to thrive. Like every other "professional," the bookie has rules that he expects his clients to follow, particularly those rules designed to keep him out of jail and in the black. We consulted our bookie buddy, Joe, on the ins and outs. Though he specializes in football, most of his etiquette suggestions work across the board.

I am a semiretired bookie, working the football season only. Over twenty years ago, I inherited the business from my brother, who died. There was this very successful business out there . . . for the taking. Not all that happy "working" for a living, I took it.

It's a very simple business, really. A customer, usually having been recommended by another customer, calls me on the telephone. To work with me, you generally need a referral from another established customer.

I give the customer an updated "College football line" and/or an updated "Pro football line." The customer either makes a bet based upon that line, agreeing to pay me an additional 10 percent ("juice") on the amount of the wager, or he hangs up and looks for another line. The line is also called a "point spread"—the number of points the ace handicappers and computer wizards of Las Vegas deem a particular team will win by. If you "lay the points" (i.e., bet that the favorite will win at least by the point spread), and your team "covers the spread," you win your bet. If, on the other hand, you bet the "dog" (i.e., underdog) and "take the points," and the favorite doesn't cover the spread, you also win.

As anyone can plainly see, it's a win-win situation. Trust me. Place your bets, friend. Tuesdays and Wednesdays are pay/collect days.

Here are a few guidelines for model behavior that I encourage all betters to follow.

1) Don't Judge a Bookie by His Cover.

The fact that sports betting is mostly illegal only bespeaks of a society mired in a "happiness is sin" mentality . . . not of a civilized, victimless contract between you, betting on the outcome of a sporting event, and me, accepting that bet.

I consider myself a professional.

Thugishly breaking a customer's leg, in an effort to collect a bet, would do nothing to enhance that professional image, now, would it?

A customer always pays me because that customer knows that I always pay him. It's as simple as that. If I'm given an excuse instead of cash, check, or money order, the customer is abruptly and forever "cut off" from his favorite pastime. Period. Want to play? Pay.

Of course, not all bookies are as professional and rational as I am, and some do have mob ties. Broken thumbs are not unheard of, so be mindful of who you are dealing with.

2) Don't Bargain.

I'm not the corner fish market. A customer cannot "negotiate" a point spread. A customer can "shop" the point spreads of various bookies (very common) and then, having found my spread to his liking, "buy" a half-point in either direction for a fee of 10 percent of the total wager.

3) Don't Whisper.

I play moderately loud music while I'm "working the phones," so as not to advertise my profession through the walls of my condo. When you place a bet with me, for God's sake, don't whisper. As you can imagine, my ability to clearly hear your bet is indispensable to the entire project.

One time, a customer was suspiciously whispering all of his "action" to me, and his wife got on an extension and screamed, "I KNOW WHAT YOU'RE DOING!!!!!"

A classic reason not to whisper.

4) Don't Bore Me.

I'm a bookie, not a bartender. I really, really don't care if you "lost that last fuckin' game because of a fuckin' fumble with three seconds left on the fuckin' clock!!!!".

5) Don't Ask Me, "Who Do You Like?"

You see, the only thing I like . . . is for you to lose. I'm not a sports-investment counselor. Or even a common tout. Know what you want to do. Don't be wishy-washy and tie up my phone line. Make your bet. Accept my heartfelt thanks. And hang up.

One time, I glanced over at the pay/collect sheet of a hapless customer—he already owed me thousands of dollars from lost football wagers. I asked him, "Why don't you try betting baseball instead?" He responded, "I don't know anything about baseball." That's the best kind of customer.

6) No Need To Tip.

My 10 percent juice will suffice. However, many bookies employ "clerks." These clerks are responsible for taking the bets. If you're feeling generous, feel free to tip the clerk, or give him a gift at Christmas.

There Are Also a Couple of Quick Rules for Bookies to Follow.

1) **Know Your Clientele.** Don't mess with "stiffs"—clients who stiff you—or anyone who might be a problem. Most of my new customers come from referrals, which helps insure the quality of my client pool. I deal with those who can afford to lose: surgeons, actors, big-time lawyers and judges. Smart bookies use discretion as to who they deal with.

2) **Keep Your Mouth Shut.** Do unto others. . . . You don't want your clients indiscriminately broadcasting your profession to the world. Likewise, respect their privacy and keep all transactions confidential.

However, if you're a local bookie and the cops come knocking at your door, it is acceptable to talk with them. They usually don't care too much about small-time bookmaking operations. Their concern is the infiltration of organized crime . . . a mutual concern of yours, too. Generally the protocol is to be cooperative, without compromising the privacy of your clients.

FANCY INTERNATIONAL GAMES

U nless you're James Bond or Austin Powers, you'll probably steer clear of these games. But here are some basic rules, just in case you get stuck in Monte Carlo on a layover or something.

Baccarat: If you're smart, then this is the game to play. The odds are really good (as far as odds go), so winning is a possibility. The dealers will teach you the game.

Pai-Gow Poker: Sort of like seven-card stud poker with a Chinese twist. They'll generally teach you how to play. Though the game has its legions of fans, it sounds like something you eat with chopsticks rather than an outlaw pastime. We say pass.

Roulette: Try to get your bet down early, before the dealer waves off betting and before they drop the ball. If you're sitting at the bottom of the table and you want a number farther away, put the chips by the dealer and ask him/her to make the bet for you. If you win, tip the dealer by putting a dollar on his/her favorite number. Don't worry, they'll teach you how to play.

Patchinko: This is a big game in Asia . . . not in America. Feel free to avoid.

HORSE RACING

I n most states, horse racing is the only form of legalized gambling available aside from the lottery. Places like California and New York offer racing year-round and support off-site betting, so you don't even have to go to the track to play the ponies. Generally, it's the pros and retired folks who gamble by day; the nighttime and weekend races bring out the amateur crowd. While we cannot possibly go into all the ins and outs of racing, here's a small stable of advice.

Betting

It's your money, so feel free to bet on any damn horse you like, no matter what anyone says. Underdogs? Fine. Sure things? Go for it. Etiquette only really comes into play when you start asking someone else for advice on a horse.

Tipping (not the horse) is the most frequently cited rule to follow when getting handicapping advice from someone who works at the track. If the guy who parks your car gives you some advice, drop him a buck. If it's the person who hands you the program, tip him, too. As in slots and cards, tipping is considered a gambling mojo. The more you tip, the better you'll do. And, if the advice brings you success, feel free to throw another buck or two to the person on your way out.

If you're a novice trying to get some horse hints from a regular at the track, it's best to follow commonsense rules of etiquette. Ask if it's okay to ask them a few questions, and be polite. Depending on the amount of information they give you, you might want to offer to buy them a drink. Since the odds are determined based upon the bets, don't be surprised if they balk at giving you their picks—it's not bad form on their part to hold out.

These same rules apply to talking with the jockeys, owners, and trainers. Most will talk with you and give you guidance if you're nice. Hell, they'll probably talk your ear off about "exacta" betting. On the other hand, some won't. Either way, be polite and gracious.

The worst thing you can do is spy on the jockeys and trainers and see who they bet on. Doing so will get you the stinkeye, or even a bloody nose.

Winning

As in a casino, if you win big, it's customary to tip the person who gives you your winnings. Again, feel free not to tip the IRS guy (stationed at all tracks). Fuck him!

DOG RACING

Hey, what does the Royal Family have in common with Appalachian white trash? Inbreeding and dog races. If you're into it, the horse racing info should help, but you'll have to get the full dish at the track.

Since the Taco Bell chihuahua came out, some tracks have been racing those rat-like canines. If you're there just for the spectacle and stupidity of it all, you're fine in our book, Jimbo.

A   FRIENDLY   GAME   OF   POKER

There's nothing more American than inviting your friends over and trying to beat them out of their money. Here is some home poker protocol that any host can bank on.

Before You Start

Before the players arrive and the cards are dealt, take care of the essentials. Who's bringing the food? Will the house be providing snacks, or will everyone chip in for pizza? Also determine who's providing smokes and libations, two very integral parts of any good poker party.

Discuss money with your guests ahead of time. Chips? Change? If everyone goes to the ATM before the game and there are no chips on hand, you got a problem, unless you're planning on playing $20 hands.

Finally, make sure the house has several decks of *new* cards. No offense, buddy, but we'd like to see those cards come out of a *fresh* deck!

The Game

Hell, the game's up to you. Wild cards? Sure. Just try not to have more than two sets of cards wild during a game. It just looks silly.

The Mark

Okay, so your brother-in-law wants to come to the party, and you figure anyone dumb enough to marry your sister is dumb enough to lose his money! Bringing in a mark to take his money is a precarious thing, since you probably know him, and he probably knows where you live! Generally, good form is to let him win a few hands before you take him to town. It's a nice thing to do, and it gives him a false sense of security. Everyone loves a good mark. Just remember: If he knows what he's doing (a popular con is to play "dumb" and feign beginner's luck), the hustler may become the hustled.

PAYING DEBTS

To reiterate, wagering more than you can afford to lose is never recommended. Nevertheless, people ignore this bit of commonsense advice every day.

If you lose a bet, pay it. If you can't, sell something, come up with a payment schedule, or offer a barter. Many a friendship (and a pair of legs) has been broken over a welched bet. Don't let your mouth make promises your ass can't keep.

Strip Clubs

THE NAKED TRUTH

"Nudity" or "in a state of nudity" means the showing of the human genitals, pubic area, buttocks or female breast with less than a fully opaque covering below a horizontal line across the top of the aureola at the aureola's highest point.

—Local city ordinance

I have always depended on the kindness of strangers.

—Blanche Dubois, *A Streetcar Named Desire*

The opening trombone wail of Sonny Lester's striptease anthem is as familiar to us as the "Star-Spangled Banner." In other words, like booze, smoking and poker, naked, jiggling flesh is classic American vice.

And it's not just for outlaws anymore. The sleazy stigma once attached to strip clubs and nudie bars has all but dissipated. These days, strip joints are popping up from the airport to the 'burbs, and more and more "respectable" men and women are deciding that these establishments are perfectly acceptable venues for entertainment (as well as employment). They're places to party, let your hair down, and get up close and personal with a 3-D fantasy.

Which brings us to the single most important thing to remember about strip clubs: They are in the business of peddling fantasies. If you want to get laid, go somewhere else. This fundamental truth underscores most of the prescribed modes of conduct in these dens of iniquity, which operate on their own stringent, often paradoxical sets of rules—rules that differ from city to city, and between male and female strip clubs.

We've focused on straight clubs featuring female dancers, with some nods to gay clubs and Ladies Only establishments where the shoe (and every other garment) is on the other foot.

DEGREES OF UNDRESS

The general rule of thumb is that the amount of clothes removed is inversely proportional to the availability of alcohol. In other words, if the girls take it all off, there will be no booze. As laws governing nudie bars are city-controlled, there really aren't any hard and fast rules. Before we get into our discussion of etiquette, here's a quick rundown of the basic types of clubs.

Bikinis and Pasties

Bikini dance clubs are the lowest levels of strip bars. Relying on descriptions like "exotic," these establishments do not permit nudity, requiring their gals to make creative use of nipple-obscuring pasties or electric tape, and colorful strands of dental floss masquerading as bikini tops and bottoms. Most feature fully stocked bars, and many have little or no cover charge.

Topless Time

Letting just the tops fly means, in most cities, that you can still serve booze. Topless tends to be the most popular type of club, since there's lots of money in alcohol and it's easy to take a horny drunk's money. Cover charges vary.

Butt Naked

Full nude is just that: au naturel. While the laws vary from city to city, many totally nude (AKA "Nude, Nude, Nude!") clubs do not serve alcohol. This dry policy makes the club 18+ friendly, and justifies a higher charge at the door.

Even if the gals are nude nude nude on stage, they might be legally required to cover up a bit before coming down on the floor to flirt with customers.

Themed

Theme clubs are all over the map. There is no alcohol served at the renowned Mitchell Brothers in San Francisco, but they do offer live, onstage lesbian action complete with foreign object penetration. On the flip side, Manhattan's gay bar/club Splash features on-bar showers, where the male dancers will literally shower nude, then strut their stuff on the long bar while toweling off. It begs the question of where the men should put their tips. Meanwhile, the famous Hollywood Tropicana boasts a full bar, lap dancing, mud and hot oil wrestling with nary an exposed nipple or nether region.

SAVE THE LAP DANCE FOR ME

Usually you can count on three (legal) activities going on in any club: stage dancing, lap/table dances and private dances.

In between or during onstage routines (stripteases, brass pole acrobatics), be prepared for dancers offstage to come over and try to get you to buy a "lap dance"—a personal booty-shaking performed just for you, at a ballpark cost of $10–$30 plus tip. Talking with these dancers, or even having a drink with one of them, does not obligate you to purchase a lap dance. But if you do opt to buy one, they'll bump and grind on your lap and even put their boobs or crotch in your face.

The important thing to remember is you have to leave the driving to the dancer. They can touch you, but you can't necessarily touch them, although this depends on the girl and the club. In the eyes of the management and the bouncer, the dancer is in charge of the dance; copping an unwanted

DRESSED FOR SUCCESS

You don't have to belong to MENSA to figure out how to see action at your local nudie bar. Look money, smell money, be money, and you'll be popular all night! Just remember: it's all a game.

Thinks she digs him for his mind and charm.

Smells enticing perfume, bought by the gallon.

In his heart, he knows that he could help change her.

This one gets a big tip!

Smells money.

Presses her breasts against his nice suit.

Feeling for wallet.

feel might get you physically introduced to the pavement. Be nice, and she'll grind you into a pulp.

Some strippers prefer that you don't bust a nut; others we spoke with really don't care. A man's got to do what a man's got to do. Just enjoy the experience, tip big, and go clean up in the bathroom.

LAP DANCE DELUXE

The "private dance" is like a deluxe version of the lap dance. Taking place in a semiprivate booth, it costs more, lasts longer and *sometimes* leads to more personal contact.

LOOK, DON'T TOUCH

Entering a strip bar gives you license to look. Don't worry about political correctness, you're in a nudie bar! Look! Titties! It's all right. The strippers know why you're there, and there's no need to be shy. Basic etiquette includes making eye contact with the gals and smiling. As the strippers are there to entertain you (and are paid to do so), looking and applauding lets them know they're doing their job. Avoid making obnoxious catcalls or anything that will make you look either underage or like a frat boy.

Lines of communication between strippers in the club are highly efficient: Slobber on one girl, slap one on the ass, or make a particularly unsavory comment, and her co-workers will know about it within minutes. So will the bouncer, who will always take the girl's word over yours.

CLOTHES CALLS

You probably couldn't care less about her attire, but she'll pay very close attention to yours.

Unless you're a rock star, it's always good form to dress well. Indeed, in a strip club, clothes definitely make the man. If the stripper thinks you're made of money, she'll give you more attention. So don't look unkempt. Wear a suit—preferably a nice suit. It's like wearing a big fat dollar sign, and the girls will hone in quickly.

Tank tops, frat guy fashions, or any apparel that reeks of un-bridled testosterone can be an instant red flag that suggests "rude" or "rapist." Make sure your friends aren't sporting this look, either, as you are judged by the company you keep.

Look money, smell money, be money, and you'll be popular all night . . . unless you're broke.

TIPPING

Which brings us to the mantra of every strip club: "Show me the money!" When all is said and done, strip bars provide a pay-as-you-go service. Tipping is only in paper denominations and does not include wrapped or unwrapped change.

You don't have to tip every dance, but it is expected/required that sometime during the evening you tip a dancer. Whether it's to com-mend a gal for her stunning interpretation of Mötley Crüe's "Girls, Girls, Girls" or to buy yourself a lap dance, the amount of attention you receive is directly proportional to the amount of money you put out.

If you're tipping a dancer, you can either place the money on the bar or on the stage itself. Some girls will encourage you to slide bills in their G-strings—just watch the straying fingers. Crumpling up bills and tossing them on the stage is acceptable but less polite—it's like throwing popcorn at the screen. Crumpling up bills and chucking them at the stripper's privates is uncool, unless she invites it. Wrapping up change in a crumpled-up bill and chucking it at her, as some repressed women-haters take joy in doing, is way uncool.

Thrifty tippers attempting to ration funds should drop their larger bills at the start of the night. Like we said, news travels fast in a strip club. If a stripper sees Hamilton, Jackson, Grant or Franklin, you will get more attention throughout the night from both her and her co-workers. Unless you're planning on returning real soon, dropping a fat wad at the end of the night will get you nowhere since . . . hell, you're leaving and they're probably not going with you.

LOCATION, LOCATION, LOCATION

If you sit at the stage, a steady flow of bills is the general protocol. If you don't tip for long stretches, the bouncer might ask you to leave

STRIP CLUB ABC's FOR THE ALCOHOL—IMPAIRED

Clip this page for an E-Z guide to strip club etiquette

A	B	C

Look poor

Don't tip

Stripper

Won't talk to you

Will tell everyone not to talk with you

Be gross to a girl

Grab at a girl

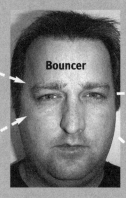

Bouncer

Will ask/force you to leave

Will kick your ass

Cops

Be drunk and get in the bouncer's face

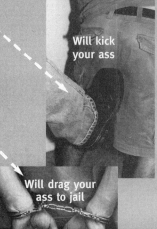

Will drag your ass to jail

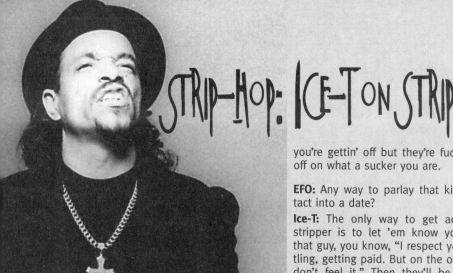

STRIP-HOP: ICE-T ON STRIPPERS

you're gettin' off but they're fuckin' gettin' off on what a sucker you are.

EFO: Any way to parlay that kind of contact into a date?

Ice-T: The only way to get access to a stripper is to let 'em know you are not that guy, you know, "I respect you for hustling, getting paid. But on the other side, I don't feel it." Then they'll be like, "Oh, you're different."

EFO: You're in a long-term monogamous relationship. Is it cheating to go to a strip club?

Ice-T: I don't look at it like that. If you're [screwing] 'em that's a whole other thing. I think it just pumps the blood a little bit. Now, what you're sayin' to the girls in the privacy of this club—I mean, if your girl heard it, I don't know if she would enjoy it.

A veritable wealth of knowledge on assorted forays into sin, Ice-T definitely knows his way around strip clubs from coast to coast. The former pimp-turned-rap-star has hosted naughty segments of Hot Rocks on the Playboy channel, which features a bevy of flesh-baring beauties, and had a pay-per-view cable show called Ice-T's Extreme Babes. Finally, the last album from Ice's heavy metal act, Body Count, includes a song called "Strippers," a wickedly humorous, highly graphic mini-exposé of these fantasies-for-hire.

In other words, he's an expert on the subject. We asked him to help us peel away some of the layers of the stripper mystique.

EFO: Who do you respect more, a hooker or a stripper?

Ice-T: At least with a hooker, you get somethin' for your money. Deep down in their minds, strippers really believe they're entertainers. Actresses! But they're just con women. They sell you a dream.

EFO: Can you elaborate?

Ice-T: You believe that they love you. They have what they call their regulars and they work 'em. If you ever get a chance to get on the other side of a stripper and talk to them as a friend, an ally, not a john, they will show you a true and total disrespect for men. And if you ever really get to meet a stripper on that level you'll never tip again, 'cause you know they look at you like such an ass, such a joke. You think

Dating Strippers: T's Tips at a Glance

1. Don't tip her! If you're in a club with her you've got a harder time. If you met her on the street, then you've got a better chance of action out of that environment. But once you're in there, DO NOT TIP HER!

2. You can't be like, "Yo, you're fine, here's some money, I gotta house, I can buy things for you ..." Puh. You're just goin' down the road the strippers want.

3. Get onto the other side of the game with her. "Don't confuse me with them." You just have to be like, "I understand, I wrote a book on strippers." Just come at it like, "I know the game but I think you're cool and you've gotta have a life on the other side of this. Is there anything that you do outside?"

4. Take her to Disneyland or something. "You gotta not be a stripper sometime. That's what I wanna know. . . . Is there a chance?" Then she'll say "Yes" or "No." You're saving yourself 2,000 bucks.

or move to a different seat. The front seats are the money seats for the girls on the stage: respect that.

If you sit at the stage, some of the strippers looking for lap dances might not come by and talk to you. They don't want to distract you from (and incur the wrath of) the stripper who's up there dancing.

We suggest sitting at a table near the stage if one is available—it's the best of both worlds.

DRINK UP

Some clubs have a drink minimum; some dancers get a percentage of the drinks purchased by their "clients."

Either way, be prepared for the girls and the waitresses to egg you on to imbibe, as drink sales are another key source of the club's income. If a dancer sits at your table, you can bet the cocktail waitress will be there in a flash to take your order . . . and hers. It's a little house hustle to pump up the bar receipts. Naturally, you'll feel obligated to pay, or risk looking like an asshole. There's not a lot you can do about it—just make sure you have enough cash on you . . . as always.

Also bear in mind the difference between the scantily clad cocktail waitress working the floor and the half-naked stripper on stage. In addition to slinging drinks, some waitresses may indeed shed for bread. But while they're serving drinks, treat them as you would treat a waitress at a normal bar or club (see "Booze" earlier in Part I). Inappropriate behavior could result in a Mai Tai in your face, or a stern warning from the bouncer.

DATING STRIPPERS

A strip club isn't a brothel or a coochie supermarket. Generally, you can't just walk in and buy a date.

If they talk with you between dances, smile at you or sit with you, it's not because they want you—it's so you'll buy a lap dance or at least feel compelled to tip them more when they're onstage.

If a stripper asks for your phone number, it's not because she wants you—it's probably so that she can call you the next time she's dancing. If she gives you hers, it might well be a pager, so that she can call you back and let you know when you can next catch her act at the club. This personal attention is all part of the game—a premium that will obligate you to dish out more cash when you show up.

BRINGING SAND TO THE BEACH

Contrary to popular opinion, bringing a chick to a strip club does not bestow upon a guy instant credibility—it does not say, "Hey, I have a girl, I'm here by choice, not out of necessity." Nor does it immediately stamp him with a cachet of open-minded hipness.

When dancers see a woman come in with a man, they assume one of the following: a) that she's a lesbian, b) that she's his girlfriend, and that he needs some sort of extra stimulation beyond what she can provide, or c) that it's a novelty date—a couple just having a laugh. For these reasons, the dancers might proceed with more caution when approaching you. In addition, the presence of a woman suggests to the stripper that she can't take her fantasy-building hustle quite as far.

But keep the cash coming, and they will get over any concerns quite quickly.

In fact, once they've sized up the situation, most strippers we talked to enjoy dancing for women, and give them better service, as female patrons tend to be more polite and leave bigger tips. Strippers, in turn, tend to be more lenient in terms of contact with female customers, as there's less threat of unwanted *gropeage*, and no threat of nut-rubbing.

FOR LADIES ONLY

Okay, ladies, you've endured 2,000 words on the chauvinistic institution of female strip joints. We thought we owed you a little fun, too. In fact, you're entitled to more depravity and debauchery than the fellas. Check it out.

Some male strip clubs, where men shed for bread, are "ladies only" or "ladies preferred." A straight male strip club catering to female guests might not deny a gay man entrance, but don't be surprised if the dancers are not as receptive. (We spoke with one male stripper who sells kisses to audience members, but only if they're female.) Otherwise, official rules for the male strip club may be quite similar to those for female clubs.

The big difference is that ladies are allowed a lot more leeway when it comes to crossing the line. Girls, if you stuff a bill in a gyrating male's undies, you can probably go for a little shaft-stroke without fear of reprimand. It takes a lot for a woman to get ousted from a male strip joint. Expulsion is only a last resort after repeat offenses.

Other implicit rules of conduct: watch the long nails, no clawing, no drawing blood. And when depositing fresh bills in the G-string, be extra careful about paper cuts.

THE PRIVATE PARTY STRIPPER

Many of the standard rules and regulations of the club go out the window once you have a stripper in your own home for a special event, the most common being a bachelor or bachelorette party. Though it depends on the stripper, you can usually get away with a lot more groping.

Standard party games include erotic, "hot seat" lap dances for a featured, soon-to-be-married guest, "feeding the kitty," "grabbing the banana," body shots, whipped cream antics, and tricks with Blow Pops and double-ended dildos. If you have special requests, discuss them ahead of time with your dancer, or with their agent or personal manager/bouncer (most female strippers will always bring along someone to watch their back in case the guests get out of line). Make sure you have plenty of singles on hand. Most also accept plastic.

Frequently, the games are pay-as-you-go, which can be awkward and momentum-killing. You might want to negotiate a blanket fee up front, including tip, so that guests don't have to keep digging in their pockets every ten minutes for large bills just to keep the party going. But even with payment up front, you'll still need lots of singles for certain games, such as "feeding the kitty" or having the stripper fish for bills strategically placed around the groom- or bride-to-be's privates.

As a guest at a bachelor or bachelorette party, it's your job to let the guest of honor have a wild time that will last them a lifetime. Get them really drunk. Let them sample the soon-to-be forbidden fruit. Pay for anything they want. Humiliate them in front of their close friends. Just don't push them into anything they really don't want to do. Tying the knot is tough enough as it is.

No pictures, no camcorders! The betrothed doesn't want this night of debauchery documented; nor does the stripper. And every guest is sworn to secrecy about any missteps over the line.

WHEN A STRIP CLUB JUST ISN'T ENOUGH...

San Francisco native Ron Newt spent years in the flesh-peddling business, amassing a bicoastal "staff" of 17 women and pulling in a 7-digit income before he hung up his pimpin' hat and went legit. Here he gives a crash course in the game that was once his livelihood. (Authors' note: Prostitution is illegal, and perpetuates the objectification and exploitation of women. We don't condone it. Just say "No!")

EFO: Are there levels of pimpdom?

RON NEWT: You've got your "ghetto pimp," your "Mexican pimp," and a "Man of Leisure." A ghetto pimp takes his girl to work on the bus. He's her broker, protecter, lawyer, all of that. The Mexican pimp—he'll sit and squat and watch outside the room or on the street corner and make sure [the girls] do what they gotta do. He follows her. He's not so sure of himself. He's scared that the girls aren't going to give him his money. The Man of Leisure just has them go. He's the master of it all. The master manipulator. She handles her business and brings [the money] to him. He has mastered the game.

EFO: What was the standard cut?

RN: 100%.

EFO: What does the girl get?

RN: I took care of them. All of their needs. That's standard for a real player. Lower level pimps make deals—60-40, that's what I hear. I don't make deals—I ain't Monty Hall.

EFO: Explain "pimp arrest."

RN: She's on pimp arrest if she's a renegade, a woman without a pimp. And if I see her, and ask her, "You gotta man?" She says, "Nah-ah." "Honey, you're under pimp arrest . . . handcuffs . . . let's go." I could do that. [But most pimps] can't do that. You've got to have the charisma, the flavor, so when you make love to them, they say, "Put the handcuffs on me, daddy."

EFO: So it's cool to sleep with employees?

RN: What? [I'm a] super mack daddy—that's what we get paid for! She ain't gonna pay me unless I do some super sex to her. I'm gonna be everything she wants me to be—if they deserve it, if they bring enough money in. If they don't bring at least $500 to a grand, ain't nothing happening.

EFO: Is it important to screw her beforehand, to test the merchandise?

RN: No, no—finance before romance. That's in the rule book. I won't touch her 'til she pays me. I'm a prostitute for her. Pimps are prostitutes. To stay, she's gotta have something that she likes, right? She's gotta like my flavor.

EFO: If a trick gets too rough with one of your girls, does he have to pay the pimp the estimated loss of income due to damages?

RN: Sure they gotta pay if they don't want to get killed, but tricks don't usually beat up hoes, 'cuz they know they're going to get killed. You hit one of my girls, it's on.

EFO: Did you handle rate negotiations with clients?

RN: They did that on their own. Pimps set the price, the girls follow instructions.

EFO: Is there any protocol to approaching a pimp to solicit the services of one of his girls?

RN: You couldn't approach me. You'd approach my woman. At a lower level, you approach [the pimp], but they might rob you.

EFO: Any kind of guy you wouldn't let a girl date?

RN: Most of the women don't like to date black men, 'cuz they want too much sex. They wanna do it all night. That's the worst problem I've ever had—black men, 'cuz as soon as you come, it's over, pardner. Every time you bust a nut, you got to pay. I don't let my girls date black men.

EFO: Because it's not cost effective.

RN: No.

EFO: Is there any understanding between pimps about not recruiting each others' girls?

RN: It happens all the time. There's no code.

EFO: What would a pimp do if a girl's holding out on him?

RN: You whoop 'em.

EFO: But not in the face.

RN: No, they whoop 'em where it can't show no scar. I ain't never did it, but if I was going to whip 'em, I'd do it with a rubber hose so it wouldn't show nothing. Or a rubber spoon on the top of the head.

EFO: What if a girl doesn't want to work— like she's complaining of a sore throat, or something else that's sore?

RN: I'd send her to the doctor, make sure everything's alright. But if she's lying, she might get fired, or something else might go upside her head. When they're tired or sick, they get to lay down. I don't dog my girls. Sometimes the vagina gets kind of sore. Those ovaries get kinda toe'd up. I check it. I'm the doctor. I'm a gyn-o-colo-gist. I do the checking myself. I take my glove, my lovely silk hand. I have little tests. You take a little earwax and put it up inside her, and if she hollers, she's got VD. That's most classy pimps who know what they're doing. When I turn a girl out, I turn her out after a physical. If the girl's on her period, and I really need my money, I tell her to get a sponge and plug it up.

EFO: Did you make 'em get an HIV test?

RN: They didn't have [the AIDS crisis] back in my day. I would if I started pimping again—hell, yeah!

EFO: Would most pimps?

RN: Nah.

EFO: When showing a new girl the ropes, do you tell her to wear a condom?

RN: They always keep a purse full of con-doms. I also teach 'em to take the trick to the bathroom and milk 'em [tug on their cock]. If any puss comes out, that means they got something. I tell them to run their fingers through his hair to inspect them for crabs. She tries it all out on me [first].

EFO: What's the biggest rule of etiquette among pimps?

RN: Client confidentiality! I can't break the code of silence.

RON'S 10 RULES OF PIMPIN'

1. Pimping ain't easy, but somebody got to do it.

2. Two for the room, ten for the cock. (Doesn't account for inflation, but you get the idea.)

3. The pimp's got to dress to impress.

4. The pimp's gotta be pretty in the face, cute in the waist, and drive a Fleetwood Cadillac.

5. Put your ten toes down in the town. (Translation: Hit the pavement, bitch, and make me some money.)

6. Always finance before romance. (Don't start porking one of your girls until she brings home the bacon.)

7. You've got to have hair fried and dyed and laid to the side. (A pimp must be properly groomed—no nappy hair!)

8. You got to fuck a bitch from side to side. (Be the super mack daddy to your ho, and she'll deliver the dough.)

9. My girl's got to sell her pussy, rob, steal and kill for me.

10. You gotta know the game from A to Z.

PART II

That was the most fun I've ever had without laughing.

—*Woody Allen*

When one thinks of traditional vice, sex is right in there with boozing, smoking, and gambling. A cornerstone of sin and debauchery, the topic would have been quite at home in Part I. But we decided to give sex its very own section because, hell, no one ever seems to get enough of it or complains about hearing too much about it. Besides, they say sex sells.

We've steered away from more conventional subjects: for instance, you won't find a suggested number of dates before making your first move. We'll leave that to more prissy protocol manifestos, and stick to the juicier, less-talked-about aspects of sex and dating. If it's not covered here, go ask your older brother or sister.

As to our methodology, all conclusions are based on data gathered from a wide range of interviews, from industry insiders (adult film stars, phone sexers, condom peddlers, "spooge booth" operators) to horny married couples to swinging singles trolling for noncommittal evenings of passion. In short, anyone who likes to screw qualified as a "sexpert." The following information represents a consensus of their opinions.

Basic Sex

THE DO'S & DON'TS OF DOING IT

Do you mind if I smoke while you eat?
—Linda Lovelace in *Deep Throat*

In *Deep Throat*, Linda Lovelace does her best to be polite and considerate toward the eager but ultimately uninspiring gentleman between her legs. Finding the request perfectly reasonable, the man says "sure" and happily resumes his futile attempts to pleasure her.

But that's the movies. In real life, Linda's innocent but ultimately telling inquiry might not be so appropriate. Or would it?

This section is devoted to such lofty debates: what you should or shouldn't say to your partner before, during or after; minimum requirements in terms of pleasing him or her; how to broach topics like sexual history or kinky fantasies, and so forth. You'll notice that the bulk of our recommendations are directed toward men because, well, women generally exercise a degree of common sense in the etiquette department, while men have a propensity toward acting like selfish, inconsiderate pricks. In addition, we've focused our attention on hetero sex rather than gay sex, though many of the rules cross over.

SAFETY FIRST

Polite sex is always safe sex.

This isn't a safe sex manual, so we won't belabor the point, but the first rule of sex etiquette is to be responsible to yourself and your partner, whether that means using discretion, wearing a condom, using birth control pills, or refraining from going home with that human petri dish you met at the bar. Keep current on HIV tests (every year or so), and if it feels like you're pissing razor blades, go see a doctor before passing that burning sensation on to a friend.

If you have an STD, please disclose it to your partner *beforehand*. It's always the right thing to do, and in certain states, it's the legal thing to do.

Mark the Pharmacist on "Safety" Issues

These days, condoms are sold freely in displays at drugstores and many markets, and there is certainly no stigma attached to buying them. Hell, having condoms in your shopping cart is like a badge of honor. Not so in decades past, as we learn from Mark, a retired pharmacist who pushed prophylactics in the 1950s, '60s and '70s. Here's what he had to say.

Back then, condoms were not a self-service item. They were usually kept in little drawers behind the counter in a sort of hush-hush fashion. We'd carry like two or three different brands, and they'd come in packs of three, twelve, or gross—twelve dozen. Generally, people would walk in the door, sort of like they were going to rob the drugstore, looking to the left, then to the right, tippy-toeing up to my counter, and in a very hushed voice, say "Pssst." And then they would either mumble something that you couldn't understand or use various, vague terms like, "Give me three 'safeties' " or "three rubbers." They'd never ask for prophylactics. Ninety-seven percent of the people who bought them were males, while the occasional woman customer would almost always say, "I'm getting these for a friend."

People would do all sorts of things because of their embarrassment. One would be to just buy a number of items, I'm getting ready to ring them up, and then out of the blue, they'd very quickly ask you to throw in a pack of condoms. With couples, the gal would disconnect from the guy, drift around, browsing, while the guy made the purchase. Sometimes people would just stand there, and look over to where you kept them, and you would have to figure out what they wanted. I'd put them in a bag—you'd never sell them without putting them in a bag.

I worked for a drug chain, like a Thrifty or a Sav-On, and we'd get commissions for condom sales. It was a very high-profit item. So you were encouraged to sell larger quantities to people, telling them that buying a "gross" was a substantial savings. That's a lot of condoms. I remember that a gentleman in the older age bracket came in and asked for three, and I did my pitch, reminding him about the bulk savings, and he said, "Sonny, I'll be dead before I use up a gross."

If you find out after the fact that you've caught one of those sexually transmitted buggers, you must alert anyone you might have exposed *and* anyone who may have given it to you, whether that means your monogamous lover, a few liaisons on the sly, or half the phone book. In other words, *all* recent partners—potential STD givers and receivers. Believe it or not, the person who transmitted it to you might not be aware that they are infected, and it's your duty to fill them in. For instance, a woman who has no noticeable symptoms herself can pass warts on to a guy. She might have no clue, and if she neglects the condition, it can lead to cervical cancer.

SEXUAL HISTORY

What you don't know *can* hurt you. Ask. It's cool to be straightforward. If you're going to be bumping uglies and putting parts in each other's mouths, a little intimate conversation shouldn't be all that difficult.

Ideally the subject of sexual history with a potential partner is broached beforehand, in a pre-naked context. Answers tend to be less than trustworthy in the heat of the moment.

If you're ready for love but you're fresh out of gloves, and your partner reassures you, "Don't worry, I always use condoms, I'm always safe, this is an exception," assume that it's not an exception. If they're throwing caution to the wind with you, you can bet it's not the first time. Feel free to be insistent on protection, or just say "no." Anyone who is 100 percent disease-free should be appreciative of your caution. If they get insulted, fuck 'em (figuratively, of course).

In bed or out, you can open up a discussion about sexual history with a general question like, "Is there anything I should know about before we go here?" or "Have you been tested for HIV?"

If a potential partner asks that the two of you go in and get HIV tested together, or requests to see a copy of your negative test results, be grateful that he or she is so concerned, and bow to the request. It's their right, and you should oblige without putting up a fuss.

CONDOMANIA

Regardless of your gender, come dressed for the party. In an age of STD fever, both men and women need to be packing prophylactics.

If you're uncomfortable about purchasing them, buy a number of items so that your lubricated three-pack isn't sitting alone in the shopping basket. It's a common practice that seems to cut down on the embarrassment.

Check the expiration date. Unlike yesterday's milk, an expired condom can leave you with a whole lot more than a stomachache.

Invest in a bottle of water-based lube—Vaseline or mineral oil can render a condom ineffective.

Consult your partner about allergies and irritations—for instance, some girls are allergic to latex condoms, or condoms with lube or nonoxynol-9. If you insist on using rubbers for blow jobs, get yourself some "Kiss of Mint" or keep a few "nonlubricated" on hand. Remember that porous "lambskin" rubbers feel great and help prevent pregnancy, but they don't do shit when it comes to HIV.

Of course, in a pinch, any rubber is better than no rubber.

BE CLEAN

No one likes a partner with a noxious odor, a discernable body film or crust, stanky breath, lice, crabs or fleas. Best to bathe before you boff.

BE SURE

Forcible entry is, of course, a definite no-no. Date rape accusations are quite fashionable these days, so make sure she's into it with a simple, direct question: "Do you want to?" If she's too wasted to give you a clear answer, refrain. Drunken ramblings do not constitute consent. Snoring is the mating call of the date rapist.

BE ATTENTIVE

While engaging in sex, it's best not to a) smoke, b) watch TV, c) make a grocery list, or d) count ceiling tiles. Such activities are liable to give your partner the impression that you're bored with their performance.

SIZE MATTERS

Probably more to guys than girls. Women are well aware of the fact that most men are sensitive about their equipment. Hence, unless she intends to be hurtful, she will never outwardly tell a man that his pee-pee is too pee-wee. In addition, she should never use descriptives like "cute," "adorable" or "my little friend" in reference to his genitalia.

Does a guy want to know about the guy before him with the huge porno pole? No.

Size queens with high standards should try to make an over-the-clothes assessment before the guy drops trou. At that point, it's easy enough to come up with an excuse without hurting his feelings.

If the man is simply below the level of acceptability, he should know enough to make up for it in other ways, whether that means working harder, investing in some tools, or taking his mouth down south. Remember: If you don't got the size, you'd better learn how to dive.

THE OFFICIAL EFO "HO" TRAVEL KIT

Condoms (three-pack)

Hair gel (for bed-head)

Alka-Seltzer/aspirin (for the hangover)

Scrub brush (Who knows what evil lurks under your nails!)

Hand sanitizer (kills germs on contact; good for all external areas)

35¢ (to call in late to work)

Cover-up stick (use as needed to cover up hickeys)

Quick bad breath relief (mouthwash, Tic Tacs, or gum)

Instant MemoryZapper (Who needs quality at 2:00 A.M.? Use on yourself or partner as needed)

Cologne/perfume (Who needs a shower?)

EFO "HO" KIT OPTIONALS:

Ace bandage—in case of injury

Mirror—to check for scratch marks

Handi wipes—good for stains in car or other miscellaneous goo marks

Febreze—cleans your clothes before someone else smells them

If the guy is a Magnum XXL, a woman can certainly ask him to "please be careful" without fear of hurting his feelings. Mr. Ed is probably used to such requests.

THE TWO-MINUTE RIDE
TO THE MOON

Guys: Relieving yourself too soon doesn't relieve you of obligations to take care of your partner. If you shoot your wad prematurely, don't make idle excuses, don't roll over and crash, and don't expect her to go far out of her way to get you all worked up again. It's not her responsibility; you've got to be self-sufficient. If you're too tired to get it up, lick her down.

Girls: After an overly succinct session, don't jump up, look at your watch and proclaim a new speed record. Be nice. Unless he's a real pig, the guy already feels bad enough. Instead, try to ease the situation with a little friendly banter.

"OH GOD, OH GOD,
I LOVE YOU!"

Everyone is in love when they're coming. Don't say it to a new partner. If someone says it to you, don't hold 'em to it.

We strongly recommend not calling out a) the wrong name, b) "Mommy," or c) "Daddy."

And . . . yes, it's okay to scream "Oh God!" even if you're an atheist—"Oh emptiness!" just doesn't have the same zing.

THE POSTCOITAL CUDDLE

Listen up, guys: Cuddling afterward is mandatory, even on a one-night stand. Exceptions: If you're in a moving vehicle or it's a cash-only transaction. Coming, rolling over and passing out is never acceptable, unless you're utterly wasted, in which case the girl might be relieved to have you off of her.

NO COMPARING
OR CONTRASTING

Egos can be fragile in the bedroom. Don't compare your lover's skill level, responsiveness, size, et cetera, to a past lover's. Guys, don't ask if you're the biggest or the best. It's a loaded question.

KNOW WHEN
TO CALL IT QUITS

Guys, if you're too drunk to rock 'n' roll, give up! Don't try all night! It's frustrating for everyone! Just pass out, and take care of business in the morning.

FAKING IT

Thou shalt not lie! Faking an "O" instills in your a partner a false sense of hope and standards, and it can come back to bite you in the ass if you plan on seeing that person again.

Faking it is really only acceptable if your partner is disposable, for example, a bad one-night stand when you're really not enjoying it anyway, want it to end, and just don't feel like investing the time and energy to discuss it. Moan, contort your face, and collapse.

ORAL PLEASURE FOR MEN
(POLISHING THE CLOWN)

Guys, don't beg for it, and don't demand it. Receiving fellatio is a privilege, not a right.

Respect the "gag" rule. That means don't ram it down her throat, or grab her head and hold it there. She's the driver; she's in control of the stick. Any thrusting should be gentle.

Let her know when you're going to climax. That way she can make an informed decision about whether or not she chooses to receive your mojo.

IMPLANTS: THANKS FOR THE MAMMARIES

Whether it's shape or magnitude that's affecting your self-esteem (or income), there is no shame in wanting to supersize your breasts. We talked to several women, doctors, and owners about purchasing, displaying and handling fake ta-ta's. Here's what they said.

BOOB BUYING

When looking for a doctor to do the job, it's best to get a referral. As with any doctor, word of mouth is better than the cheesy ad in the yellow pages. When you decide on the doc, feel free to ask as many questions as you'd like. It's also not uncommon to check your doctor's qualifications with the American Medical Association to make sure they're certified plastic surgeons, rather than general doctors performing the procedure.

Always invest in the best. A $3,000 estimate is a red flag that you've got the wrong doctor. Expect to pay $5,000—$6,000 for your new friends, or roughly $3,000 per boob.

Picking out your new boobs can be as easy as bringing in a *Playboy* and saying, "I want these!" The really important thing is to try to stay in proportion to your bod. If you're 5'1", don't go for a double-E cup, unless you're planning on going into the business (see "Strip Clubs" in Part I and "The Porn Star" in Part V). A good doctor will let you know what's too big, or too small; trust her/his judgment. And don't settle for silicone. They're dangerous. Saline ta-ta's are the safest.

After the surgery, be prepared for recovery time; it'll be about a month before they're ready for action.

If you plan to have kids, do it before you get your surgery, thus avoiding the danger of giving the child lockjaw.

NEW KIDS ON THE BLOCK

Once they heal, it's business as usual. Have your lover squeeze 'em, suck 'em, and bounce 'em about; they're yours to enjoy. They're not going to pop or rupture from use. You can expect them to be harder than the original breasts, but if you find them getting really hard, you may want to see your doctor.

Many women find themselves becoming exhibitionists with their new synthetic enhancements. But never show your new breasts in a public place, unless you're getting paid to do it.

If you are a friend (or are becoming a new friend) of someone with freshly made mams, you can ask to see, even touch. If you're not a friend, it's considered bad form to ask if a woman's breasts are real. If she brings it up, feel free to tell her "nice work."

FINALLY . . .

You may want to warn friends and family beforehand about your jump from a medium to XL. Family dinner with the folks is one of the few places your newly magnified mammaries might be unwelcome guests.

Don't be a wuss about kissing her afterward. It's a nice way to equalize the exchange of bodily fluids. It also makes you look progressive.

Gals, watch the teeth. And, if possible, try to swallow. But if you're just not in the mood, try not to spit it out in front of him. Excuse yourself and go to the bathroom. Rinse or flush if necessary.

ORAL PLEASURE FOR WOMEN (LICKING THE CAT)

Gals, receiving cunnilingus is generally a woman's right, not a privilege . . . unless of course you're on the rag, at which time it is *definitely* a privilege.

A man's stubbly facial hair can be hard on the skins. Excercise due caution, fellas.

If a man goes down on a woman and she accidentally farts, should the guy a) pinch his nose and yell, "Pee-uuu! Grab the gas mask!," b) ignore it, or c) add a little levity to make her feel comfortable?

We say "c."

BATTERY-OPERATED

A new lover might be turned off by a dildo or motorized accessory that's been used on your previous partners. A brand-new "foreign object of penetration," freshly unwrapped from a hermetically sealed, plastic shrink-wrapped package, is always preferable to some stained, crusty item that you whip out from under the bed.

But purchasing new equipment for each new romantic entanglement isn't necessarily realistic or cost-effective, particularly if you have a high turnover rate. In fact, most vibrators *will* outlast most relationships. You wouldn't throw out your bed, would you? Just remember to scrub all tools and instruments, along with their various heads and attachments, with soap and water after each use. In addition, it's not unheard of to sheath a dildo with a condom.

If the gal wants or needs more and the guy just isn't up to it, or she just needs additional help to get off, it's perfectly acceptable for her to pull out her vibrator. Of course, she should be sensitive to the fact that some men might be uncomfy and insecure about it. Tact dictates that she doesn't just roll over, plug it in, and go to town on her own. She should invite the guy to be a part of it.

THE ONE-NIGHT STAND

Etiquette doesn't have to go out the window entirely (see "The Post-coital Cuddle" earlier in this section), but expectations should be greatly diminished on both ends.

Go to their place if possible. That way, your pad is not soiled, and you can leave whenever you want.

If you've agreed beforehand that it's a one-time thing, respect that. Don't track the person down in the phone book and give 'em a ring at home—you don't know who's there, and you could really interrupt his or her life.

When it comes to casual sex, sleeping over is not a given. You can ask, but don't assume that it's okay.

MÉNAGE À TROIS

Always a thorny subject. If it's a male–female couple pulling in an extra gal, the female picks the extra woman. If the male seems too eager, it might make his mate feel insecure, inadequate, etc. Of course, the male must approve of the extra woman.

If it's a male–female couple pulling in an extra guy, the female *still* gets to pick, again with the male's approval.

It's like the "advise and consent" rule between the President and the Senate. The selection comes from the woman, but the consent comes from the man. If you're unclear as to the rationale, we suggest you consult a psychology book on the differences between men and women. (Also see "Swinging" later in Part II)

CHEATING

Of course, you *shouldn't* cheat. But if you do, should you always disclose? If you really love your spouse, boyfriend or girlfriend, should you tell them about that time you went astray and acted on your temptations? Should you risk the relationship that's really important to you, and risk hurting the person you care about very deeply—simply to assuage your own sense of guilt? In an intimate relationship, should truth and honesty be placed above all else?

MAKING THE BREAK

A Heartbreaking Femme Fatale on "The Dump"

Cuttin' 'em loose. Kickin' 'em to the curb. Dumping their sorry ass. No matter how you phrase it, it boils down to the same thing. Person "A" rejecting person "B." It always hurts, and, as they say, it's always hard to do. So to make it easier, we consulted an expert: Sandy P., a free-spirited young New York actress who believes that variety is the spice of life. After eight marriage proposals, two suicide threats, and a trail of broken hearts, she's mastered the "art of the dump." Here are her suggestions, which we think apply to both sexes.

1. Never in a note. Never on the phone. That's just cowardly.

2. Go to them, don't make them come to you—common courtesy. You don't want a sniveling ex-lover lingering at your house for hours, begging and trying to work it out. That's never any fun. I prefer to do it at their place of residence—their turf. They don't have to drive anywhere afterward, they've got their phone to call friends for support, and their own bathroom if they have to heave.

3. Not at a bar, particularly a bar they have to drive to. It's irresponsible—you don't want an alcohol-related accident on your conscience.

4. Be compassionate, but be swift and resolute. Think about what you're going to say ahead of time. And no waffling. Make it as quick and painless as possible. In centuries past, the executioner always sharpened his blade before the head went on the chopping block.

5. Be honest, up to a point. In other words, you don't have to tell them everything. I try to make it about me, not them—"You're great, but the timing's off," "I'm just not ready for a commitment," etc.—anything to give their fragile egos a break. Of course, how much you disclose is highly subjective. As a rule, I tend to keep things like deficiency in the sack or bad hygiene under my hat.

6. The good-bye screw is always a temptation. Men seem to want it no matter what, even if you've just put their heart through a meat grinder. Avoid if possible. It can give a false sense of hope, and it might make you question what you're doing, especially if they're really good.

7. Bring all their stuff that's accumulated at your house with you at the time of the breakup, including keys. Ask for your stuff back on the spot. Prevents that icky, uncomfortable second meeting. Also guarantees that he or she doesn't burn your stuff or chuck it out the window. This is another good argument for rule number 2.

8. All naughty pix or tapes should either be destroyed or confiscated. You never know where they can end up.

9. Dropping them a short 'n' sweet note or a message on voice mail to check in, to let them know you're thinking about them, is a nice gesture. And they might not talk as much shit about you.

Fuck if we know. Just make sure that if you cheat, you do it safely. You're jeopardizing the health of your partner as well as your own.

If you suspect a mate of cheating, don't make ultimatums or threats of breaking up, impending emotional breakdown, suicide, castration, etc., as this will provide little incentive for your partner to let the cat out of the bag. Instead, let him or her know that it's okay to be honest, that you'll do your best to work it out, that you just need to know, and that they'll get points for telling the truth. In such a reassuring climate, the cheater should 'fess up to the sin.

Then dump his or her two-timing ass.

" E X "   S E X

During a dry spell, it's perfectly acceptable to recycle your exes—sex with an ex is better than no sex at all.

When it comes to casual shagging, though, close acquaintances and immediate relatives of your ex are usually off-limits. There are just too many other fish in the sea. At the very least, try to wait until he or she has moved on to another serious relationship before you start making moves on best friends, siblings, etc.

J A I L B A I T

Just say "No!" for a number of reasons. They can get attached too easily—and you can get prosecuted. Besides, there isn't that much of a difference between a sixteen-year-old and an eighteen-year-old. The other option is to go to a county or state or even country that does permit sex with sixteen-year-olds. But we (and our publishing company's legal department) can't condone sex with minors. Bad, bad, bad.

Sex with *coal miners*, as long as they're of legal age, is perfectly acceptable.

You should check up on your new lover's age if he or she a) has an 11:00 P.M. curfew, b) is driving his or her parents' car, c) carries a book bag, or d) invites you to the prom. A tactful approach is to take him or her to a bar or club with a strict door policy, and put the onus on the barkeep or bouncer to figure it out.

Ignorance is not an excuse, at least in the eyes of the law. But if you do your best to ascertain whether a new partner is of age, and they really bamboozle you with, say, a fake ID, it generally does provide a basis for defense against any nasty statutory rape charge that might pop up later.

VIAGRA

Let your partner know in advance that they're in for a very, *very* long ride. Make sure you both pee beforehand, and pack accordingly: a large jar of lube, and lots of water to combat dehydration.

Leave the nitrous poppers behind. Poppers and Viagra don't mix.

Finally, consult your doctor before using it. Viagra can be hard on the body, especially if you're on some other nitro-based medication, and dying on your partner is really selfish and uncool.

FROM SEX SHOPS TO CYBERING

Annual porn revenues equal the gross national product of many a Third World nation.

—Hustler

For incredible buttery nipples, click here!
—Online solicitation for adult website

This section deals with the business of sex—the sex found outside
the bedroom, the sex that's prepackaged, on public display, and
available for mass consumption.

We start with X-rated theaters and the different tiers of smut
shops. Remember, this isn't Wal-Mart, and the rules of engagement
with the merchant and fellow patrons can be tricky.

We also delve into phone sex and cybersex. In this era of STDs
running rampant, both have become popular options for getting off,
raking in combined profits in the neighborhood of $1 billion in the
United States alone. Phone sex has been around for quite some time,
and has become a corporately organized enterprise with prescribed
modes of conduct for those on both ends of the line. Meanwhile,
"cybering"—essentially phone sex with a computer—is the latest rage,
and cyberporn has become the single most profitable business on the
web. In the age of sex.com, any modern-thinking outlaw will find the
following information invaluable.

SEX SHOPS

Sex shops range from smutty bookstores with "spooge booths" to
higher-end retailers specializing in erotic tools, toys, and garments. The sleazier the establishment, the more you can get away
with, but we've provided some guidelines of model behavior.

Not a Meat Market

Nicer erotica shops—The Pleasure Chest in Hollywood, New York's DV8, for example—are for shopping, not cruising. Don't approach other customers, offering unsolicited advice about the various tools and toys as a pretense to flirt.

Lower-brow shops, particularly "mop shops" with private XXX video screening booths, may be more tolerant of such behavior.

Most sex shop employees dig sex, and a little flirting is okay. But tread lightly, be cool, and keep it appropriate. Don't assume an employee is easy or kinky.

Moreover, entrance does not automatically give you license to lay lurid details of your sex life and fantasies on a sales associate. Some might be cool about you airing dirty details, but others may not want to hear it, particularly if you're a real creep (you know who you are).

Anonymity, Please

If you spot someone you know at a sex shop, think twice before approaching them. It might be a naughty little hobby they'd prefer to keep secret.

Stupid Questions

If you have genuine questions about the merchandise, don't be inhibited to ask a store associate, but be specific. You look stupid asking something like: "I have this girlfriend, and I want to rock her world. What should I buy?" Do some homework ahead of time. What color do you want? Size? Texture? Do you want it to vibrate?

Another popular but very ignorant question: "Is this a gay store? Where's the straight stuff?" Don't be square: Creative sex and sex toys are fun for all orientations.

Sizing Up a Ring

You cannot try on a cock ring before purchasing it to see if it's too small. And you can't test out a dildo to see if it's too big. Bring your size requirements in with you.

You can't try out the whips. It's a safety issue. You could hit another customer in the eye. You can, however, sample a paddle, just not too zealously. You can also try on a strap-on over your clothes, either in plain view or in the dressing rooms, as long as you keep it hygienic.

Some erotic accessory stores will only allow one person in a dressing room at a time.

No Playing with the Merchandise

Be considerate of other patrons. Sex stores hate it when drunk college kids come in on a weekend night, laughing and making fun of the dildos. A serious shopper might feel uncomfortable about buying "The Big Plunge Play Set" if you're jeering at it.

Please refrain from the following escapades, which have all been overdone, and long ago ceased to be funny:

- Sword-fighting with the dildos.
- Letting the dildo hang out of the fly of your pants.
- Penetrating the blow-up dolls.
- Juggling the Ben Wa balls.

Window-Shopping

Just because you walk through the door doesn't mean you have to buy something. No pressure. "Novelty" treks—like going into a sex shop with a date just to be wild and wacky—are fine, as long as you explore rather than ogle. Again, the key is to be respectful of other shoppers.

Looking for a part-time job? A gig with flexible hours and the option to work at home? Try phone sex. Here are some helpful hints to help you become a smooth operator.

1. Talk. As much as possible. For as long as possible. Even if the caller is silent, it's your job to keep him or her on the line and rack up those costly minutes. Go slowly, with as much teasing and verbal "foreplay" as possible, to get more buck for your bang.

2. If you're working out of your house, playing with yourself is a great way to add an element of realism to your dialogue. But it's perfectly acceptable to mop the floor, do your nails, pay your bills, etc., as long as you do it quietly, without interrupting the caller's fantasy.

3. Don't eat on the phone or chew gum. And don't fall asleep on the job.

No Returns

Unless your motorized accessory has some sort of manufacturer's defect, don't expect to be allowed to return or exchange it. Ditto for dildos or any other object of penetration that's no longer in its hermetically sealed packaging.

4. Don't hang up, even if a guy is venturing into forbidden phone sex territory (such as rape). Generally, calls are fielded and redirected by an intermediary operator by way of a special "bridge." It's their job to screen and disconnect. If you hang up, you might disconnect all the other calls being bridged through the same system.

5. If a caller asks for a specific person who doesn't happen to be working at the time, it's cool to field the call. Most services pay their employees hourly, so there's usually no major competition for clientele.

6. Be mindful of customer service. Many phone sex companies encourage their employees to keep a log or diary about their callers—their age, appearance, what they like. It makes the caller feel special, and adds to the fantasy. You might also want to set up a P.O. box so that lonely clients can send you mail.

7. Never give your real full name, address, or phone number, though some phone sex operators use their real first name. And never ever ever agree to meet one of your callers, no matter how nice and normal their voice sounds. Anyone getting off via Pac Bell clearly isn't "normal."

No Jerking

Only the sleaziest of stores will tolerate someone masturbating by the book rack. If public pudpulling is your thing, try a "spooge booth" or "mop booth."

S P O O G E B O O T H S

Found in accessory shops and dirty bookstores, a spooge booth can be a private cubicle or stall where you can watch XXX movies, or where a curtain goes up to expose one or more strippers behind a Plexiglas window, who chat with you or dance about provocatively.

Often, posted signs will say "ONE PERSON IN BOOTH ONLY" so as to prevent a couple from getting down on store property. Sometimes this rule is enforced, sometimes it's not. Depends on the store and the hour of the day.

A decent store will have a paper towel dispenser located near the booths. Use the towels to open the door of a booth without touching it (who knows whose hands have been on the handle) and to remove any sticky residue that might be on your own hands.

If you're cruising to trick with someone at a spooge booth, glory hole, or gay bathhouse, asking someone's name can be taboo.

Generally, these dens of iniquity are about anonymity. You're far more likely to leave with something contagious than with a soul mate.

Don't ask spooge booth patrons if you can interview them for a book. We discovered they don't like that.

A NIGHT AT THE THEATER

Porn video has rendered the XXX porn film theater almost obsolete. Only a few of these once-prominent institutions of smut have been left standing.

Some are recognized pick-up spots, generally gay pick-up spots, termed "ant farms" because of all the people shuffling from row to row looking for action.

If you're there to watch the flick, it's supposed to be a silent viewing experience—hootin' and hollerin' at the screen, screaming "Go! Go!" and cheering for the leading man or woman is not appropriate.

Often, laws against whacking off in a dark XXX theater are not enforced, and no one will say anything if you get busy. But you never know. Just ask Pee-Wee Herman.

RINGING YOUR BELL WITH "976"

Feeling alone? In the mood for a little friendly conversation? Well, you can dial up Mr. or Ms. Right right now! Just grab your local weekly newspaper and flip to the back, where you'll find tons of phone sexers who are standing by to help you ring your bell.

Some phone sex services charge you directly through your phone bill ("900" and "976" numbers); others require a credit card. Most sex talkers work through a service of some sort: either they're working in cubicles in an office, or an intermediary switchboard operator has fielded your 900 call and has redirected it to their home phone via a special "bridge."

You're supposed to be a legal adult to partake in phone sex, but for the most part, anyone with a phone or credit card number can call in for love.

Specific Rules for the Caller

When you dial up, we suggest not using your real full name, or giving out your real address. Calls may be monitored by the silent intermediary operator—you just never know who's listening.

Once introductions are made, a caller need not be shy about jumping directly into his fantasy. If a guy asks, "Do you have big boobs?" the woman on the other end knows enough to say, "Why yes, they're huge." Or the caller might simply begin detailing a fantasy, while the callee fans the flames of passion: "I want to be in a threesome right now." "That sounds great. I'll be in the middle, touching both of you."

You can call up by yourself, or with a friend or lover. You can be on an office phone, a cell phone or speakerphone. They don't care. It's your dime.

It's perfectly acceptable for a repeat caller to request a specific callee. On the other hand, don't feel compelled to be faithful. Most phone sex employees are paid hourly, not per call or by commission.

Phone sex is kind of like a therapy session without the time limit: you can talk about whatever you want, or you can choose to be silent. Describe any fantasy that tickles your fancy, as graphically as you like, but bear in mind that if you're detailing a scenario that's overly violent ("I want to rape you"), you run the risk of being disconnected by the intermediary operator, who randomly checks in to the various conversations. The operator is the one who decides if a caller is going too far. At times, the callee might try to coax a distasteful fantasy into a different, more acceptable direction: "I don't want to talk about that, it doesn't turn me on. What if we talk about this instead?" Other times, the callee will just roll with your fantasy, no matter how heinous. Again, it's your dime.

Ask them too many questions about their rate of pay, the company they work for, and other details that might make interesting material in a book, and you'll be disconnected.

Feel free to come as quickly as you like. Time is money, and, like we said before, it's your dime.

If the callee has done a good job arousing you, always say "Thank you" before hanging up. It's just common courtesy.

CYBERSEX: "TURN ME ON, I'M A SEX MACHINE"

Between singles chat rooms and "cybering" (online screwing), XXX websites and cyber-teleconferencing, your hard drive is a veritable sex machine, a "pornocupia" of naughty fun capable of bringing your fantasies onto your screen and into your home with total anonymity.

Not only that, it's pure fantasy. You can add three inches to your height or length, ten years to your age, or $100K to your income. Janitors can become lawyers. An A cup can swell to a C cup. You can also switch your gender or sexual orientation. Just remember that your chatmates can do the same.

In short, when it comes to online hookups, there isn't a high premium placed on truth and honesty. It's one of the few realms where misrepresentation and an aptitude for creative lying are accepted, condoned and appreciated.

Cybering 101

Want to pop your cyber-cherry? Start with your online "profile," the personal fact sheet that other members of your online service can access to find out more about you. We suggest you do not give your real address and phone number. Feel free to be totally honest about your age, occupation, hobbies, etc. . . . unless you're a totally boring loser, in which case you should lie and tailor your profile to the kind of person you want to attract. Want to meet a guy with a hot bod? Say you're an aerobics instructor. Want an intellectual chick? With one swipe of the keys, you can become an art professor with a Ph.D. Then add a lascivious twist to your profile, just to let the cyber-world at large know that you're open and available.

Next, go to a singles chat room. A room entitled something like "Looking for Romance" or "Young and Lusty" will fit the bill. Traffic is highest on weekend nights after bars and clubs close, when unlucky, lonely or just plain horny people are trolling cyberspace for companionship.

People in a chat room will frequently ask for an "age/sex" check, or an "age/sex/location" check, in which case the other guests in the room respond with something like "19/M/Los Angeles." Or, if you're looking for something specific, you can say, "Any 18+/F in here?"

SWOLLEN IN CYBERSPACE

We took a little trek into a singles chat room, where we hooked up with a hot thirtysomething blonde, took off to our own private chat room, and conducted a little hands-on research about "cybering."

EFO: Do you regularly meet people via chat rooms?

Sexy69: Yeah!

EFO: So, is there any protocol, or rules of etiquette—do's and don'ts that you can fill me in on? I'm authoring a book—sort of like *The Preppie Handbook*, but about sins and subcultures. Working on the sex chapter, and I thought I'd include stuff on cybersex, cyber pick-ups.

Sexy69: Have you ever tried it?

EFO: I've never "cybered."

Sexy69: Don't knock it 'til you try it. I'm 32 and blond.

EFO: How do I know you're not lying?

Sexy69: Check my profile.

EFO: But can't a profile be totally fabricated? And, is it cool to lie when trying to meet someone to "cyber"?

Sexy69: I prefer the honest route.

EFO: Should you not cyber with an underage person, or does it matter?

Sexy69: Pretty much anything goes, but I wouldn't.

EFO: Is there any way to check if someone is lying about age or gender?

Sexy69: No, unless you talk to someone long enough to catch them lying.

EFO: Do most chatters try to get to know someone before "cybering"? Are there any taboos—things you shouldn't do?

Sexy69: Anything goes!!!

EFO: If you meet someone in a chat room and "instant mail" them, is it uncool to keep their e-mail address and contact them at another time?

Sexy69: No, but use your discretion.

EFO: When's the last time you cybered?

Sexy69: Months ago, can't really find the right one!

EFO: What do you look for?

Sexy69: I don't really know, it just happens.

EFO: I like a woman with lots of verbs and capital letters, personally.

Sexy69: What do you mean?

EFO: Bad cyber joke, I guess. Trying to be witty.

Sexy69: Okay, I thought I'd have to do an age/sex check on you!

EFO: Well, for the record, 32, male, straight. Sexy—when you're chatting, do you get turned on?

Sexy69: Sometimes.

EFO: I am right now. No idea what you look like, who you are, but I am excited.

Sexy69: Me too.

EFO: What DO you look like?

Sexy69: 5'7", blond hair, blue eyes. You?

EFO: 5'6", green eyes, brown hair—very short right now, just had it hacked off.

Sexy69: Mine is long.

EFO: What are you wearing right now?

Sexy69: Nothing, it's almost 3:30 A.M.!

EFO: What do you smell like? Any particular perfume?

Sexy69: Calvin Klein. You?

EFO: No cologne. Never been a big fan of it. My penis is starting to swell.

Sexy69: Mine too!

EFO: Your penis is swelling?

Sexy69: Yeah, it's huge! I can't keep my hands off of it!

EFO: Oops, I thought you were a woman!

Sexy69: Dumbass! Very funny. I thought I told you.

EFO: I must not have been paying attention. Kind of a shock that you have a dick! I might just have to use this little exchange in my book—changing the cyber handles, of course, to protect the innocent.

Some people will brazenly type in something like: "25/M wants to cyber with hot 18+/F." Others might ask a specific guest in the room what they're wearing. It's not rude to be so forward, but it can be construed as desperate.

We suggest getting involved in the communal conversation. Be effervescent. Be original and witty. Keep a dictionary and a book of famous quotes close by for easy reference. If someone else's words of wit catch your attention, address him or her directly and start your own little conversation. You can ask them for an age/sex check. You can also pull up someone's profile to find out more about him or her, or at least what they want you to find out.

No online cock-blocking! If two chatters seem to be making a really nice connection, don't butt into their conversation.

If someone interests you enough, send them a private "instant message" or invite them into a "private room," where the two of you can get to know one another one on one. After a while, asking them what they are wearing, what they smell like, etc., is a good segue into sex talk.

Be creative. And accurate. The best cyber-lover has a way with words and is a proficient typist—preferably with one hand.

After you're both done, no cuddling or coddling about the quality of performance is necessary. And there's no need to keep in touch—you can dot.com and go, so to speak, with no worries about commitment, disease or what your friends will think. Just wipe off the keyboard and hit the "Shut Down" command.

If someone you're not interested in sends you an instant message or extends an invitation to chat privately, simply tell them, "No thank you, I'm not interested." It's as quick and painless as the click of a button (or two or three keystrokes).

If someone you solicit voices a lack of interest, leave 'em alone. Nobody likes a cyber-stalker.

Netting a Lover in the Flesh

Some people cruise local chat rooms in the hopes of actually getting a live, in-the-flesh date. Here's a quickie guide to the protocol.

First off, remember all that stuff we said about lying about yourself? Please disregard. If you're taking your cyber affair into the real world, the rules change. Clear up any drastic inaccuracies on your profile before you meet, as he or she will be extremely disappointed (and pissed off) when they show up and discover that their hot, twentysomething cyber-babe is really a pimply-faced, prepubescent troll. Any major breach of honesty could end the date immediately.

More important, be careful. We can't emphasize this enough. Maintain barriers. Keep your guard up. Give personal information out very slowly and discreetly. Carefully move from the computer to the phone. When you finally meet for the first time, make it at a well-populated public place. If you have any doubts, check out the grisly movie *Strangeland*, about a small-town cyber-predator on a rampage.

www.smut.com

Anyone with e-mail knows about the thousands and thousands of adult websites available to the public.

Before they let you in to see the goods, most will make you read a brief waiver, in which you agree that you are of legal porn-viewing age, and that explicit Internet material is legal in your area. If you say you're underage, your entrance will be denied. That's the responsibility of the site, at least in the United States. Many sites demand a more stringent "adult check" that requires a credit card number.

Most sites will entice Net surfers with offers of free XXX pix, free XXX video links, free XXX everything. Just remember: Nothing is really free. They'll let you preview a few photos as a tease, but a solicitation for a paid membership is never far behind. If you sign up, they give you a password that acts as the keys to the kingdom for a designated amount of time. Most sites are month to month.

Be careful about giving your credit card over the Internet. As with all online commerce, make sure that the site is "secure," and that your information can't be intercepted by a third party.

A good site will charge your credit card discreetly, under a generic name or harmless abbreviation, so that your wife, husband or parents won't know what you're paying for.

The Internet is far less rigid than other porn mediums in terms of restrictions about content, largely because the material comes from all corners of the world, where laws vary greatly. Online fisting may be illegal in the United States, but the website based out of Amsterdam can make those painful photos available to you. Ultimately, your hosting service is responsible for keeping content legal, so don't stress about checking out the wrong stuff.

Child porn is an exception, and we strongly suggest that you steer clear of it. The U.S. government is very strict about this, and to patronize sites promising underage kids is criminal—kind of like patronizing a prostitute. Some servers and government agencies have even set up sting sites. Log on just for curiosity's sake, and you might receive a mean note from AOL, the FCC or the FBI. Just keep out.

Porn teleconferencing and video streaming let you chat live with the naked people on your screen. You can ask them to bend over, pleasure each other—all sorts of great stuff. When you first log on, it's quite standard to ask the girl or guy on your screen to wave or jump up and down, just to prove that it's really live. Threatening or overly abusive conferences might get you disconnected, but for the most part, it's no-holds-barred. Type your mind.

Alternative Sex

A WALK ON THE WILD SIDE

I've tried several varieties of sex. The conventional position makes me claustrophobic and the others give me stiff neck or lockjaw.

—Tallulah Bankhead

I enjoy getting dressed as a Barbie doll.

—Vanna White

If missionary is getting old, "vanilla sex" leaves a plain taste in your mouth, or you just have an urge to inject your lovemaking with something new, something "alternative," this is the section for you.

We're not suggesting you start engaging in "blood sports" or flinging excrement at your lover. We're talking about simple, entry-level S/M role-playing and other fetishes that can add a little color and variety to your love life. These days, fooling around with a paddle, whip, or cuffs, donning a dog collar or licking a woman's stiletto high heel are hardly taboo or deviant. In fact, for a sizeable chunk of mainstream society, they're simply an adventurous bedroom detour or part-time hobby. Not only is the paraphernalia highly accessible, but initiates can also find tons of books, magazines and websites devoted to virtually every kink under the sun. They can even set up an appointment for private instruction with a pro (see "The Dominatrix" in Part V). The important thing to keep in mind is this: Even at entry level, such activities should be enjoyed correctly and safely.

A dungeon of fantasies awaits. Enter with an open mind, and we'll give you a few lessons in etiquette you won't soon forget!

IT HURTS SO GOOD

There's a huge difference between naughty sex and S/M. Naughty sex is a spontaneous slap on the ass in the heat of the moment, or buying some fur-padded cuffs as a gag gift.

Real S/M is a calculated series of systematic, punishment-and-power role-playing, geared toward more of a mind-fuck than an actual fuck. It's the difference between improv and stand-up, and if that's your kink (leather face mask, the whips, etc.), *well, right on!* Bust out of the norm and break out the riding crop.

The key thing to remember is that it's largely about fantasy. While this crime-and-punishment "play" takes its name from the truly evil Marquis de Sade, modern S/M (not S&M) is based more on enjoying the titillation of a dark sexual fantasy than the sheer delight of torture (de Sade's main kink). In this sense, it's actually the slave (AKA "Sub," "bottom") rather than the master ("Dominatrix," "top") who controls the play—they tell you when to stop. The goal of the whole thing is to explore the boundaries between pleasure and pain, domination and enslavement, without doing any real damage.

And it ain't cheap. Be prepared to spend bucks on elaborate clothes and equipment. Etiquette demands that you not only play your part, but that you look the part to complete the aesthetic.

Safe, Sane and Consensual

Safe, sane and consensual is the mantra of the serious S/M crowd.

Practicing S/M safely refers to taking all proper precautions against STDs. If you're HIV-positive, bring that up first. Safety also includes proper handling of the whips and restraints. Remember: You could poke an eye out with that thing!

Because you're dealing with, frankly, torture devices, the sane rule demands that you not be under the influence of any substance that could impair your judgment or pain threshold: *Physician, know thyself.* "Sane" also means that you never play with someone who doesn't have a full deck. Bust out the ropes with a disturbed postal worker, and you're just asking for it.

Finally, consent to an S/M relationship is not only a rule of etiquette, but a rule of law. In all states, it's both bad form *and* illegal to hit your spouse without consent (even after the Super Bowl, even if they had it coming to them). If one partner is not into the idea, just don't do it. Know the expectations, rules and boundaries before you take out the cuffs.

Testing the Waters

If you've never done any S/M with your partner, it's best to talk it out before you reach for your new riding crop. Gauge if they're interested. Go rent *9 1/2 Weeks* and see if it turns 'em on. If it does, start exploring.

If not, either give up the idea or explore a different relationship.

If you're into the scene and want to find out if someone else is, feel free to drop a few mind bombs: "Have you read *The Story of O* or *The Reclaiming of Sleeping Beauty*?" If the answer is "yes," then you're going somewhere. If you need more info, drop insider terms like "vanilla sex" or "play" and see if they register.

It's never considered bad form to be direct with a question like, "Are you into S/M?" Just don't be surprised or angry if the answer is "no."

A good clue that someone's into the scene is if they're wearing any kind of collar with a ring on it, like a dog collar. It could be a fashion statement, but it's widely accepted among S/Mers as a signal that you're a Sub. If you wear a collar, don't be surprised if someone tries to yank your chain.

If you're feeling ballsy and want to ascertain your lover's interest in S/M play, just go for broke. Plant a note with your lover

Dr. X: The Back-Door Doctor

Sodomy has always been a delicate issue, legally, morally and physiologically. So we asked an expert in the field: Dr. X*, proctologist to the stars. With a client list boasting movie and music megastars and Hollywood up-and-comers of all orientations, Dr. X has seen it all, and he's more than a little concerned that our readers tread gently when it comes to back-door antics. Here's what he had to say . . .

Butt sex is generally not something you try the first time you go to bed with someone. I would recommend testing the waters first, particularly if the receiver is a novice. Warm up to it by rubbing or penetrating the area with your fingers during regular sex. Watch the fingernails, and please take off any rings that might catch.

If, after a discussion with your partner, you decide to go for it, make sure to use lots of lube, care, and caution. Always let the receiver back into it, and stop immediately if he or she is in too much pain. By the way, guys, if you're open-minded enough to let your girlfriend use a strap-on on you, buy a dildo that approximates the size of your own love muscle, rather than one of those pencil-sized deals. In other words, take it like a man. She does.

Once you go there, you stay there. No back and forth. After entering through a person's back door, you don't get to use the front entrance without cleansing—that's a big neon "Welcome" sign for infectious germs.

Finally, if you anticipate back-porch guests, do your best to move your bowels before hand. You don't want your partner to bump into anything brown.

*Anonymity requested

telling him or her to be showered, shaven, and in a sexy outfit at a given time of day, and then implement an entry-level fantasy. Just go slow, and don't go overboard with the restraints or spanking.

Vanilla Sex First

S/M is not always sexual. A number of people play without sex. But if sex is going to be part of it, a second prima facie rule of S/M is to start with "vanilla sex." Learn to crawl before you stand, learn to stand before you grovel at someone's feet. Remember, it's a long night. If things work out, you can try out the shackles later.

Communication

Find out what both you and your partner like. Sounds simple enough, but etiquette dictates that if you are to receive pleasure, you must reciprocate by pleasuring your partner (whatever that entails). And conversely, if you or your partner are not turned on by one or the other's kinks, lack of communication could lead to problems in the relationship.

Safe Words

To ensure your safety, make sure you have established a safe word that, when uttered, will alert your partner to cease any activity causing too much discomfort. "Stop!," "Ouch!," or "No!" don't work because they're part of the fun. Come up with something generic like "red," and when your partner says "red," stop what you're doing *immediately*.

It is a profound violation of S/M etiquette for the Dom to resent the Sub for using the safe word. The safe word exists to ensure that no one gets really hurt. A Dom is expected to be gracious and attentive to the slave, especially when the slave has reached his/her limits. If the Dom does not respect these limits, the Sub should start looking for a new master, or a cop.

Etiquette *after* the utterance of the safe word varies. Some use it as a signal to stop and move on to something else; others see it as a stop sign for the night. The choice is yours.

Marks

It's always best to outline in advance the areas on the body where you can and cannot leave marks. Etiquette dictates that you respect these zones. If, by chance, you do leave a mark in the wrong spot, apologize to your Sub and get him/her a turtleneck or cover-up stick.

Neighbors

Respect thy neighbors. If you love it loud, consider investing in some soundproofing. If not, keep it quiet or they'll call the cops, who may get the wrong idea if they find your mate bound and gagged.

The Quest for Dominance

You can never tell who's top/bottom until you get there. Maybe the boss likes being boss all the time; then again, maybe he might like to wear diapers on his off days. If it's a new relationship (or you're just testing this out), you can experiment, with each of you trying out the Sub and Dom roles. Comfort level will let you determine who's on top. If you're a Dom by nature, you may sometimes have to break in a new Sub. If you're a natural Sub but your partner is new to the scene, you may have to assume the role of Dom for the first few play sessions so that your future master can learn the ropes.

Practice, practice, practice! The Dom is expected to be a master of the tools, not the slave. The better your technique, the more pleasure you produce and the less likely the chance of injury. Never hit someone with something that you haven't tested out on yourself first. And test your instruments at different speeds so you can begin to gauge how it will feel in field use.

Once you bring your Sub into the mix, work with them to find out what they can and cannot take. Experiment with various toys to find out what you both like: hairbrush, cat 'o nines, paddles—there's always the right tool for the right job. Get some books on the subject and practice your strokes together: overhand, punching and backhand.

Hot Under the Collar

Many S/Mers use a collar to indicate when play begins. If you're the Sub, at any given time your Dom can place the collar on you, and you're obligated to obey . . . or face the whip!

The collar acts like the S/M marriage contract. Whether you keep this contract at all times is up to you. Obviously, if you're under the weather, the contract is open for negotiation. If your master is a good one, they will realize that you're not well and won't go there. Part of the fun of this contract, however, is that it keeps the Sub on their sexual toes at all times.

Obeying Your Master

Okay, so it's sort of half the fun to be bad. Heck, if you don't deserve a good beating, why be a Sub? It's a situational ethic. Depending upon your desires, you can either do as your Dom says (licking her/his boot, etc.), or you can refuse. Realize that if you disobey, you will be punished. *Thwap!!!*

But while your master is in charge of punishment, you, the Sub, are in control of the outcome. The irony of S/M is that ultimately, it's the Sub who can use the safe word and shut things down. It if hurts too much, good. But if it really hurts, use the safe word.

Playtime

Once the play begins, you must stay in character and not break the spirit of the scene. If you call each other Master and Slave, keep that up. You're acting out a role in an erotic masterpiece. Don't answer the phone, think about your job, or bring in anything that might wreck the mood.

Gag Me with a . . . Gag

When using any gag, the best etiquette is to make sure the material is clean and that the Sub can breathe well through the nose. Remember, a Sub cannot utter the safe word when gagged. A Dom is expected to instruct a gagged Sub how to invoke safety by some gesture, or through routine inquiry. The more restrained a Sub is—verbally, visually, physically—the greater the Dom's responsibility to monitor the Sub's limits.

Fashion Tips for Your First Fetish Ball

James Stone, organizer/promoter of L.A.'s annual Fetish Ball, among other fetish events, and one of the original founders of the city's notorious Club Fuck!, certainly knows the ins and outs of fetish fashion. The following are his helpful hints about leather, lace, latex and other "sin-thetics" of choice.

When in Rome . . .

No street clothes, please. It breaks the fantasy. Just throwing on a dog collar as a token and then wearing jeans and boots, or some other normal outfit, won't cut it either. It's a dead giveaway for a novice. Go all out. Let your hair down.

Old Standards . . .

For guys, a good pair of black leather jeans, no shirt is classic and easy to put together. For gals, rubber dresses and corsets never go out of style. Of late, the "pony girl" ensemble is pretty popular—bit in the mouth, attached to head apparatus with a plume for flourish.

Keep It Tight, But Keep the Cellulite Out of Sight. . . .

Baggy leather, rubber, or PVC doesn't cut it. Keep it tight, form-fitting and sexy. The idea is to look hot. Of course, if your belly is pouring over your painted-on pants or your back fat is squirting out of your itsy-bitsy corset, that's not much of a turn-on. The calorically-challenged might want to skip the really tight stuff and go for another look.

If You're Hung, Flaunt It . . .

Same goes for T&A. Merchandise those massive mammaries and bare those taut butt cheeks. Caveat: be mindful and respectful of the house rules with regard to exposure of genitalia. The police and the ABC are quite strict about nudity in places serving booze. At my events, girls have to cover their nipples with electrical tape or pasties; guys have to package their jewels in some sort of little thong or bikini undies. Cover up—it's the law.

Don't Mix and Match . . .

This is a personal thing, and some might disagree, but I'm a purist. If you're sporting leather, wear all leather. If you're in rubber stick to rubber. No leather pants with a latex shirt, for example. Mixing leather, textiles and synthetic fabrics is, in my opinion, something to avoid. It's like wearing a brown belt with black loafers.

Accessorize Properly . . .

Wearing whips, paddles or cuffs attached to your belt is too forced and screams "novice." Generally, no flogging is allowed in public, but the rule is not rigidly enforced. If you bring cuffs, also bring the key. Calling in a locksmith in the middle of the ball always puts a damper on things.

If your Sub is allergic to anything, or it's cold and flu season, skip the gag.

Blindfolds

No peeking! A Sub is expected to tell the truth as to whether the blindfold completely obscures vision. A Dom is expected to protect the safety of a blindfolded Sub. As the Dom, you can make a Sub crawl around blindfolded on the floor of your basement for you, but it's up to you to make sure there are no nails, broken glass or other dangerous obstacles in the way—unless you really are a sadistic perv.

Home Alone

Don't leave a bound, gagged or blindfolded Sub alone in a room unmonitored. Even the mildest of restraints can lead to tragic results. If leaving them alone is part of the schtick, check in frequently to make sure all is okay.

Toys

From paddles to dildos, toys are an integral part of S/M play. Keep them clean, have a good supply of lube on hand and make sure you have plenty of batteries around.

As a general rule, we recommend avoiding anything that's not designed to go in, as well as anything that can't be easily removed. That includes loaded weapons (see "Guns" in Part III), glass bottles, flaming gerbils and other livestock. Think about how you'll feel showing up at the emergency room with a bottle stuck up your ass. Just think about it.

Clothespins

Use the spring-mounted ones, and close them SLOWLY. It's always good form to try it out on yourself first so you know how it feels.

Candle Wax

Three key rules govern the use of candle wax. Follow them carefully, or someone may get burned. 1) Use only paraffin and not beeswax candles, as beeswax has a higher melting point and gets hotter.

2) Start dripping with the candle higher and lower gradually as the play continues. The higher the candle, the cooler the wax is when it hits the skin. 3) When pouring the wax, don't just turn the candle upside down. Let the melted wax stream down the candle, thus giving it a chance to cool. Remember, this is supposed to make you hot, but not flesh-scalding hot! Have an ice pack in the freezer just in case.

Check Your Role at the Door

S/M fantasies are indeed fantasies. Many day-to-day relationships find themselves skewed in S/M play, with bosses wanting to be spanked by their secretaries. Both the Sub and the Dom are expected to check their roles at the dungeon door. Just because the boss gets his ass tanned once in a while doesn't mean he's not the boss in the boardroom. Your wife may allow you to string her up and beg you to sodomize her with the ice cream scoop, but afterward, she's still your wife, not your slave.

Later That Night

When you're done playing for the evening, make sure to check for any bruising or cuts.

Nursing emotional wounds is also important. S/M can be an intense psychological workout, and after play is over, it's time to reward and reassure. If your Sub wants to worship a part of your body as a reward, that wish is granted. If your Sub needs a hug, oblige. Since S/M should be a part of a loving relationship (or it's called spousal abuse), show that love in a tender way at the end of play. Take your slave to dinner or something.

Make sure to talk about the play the next day to debrief on what occurred.

Seeking Professional Help

If you've got the kind of dough that will afford you a professional Dom or Sub, expect to have a good long sitdown prior to any whips or chains. Feel free to spell out exactly what you want out of the experience, and they'll let you know the rules and how much it'll cost. Since we're leaving the actual etiquette to the pros (it's situational and depends on your bent), we'll stick to the more or less universal rules of engagement.

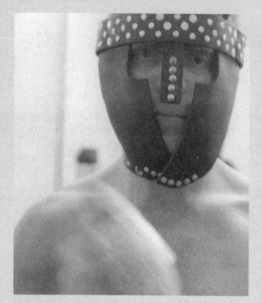

Damien is a professional dominatrix with some experience as a pro Sub, too. Though he has a girlfriend, most of his clients are men.

HE SAID / SHE SAID

EFO: Most of your clients are guys. Why?
Damien: Guys just pay more.
EFO: Why?
Damien: They're just horny muthafuckers.
EFO: Do the same rules apply for male and female Subs/clients?
Damien: I tend to be tougher on men, but the rules are the same.
EFO: What's the rudest thing a client/Sub could do during a session?
Damien: Topping from the bottom. When they tell you what to do.
EFO: Do you tolerate that?
Damien: No, I'll whoop 'em.
EFO: What about the theory, the customer is always right?
Damien: When you have clients, basically they're paying, and it's kind of like a massage, and they should, at least in part, get what they want so they'll come back. So hopefully ahead of time you talk about what they're into, what their tastes are, and during the session you just take control. That's part of the deal. You can tell me everything you want before we start playing, but once we start, you can use your safe word, and that's about it.
EFO: Does it tick you off if they expect sex?
Damien: There's never that expectation in this scene. They're lucky if you let them get themselves off. But again, they're paying, so you usually try to let them get off at the end. But if I told one of them, "You can't get off, just go home," they would do it and wouldn't be upset.

EFO: Do you facilitate that?
Damien: No, I make 'em jerk off.
EFO: Have you always denied clients who've asked you for sex?
Damien: I have gone down on people or given them a hand job.
EFO: Is sex with clients considered unprofessional? Would other pros look down on someone that, say, gave a client a blow job or hand job?
Damien: Yeah. They wouldn't respect you. Sex with clients is a big no-no. And it's a small group of people, and everyone seems to know each other. So if you get a reputation as someone who has sex with clients, that's a bad thing.
EFO: What if the fantasy doesn't meet expectations? Is there a money-back guarantee?
Damien: No way.
EFO: How about rules for the Dom?
Damien: Always respect the safe word. As a top, it's definitely my responsibility to know what it is before we start playing. And once they use it, you have to immediately untie them.
EFO: What about Subs who don't use their safe word, even when things are getting too heavy?
Damien: I'm always looking out for that. There are people who are stubborn. Mentally, they can take more pain than their body can. I think having been a Sub makes me a better top. Even if you're naturally a top, I think it's extremely important to spend some time on the bottom so you know what you're inflicting on them. A lot of women who do this have spent no time on the bottom, so sometimes they're unduly harsh.
EFO: What if you're feeling really pissed off right before a session?
Damien: It is a good stress reliever, that's for sure.
EFO: Is their a sliding scale for session fees?
Damien: No, everyone has an hourly rate. For a long session, you can get a bulk rate . . . a volume discount. But no frequent flyer miles.

Shawna Kenney helped pay her way through college as a professional Dom. Unlike Damien, Shawna worked as an employee for a specific dungeon.

EFO: How did you get into this line of work?

Shawna: I started as a dancer, but I hated it—too submissive for me. So I scanned the want ads, and saw one that said, "Get Paid for Being a Bitch."

EFO: So you've never been hired as a Sub?

Shawna: No, I'd never do that. We had one submissive [on staff]—she took all the spankings.

EFO: What is the rudest thing a Sub/client could do during a session?

Shawna: The no-shows are really annoying. A lot of clients call and then chicken out without calling back to cancel.

EFO: And the rudest thing once you're in play?

Shawna: Subs who try to top from the bottom. I always had a little consultation with clients before the session, and I didn't mind adhering to their fantasies. But I didn't really care to follow a script. And a lot of people's fetishes are so specific in their mind, and they think you're there to just act it out. That's really fucking annoying. But ultimately, you have to please them if you want them to come back.

EFO: So ultimately, the customer is always right?

Shawna: Most of the time.

EFO: What happens if they forget to address you as Mistress?

Shawna: They'll get slapped. And if they do it more than once, they'd be ordered out of the session.

EFO: Ever smack around a chick?

Shawna: No, I wouldn't. I think men deserve it more. Women put up with enough shit in everyday life.

EFO: Did you ever have an awful day, like get dumped by your boyfriend, then go into a session with a client and kick some ass?

Shawna: I've never been dumped, but it was a great way to get out aggressions.

EFO: Is it bad form to take out your anger toward the male species on your slave?

Shawna: No, it's fine, whatever motivates you.

EFO: Were you pissed if a client asked for sex?

Shawna: Just the fact that they are being submissive and coming to a dominant woman, right there they are unworthy of touching me. Unacceptable. They should know better—it's not an escort service.

EFO: Is sex with clients totally frowned upon? Does it cheapen the trade?

Shawna: I don't think so, but the woman that ran my dungeon forbade it. A lot of professionals do think it cheapens the profession. If it

were going to happen, it's got to be the dominant person who makes the move. A slave should know his place.

EFO: Did you let them get off?

Shawna: If I liked them. I would not touch them. But I might order them to play with themselves. But I would definitely let them know that it was up to me. If they'd behaved well for the hour, I may allow it.

EFO: If a session is going longer than the original session, do you cut it off like a shrink, or do you prorate?

Shawna: The dungeon did.

EFO: Are clients expected to tip?

Shawna: Never expected, but it's really sweet, and a Dom will remember it.

EFO: What about Dom etiquette?

Shawna: Every dungeon has its own rules. If we were caught doing drugs or dating a client, we'd be fired.

EFO: Do you agree with the drug thing?

Shawna: Yeah, you need to be aware. You don't want to maim or kill anyone.

EFO: What's your responsibility to your slave, like if they don't use their safe word?

Shawna: My personal rule was, once I drew blood, it's over. It's just messy and dangerous. I was caning one guy, and he got welts and started to bleed, so I tried to order him to do something else, but he begged for more caning. I said, "Shut the fuck up, put your pants on."

EFO: Is it rude for the slave to request a certain safe word?

Shawna: That's too much to demand of the Dom. I give the safe word.

EFO: Any other pet peeves with clients?

Shawna: Not washing properly. They usually get naked for these sessions, and if they're not clean, we would send them away. In addition to the cleanliness issue, it's very nice if a client coming in for dildo training has an enema beforehand.

EFO: Can they bring their own dildo?

Shawna: Sure, B.Y.O.D.

Try to be on time with your appointment (like shrinks, your hour starts at the prescribed time).

If you see your Dom/Sub on the street, you can say "Hello," but don't bust into a fantasy. On the clock, you can worship; on the street, they're civilians, and may not want to be "outed" in a public forum.

Finally, don't think of a professional Sub or Dom as a hooker. It's the rare pro who will actually have traditional sex with you. If coming is your aim, ask first. As always, it's poor form to shoot your load at the wrong time and place. (See "The Dominatrix" in Part V)

FETISHES

When we asked a friend of ours how to spot the poseurs at his fetish club, he replied: "It's tough because you never know what kind of fetish they have. Maybe their fetish is to dress like a narc and be a voyeur. Who knows?"

Generally, the term "fetish" can be applied to any non-vanilla sexual practice, but is usually reserved for more than the casual kink. Like we said earlier, a smack on the butt during sex can be kinky, but until you're breaking out the riding crop, it's not fetish. Since there are so many different kinds of fetishes that may or may not be mutually exclusive, our coverage is far from exhaustive. Here are some fetish highlights, and their accompanying rules.

Foot Fetish

One of the more popular kinks in the book, the foot fetish can manifest itself as either a worshiping of the boot (or high heel) or the actual foot. Always ask before you lick, and try to make it shine.

Some men dig being stepped on by women in heels. If you're that woman (or facsimile), feel free to step as hard as you wish. If they ask you to stop, do so. Those with naked foot fetishes suck on the toes and tootsies as if they're giving oral sex. Some like a clean foot; others like it dirty.

Voyeurism

Since the core idea of voyeurism is to look without getting caught, it's always bad form to look like you're staring, even if the person you're staring at wants you to stare. So look, but just don't look like you're looking.

Transvestites

The main rule for dealing with transvestites is to deal with them as members of the sex they choose to emulate. If he's now a she, refer to her in that gender. Dykes strapping down dildos should be addressed as "Sir," or you might have a fight on your hands.

Conversely, if, say, you're a woman trapped in a man's body, and you win a new boyfriend based on false pretenses, false eyelashes and fake boobs, please disclose to said boyfriend before things go too far—and not on *Jerry Springer*.

Fetish Clubs

The more you get into a particular fetish, the more you might seek out local clubs that specialize in that fetish. Club rules vary, but here's a few all-purpose tips.

If you're just going because you're curious, fine. But try to dress the part. All clubs have an aesthetic, whether it be high-heeled pumps, leather, latex or Saran Wrap. The better the club, the more stringent the dress code will be to keep the amateurs or looky-loos at bay. Proper etiquette requires that you respect that.

If you're merely a perv going for a sneak peek, go to a strip bar where you pay to see naked girls. In fact, it is expected that you refrain from activity that interrupts the fantasy the club tries to create.

If someone asks you to whip them, go ahead. If there are public floggings going on and you're in the mood for a beating, make sure the whip is clean prior to the first strike. While the odds are pretty huge that you won't contract a deadly disease from a whip, it's best to play it safe when you don't know the guests.

If you're a guy, never go into the women's restroom without being asked. Sure, it's a fetish club, and wild things happen there. Sex in a toilet stall? Why not?! Just make sure you're invited.

Many fetish clubs, particularly more mainstream, large-scale "fetish balls," do not allow sex on the premises. It's a legal thing. While a "no sex" rule may not be rigorously enforced, be mindful and be discreet.

Some fetish clubs will let voyeurs watch as long as they don't talk to anyone or make catcalls. If these rules are broken, said voyeur might be kicked out of the club or flogged.

ORGIES

If you're someone who believes that the more the merrier, there's always the Bacchanalian flesh fest known as the orgy. Think of it as an all-you-can-eat buffet with naked people.

If you are in a relationship, discuss it with your mate first. If the two of you plan to attend the orgy together, make sure both of you are comfortable with the idea. Lay down any ground rules ahead of time (see "Swinging" later in Part II).

You don't have to check your free will and standards at the door. If someone you really don't like tries to poke you where you don't want to be poked, that's cool. You can say "No, thank you." But overall, your presence at the orgy implies a certain degree of consent. Depending on the location and who's hosting, you can gauge the type of folks you'll be getting naked with ahead of time. Still, if you're feeling choosy, this ain't your scene.

Watch your backside. Like we said, you don't have to do anything you don't want to do. Some of your orifices may be off-limits, and that's cool. Just remember that other guests might expect free reign, and might not stop to ask.

Kissing and cuddling are acceptable, but not required.

In terms of safety, orgies are a bit of a crapshoot. Condoms may or may not be required; demanding someone's sexual history while knee-deep in a tangle of flesh is generally not appropriate. For your part, make sure you're not passing any nasty STDs on to your partners—you're liable to start an epidemic.

Go the distance. Coming and going is bad form.

Usually, what transpires at an orgy is sacred. It all stays in the room.

FISTING

If hand-to-hand combat is your kink, the first thing you need to get used to is taking care of your nails. A well-manicured hand is the preferred course of action. As the linings of both nether regions are—to say the least—tender, it's best to keep your nails not only short, but without dirt or jagged edges. Otherwise, glove both hands with latex. Lube your hand before you start, then go very slowly. Work your way up to full hand penetration and then go for it in a tender manner. If you've just fisted someone or have been fisted, you should make sure to have safe sex, as damage to the lining of the anus makes it more open to STDs.

WHAT'S THE POOP?

Hey, if you're into excrement, that's fine with us—you're probably a lawyer or politician.

Keep in mind the safety concerns that go along with that. Giving or taking, it's hard to get HIV, but if the pee-er has an infected bladder, the person taking the shower might catch something. Never pee into an open cut. And if you're into eating scat (shit) or love rimming, brush your teeth *afterward*. Don't brush your teeth or tongue three to four hours before play, as you may open small sores in your mouth and make yourself more susceptible to disease. And hey, keep the garlic and asparagus intake down to a minimum, unless that kind of nose-wrinkling pungency is kinky to you, too! Finally, it's considered very bad form to penetrate the vagina with anything that recently penetrated the anus. You can transfer viruses and germs that way. The best policy is, don't shit where you eat.

GAY PLAY

In these progressive, "anything goes" times, "the love that dare not speak its name" has actually become rather trendy. A little experimentation is not only okay, it's considered a badge of open-minded hipness. Just because a dude fondles another guy doesn't make him a homo. Just because a chick cuts a rug with another chick doesn't make her a dyke. So go for it. Satiate that curiosity. We won't tell.

We do, however, have a bit of a problem with folks who use "experimentation" as a pretense. If you're on your way out of the closet, calling yourself bisexual is considered by some to be a cop-out—a refusal to commit to a change of lifestyle. Fact of the matter is, most of us do have a preference. We say, do what you want to do, and who you want to do, but don't bullshit about it.

If you're in a heterosexual relationship, don't assume that sleeping with someone of the same sex isn't really infidelity. Some sig-o's consider it cheating, others don't. Our opinion is that it's cheating unless we get to watch.

Swinging

THE MORE THE MERRIER

Variety, multiplicity are the two most important vehicles of lust.

—Marquis de Sade

Take my wife, please.

—Henny Youngman

Two's company, but three or more's a party!

Swinging is more than just experimental, alcohol-induced participation in a threesome or orgy. Also known as "the lifestyle," it's a distinct subculture with its very own unique set of rules of etiquette, and therefore merits its very own chapter.

Swinging entails a couple (usually seriously involved or married) engaging in romantic affairs *together*. Gone are the days of lying about what you're doing late at work. The term "cheating" is rendered obsolete. Now you're a team, prowling the night hand in hand, side by side. You can swing together, doing the group thing (open swinging), or you can go for the more traditional swapping, whereby you and your partner each have your fun in separate rooms (closed swinging). You and your mate get to choose. Just make sure that jealousy doesn't rear its ugly head.

We've listed the following guidelines in the hopes that you and your betrothed might achieve the loftiest of romantic goals: to have your cake and eat it, too!

TO SWING OR
NOT TO SWING

The cardinal rule of swinging is no jealousy allowed.

Swinging is strictly for dedicated couples who are so secure in their relationship that they will allow their partner to explore sex with others. If you have a jealous bone in your body, this lifestyle will last about eight minutes, and could cost you your relationship. Don't do it. There's no shame. But if you're into actively pursuing a more prurient path, then this is your cup of tea.

KEEP YOUR PRIORITIES STRAIGHT

Always take care to see that your primary relationship is taken into consideration in any swinging situation. Make sure your partner knows where the true love lies.

LAY DOWN THE LAW

Establish personal boundaries with your sig-o. What are you both comfortable with? First base? Second? Third? Home? If a man can't deal with his wife banging another dude, she is expected not to swing that way. Maybe he can only handle her being with another woman. Set your limits, stick by them, and move on.

If jealousy arises, you must restrain yourself until you can politely extract yourself from the situation, and resolve things with your main squeeze in private, as a couple. Such troubleshooting should always be conducted one-on-one. If a tactful, immediate withdrawal simply isn't an option, make the best of things and discuss it after the session.

Once you've established your own couple rules, you must establish rules with any additional players (they have their boundaries, too!). Make an oral contract: "You can lick my husband from his hips to his head, but no penetrations."

No peer pressure. If someone in your little three-way, four-way or eight-way isn't comfortable, it's bad form to push 'em.

PLAY SAFE

As in safe sex. Unfortunately, the swing scene isn't as safety-conscious as we might like it to be. Feel free to ask about sexual history, or insist upon safe sex practices like condoms or dental dams.

BE DISCREET

Like S/M and AA recovery, a main tenet of the swinging code is, ironically, discretion: "You can fuck my wife, just don't call us at home." First names work fine, and you never want to talk about your partners outside or even inside the scene. Never "out" people in their professional life: "Oh, Hillary, she swings." Bad form. Proper etiquette means keeping things on the QT at all times.

FLYING THE RED FLAG

As in the S/M scene, "safe words" or "actions" act as red flags to your mate that you're not interested in a particular situation or scene. Establish a word (like "red") and an action (like a tug on the ear) prior to going into *any* swinging environment. If your partner makes the move, cease, desist, and leave as soon as possible.

GETTING INTO THE SWING OF THINGS

When you encounter an interesting couple at a swinging soiree, make sure to talk with both members of that couple. If you're only interested in one, perhaps you should move on. As in all social situations, talking to only one member of a couple is rude. Indeed, it's worse in a swing situation, since you're rude, *and* you want to fuck their partner.

If you're approached and you're not interested, be polite and say so. If someone tells you they're not interested, just accept it.

EVENTS AND CLUBS

Private clubs and parties are one of the better ways to enjoy the swinging lifestyle (these parties can be found in alt.sex chat rooms on the web, websites, and in swinging magazines). They usually take place at a private residence and have an admission price.

Decorum suggests that you call ahead and make reservations. If you can't make it, it's proper form to call again and cancel. Many party hosts will use the reservation call to inform you of the house rules, which can vary. Etiquette requires that you abide by all of them. If you don't like the rules, find another party.

Rules of the House

Feel free to ask the host of a swinging event the following questions:

- Is there a dress code?

- Do they allow single men or women, or couples only? (Hint: usually single women are okay.)

- Do they allow bisexual men? (Many don't, as they see swinging more as a man/woman/woman thing.)

- Do they allow on-site swinging? (Can you do it in the house?) If so, are there any off-limits areas (like pools and Jacuzzis), and is there videotaping in any room?

Usually these homes will be decorated (and party-proofed) for the event. Nonetheless, do try to keep any bodily fluid off any fabric prone to staining (like the curtains). It's also proper form to ask before you take any drugs (see "Being Blunt" in Part VI).

If you don't like the people or the scene, simply leave, but don't expect a refund.

THE DOUBLE STANDARD ON DOUBLING UP

No doubt there's a double standard applied to male and female swingers. For the most part, if you're a decent-looking female on her own who likes the group thing, you'll have no problem gaining admittance to a swingers club. If you're a lone male, then you're considered "single," and are usually not eligible to swing.

If you're just a guy looking for some wild sex, do not bring a pro to an amateur event. And don't bring in a ringer who isn't a swinger. It's called bringing a "ticket," and it's the surest way of becoming the most hated member of the club scene. You will be asked to leave; you

will probably get blackballed from future events. If you're a guy looking for concourse intercourse, you'd best find yourself a female
swinging partner.

DATING COUPLES

If you're really into swinging, you might ultimately find yourself dating another person and/or couple. Dating another couple is like regular dating, but on steroids. "Do both of them like me?" "Are we
attractive to them?" "Do they like me better?" "Well, I like her better."
"What if they break up?"

General dating principles apply. You're expected to call once in a
while just to say "hi" and see if everyone's fine. You're expected to be
kind and attentive to the personal needs of everyone. You're expected
to surprise each other with the occasional gift (a swing set?).

Some rules of dating don't apply. For example, you're not required
to meet the other couple's family. You're not expected to be monogamous or faithful to the couple you're dating. And you can dump them
and move on without feeling like you've left them all alone.

PART III

The Accessories

Give us the tools, and we'll finish the job.

—*Winston Churchill*

It's tough to be outlaw in a cardigan, bow tie and penny loafers, behind the wheel of your parents' old station wagon.

The fact of the matter is, most of us aren't really bad-to-the-bone "outlaws." Nope. But we can certainly dress the part. The following pages outline the usage etiquette for some of the tools of the trade—the proper accoutrements—for fringe behavior and lifestyles, from weapons to wheels. It is our hope that by the end of this section you will have more than just an approximate idea of how to handle them correctly.

MARKED FOR LIFE

Out, damn spot. Out, I say!

—Lady Macbeth

Inka-dinka-do.

—Jimmy Durante

Since the dawn of time, body art has been a rite of both religious and ornamental value, from the 5,000-year-old iceman who exhibited tattooed stripes on his back and a cross on the back of his knee, to the tattoo craze spawned by Captain Cook's adventures in Polynesia, to the "modern primitives" who populate today's various fetish and music scenes.

Tattoos have always been one of the most provocative ways to adorn the body, as well as *the* red badge of the rebel, outlaw or sinner. Old-school tattoos of anchors and pinups have been replaced by new-school comics, life-like pictorials, tribal designs and gang-banger insignias. Let's hear it for progress.

These days, you don't have to be Dennis Rodman or Tommy Lee to face the needle. With the practice widely accepted by mainstream society (passing the 3-year "fad" span), it looks as if tats are here to stay. Good thing, 'cause once you go for it, you're marked for life.

ASKING QUESTIONS

The most misunderstood rule about tattoo etiquette is this: It's perfectly okay to ask questions.

Tattoo novices are often shy about getting information about the process. Acting like you know what's up might seem like the "cool" thing to do, but as most tattoo artists will tell you, you can't ask too many questions. In fact, many artists are shocked that folks don't ask more. "Most people take more time picking out a shirt in the morning than they do picking their ink for life!" one ink-slingertold us.

THE RIGHT STUDIO

Nor do most first-timers look into the qualifications of the artist who's doing the work. Remember: You are a consumer employing an artist to permanently maim your skin. As such, you have the right to check the credentials of said craftsman, and the working conditions of his studio. It's not bad form to make an inquiry and take a look around before you buy. If you don't like the art on the walls or in the books, or are concerned about the cleanliness of the studio, walk out. There are plenty of places to get a tattoo.

The first thing you should check out are the working conditions of the artist. Make sure all instruments are clean and sterile. Make sure the artist wears gloves (frankly, it's more for their protection than yours). If you don't find the conditions acceptable, leave.

Next, take a look at the "flash" (non-custom art displayed on the wall) and the book of tattoos. If you see something you like, feel free to ask who actually penned it. As long as you're not being a pain in the ass and/or interfering with a tat in progress, a "reputable" tattoo artist will accommodate your questions like any other merchant looking for a sale.

It's best to find an artist who's an artist first, ink-slinger second. Maybe they just have a needle fetish, and can only really trace from a book of flash (licensed, prefab designs and sketches). It's good to ask.

If you're still unsure, shop around. Ask your friends where they got their tattoos. Usually word of mouth is the best way to find an artist.

One last way to find an artist is to find a tattoo you like, and ask the owner where they got it. Most inked ones will be more than happy to tell you who did the work. It's never considered bad form to admire someone's tattoo; just don't ogle.

If you like your artist, recommend them to your friends—that will endear you to the artist, and they may even give you a discount on that full-back dragon you've been dreaming about.

THE RIGHT INK

Save everyone a lot of time and have some idea of what you want before engaging an artist. You know how much it pisses off waiters when you don't know what you want? This is worse. If you know you want a tat, give the design some thought first. Ink-slingers are not licensed therapists (usually) and they don't know you at all. Don't agonize over what to get *while you're in the tattoo studio.*

If there's a picture in a book you like, bring it with you. If you have an original idea, most artists will work with you to get that idea on paper. If you're just putting words on your body, get a sample of the type you want used.

Tattoo artists like people who can either verbally explain the design they want (they want to make you happy) or bring a design in with them. It simply takes the guessing game out of the equation. As with any artisan, respect them enough not to waste their time.

Try to resist the temptation to ask the artist what he or she thinks about your choice of tattoos. Etiquette dictates that they humor you and your artistic choice: "Yeah, it looks really tough!" If you want their help, ask them things that are more art-specific. For example: "How do you think this image will translate to skin?" "Will the lines hold?" "How about the size and placement?" These are good questions.

Finally, while it's not bad etiquette to choose flash art from the wall, some see it as a sign of the amateur ("Flash is trash"). Show some creativity, damn it, and think for yourself.

MONEY MATTERS

Do not haggle with the person holding the big needle to your skin! It is horrible form to question the integrity of an artist's pricing policy; the price is based upon their years of experience. If you can afford it, pay it. If you can't, either see if you can have some of the work done now and some later, or put off the work until you have the jack. If you are really into getting a tattoo and you're a few bucks short, the artist might take pity on you (remembering when they, too, were inkless) and cut you a deal.

One of our interviewees told us about the gang-bangers who frequent his shop. While there are some gang members who pull flash off the wall and haggle the price, other gangstas—in particular, Hispanic members—pride themselves on paying full price for their tats. It's like a status symbol, with the bigger ones showing off how much dough they can afford to invest in their ink.

MAJOR FAUX PAS

If you're going in for your first tattoo, don't act like you know it all. You don't. Amateurs do the following: get drunk (and thus bleed more), flinch or throw up (because they're drunk), get tattoos of their (soon to be former) girlfriend's name, get diseases (because they haven't properly checked out the studio beforehand), and, worst of all, get bad tattoos (because their judgment is impaired). Woody Woodpecker with a cigar or "Sonny & Cher forever!" are proof positive that the bearer was pickled in the ink-slinger's chair.

SIZE AND LOCATION

Size does matter. There is no clear-cut answer to how big your tat should be, but it should fit the place where it's drawn. Disproportionately small tattoos are the calling card of the initiate. Either they were not sure they wanted the tattoo, or they didn't bring enough money to cover good work. Ask the artist their opinion on size; they're not going to try to convince you to go bigger just so they can make more dough. As with any artist, they know their medium, and will have a better idea of proportions than you. If you find that you cannot afford bigger work, don't haggle. Ask if you can just get the outline done, or make an appointment to come back later. There is no shame in leaving; an artist will respect you more for waiting to do it right.

Where you put your new tat is more or less up to you. Tattoos on your face, hands and neck, however, might blast more attitude than you want. If you work with the public, you may want to avoid such conspicuous locations and go with more traditional (obscured) placement. Indeed, most reputable artists will not tattoo your face or hands unless you're sleeved (meaning your tattoos reach your wrists). They don't want to scar you for life unless they know you're committed to the art. Respect that.

Moreover, many won't tattoo a pregnant woman. While the risk is minimal, the concern is that the ink could somehow pollute the bloodstream and hurt the baby. They just don't want to be responsible. If your tattooist takes this stance, don't try to sway him. Holding off for a few more months won't kill you. Besides, with all the water retention that comes with pregnancy, the inked image can become distorted once the swelling goes down. Better to wait.

ART SURVEY COURSE

Tat art is highly subjective, and we're down with anything that's done well and with imagination. Still, we've outlined a few definite do's and don'ts, from classic cool to classic fool. Choose wisely, as you will have to live with any poor decisions for a very, very, long time.

Kanji (Japanese script) and barbed wire are hip, perennial faves, but they're also kind of trendy. Dare to be different with Sanskrit text or a seam down the leg.

Tattooists love to do the traditional stuff. You can't go wrong with flaming hearts, anchors, vintage sparrows, or pinups. Mom hearts are cool, but skip the boyfriend/girlfriend tat . . . just ask Roseanne Barr.

PLEASE: No Hotstuff Devils, Tasmanian Devils, or Woody Woodpeckers with a cigar. If you go the toon route, keep it cult or put a dark spin on it. Japanimation (anlmé) is also pretty hip.

Bold, macabre imagery can blast a whole lot of 'tude. Just make sure you can back it up, or you risk looking like a poseur.

Dragons are hip and colorful. They're also quite detailed, so make sure the artist knows what he's doing.

No one will fault you for sporting a good tribal design. But remember that heavy "blackwork" can require multiple visits to complete.

Artists cringe when asked to do dolphins or unicorns. Likewise cutesy flowers, suns, moons and teensy-weensy butterflies on the ankles—a favorite among sorority chicks. Rule: If the tat you want looks like it came out of a box of Cracker Jacks, don't get it, ok?

While it's cool to tout a bid in jail with a "hand-poke," it's not cool to brag about your stay in BH. Next to ink that says, "I've got a small dick," we can't imagine a worse tattoo than the one shown here on the right.

DON'T ARM YOURSELF

Guns and tats sometimes go hand in hand (there's a reason why cops are always asking if a suspect had any "identifying marks"). If you carry a firearm, proper decorum dictates that you ask your artist to store it while he's working on you, out of respect. Most tattoo shops have weapons of their own in case of any trouble while you're under the needle, so you're in reasonably safe hands.

YOUR POSSE

If you bring along a posse to watch (which you shouldn't, 'cause it's lame), ask the tattooist's permission. Usually, they'll let one person hold your hand or take pictures (also lame), but odds are they'll make most of your crew wait in the lobby.

GETTING INKED

Eat something an hour or two before going under the needle, since you might be there for a while and you don't want to pass out—which is always bad form.

Also make sure you're sober, because, like we said, alcohol will make you bleed more—whether it's from the needle or the punch in the face from the biker chick whose ass you've been staring at for a half-hour.

If you have an itch, alert the artist so they can stop working. If you jerk around without warning, be prepared for mistakes.

After the work is done, an antibiotic cream is applied to the area, followed by a bandage to keep the area dry for a while. Your tattooist should tell you how to care for it. If they don't, ask.

THERE'S NO CRYING IN BASEBALL

How much do they hurt? While it's a fair question, the answer is difficult to explain. How do you describe a Picasso to a blind man?

It's pain, but not *pain* pain. If you start scratching yourself pretty hard in one place for a while, you might get a sense of what it feels like.

Of course, where you're getting the ink—and its proximity to bone—will increase or decrease the amount of pain involved. It's a simple equation: More cushion from fat or muscle = less pain. A tattoo on the buttocks doesn't hurt that much; a tattoo on the ankle hurts more.

The pain of the tattoo should stop when the needle stops. If it doesn't, see a doctor. If your face is starting to turn pale or you're feeling dizzy, mention it to your artist. If you faint in the chair, it can mess up the work.

Finally, Tom Hanks's line about there being "no crying in baseball" applies equally to tattoos. Don't do it. Be tough.

TIPPING

While tipping is not mandatory, it's always a great way to show appreciation. Ten percent will do. It won't get you better service (they're professionals, after all), but it will let them know that you are happy with their work.

INK STAINS

Bad tattoos can, unfortunately, be par for the course. If you're unhappy with the work, most tattoo artists will work with you to make it more to your liking. Don't be afraid to say you're disappointed, but you might want to be gentle. If you intend to ask the same artist to fix it, something like, "Maybe this didn't come out the way I wanted" will suffice. If the art just plain sucks, you should find another shop and pay the dough to have it fixed by someone more qualified. Make sure not to bag on the original artist who did it; local tattooists often hang together, and the two of them might be fast friends.

If the bad art is really *your* fault, as in a poor or drunken choice, you will be asked to pony up more cash for any repair work.

As a last resort, there is laser surgery. It's a costly fix-it, so do your best to avoid getting to that point.

SHOWING OFF

After you get a tattoo, showing it off is part of the fun. Heck, the artist might even want to take your picture for their book (always say yes). The most important rule of exhibition etiquette is this: don't show off your ink to someone who's not interested. If the answer to the question "Do you want to see my new tattoo?" is "No," please keep your left butt cheek covered.

If you are going out and want to show it off, wear a tank top. If you're overweight, we cannot condone this. Feel free to go shirtless at a tattoo convention or at gay bars.

If your employer frowns upon ink, cover it up by wearing suitable clothing. If you wear white shirts, you may want to invest in undershirts so it doesn't show through.

THE FINAL NEVER

Probably the worst thing you can do is bag on somebody else's tats. If they ask you what you think, try to find something about it you like. Making fun of someone else's tattoo is like telling a mother that her kid's ugly. You'll get a well-deserved ass-kicking, or at the very least a serious dose of stinkeye.

Piercing

LIVING ON PINS AND NEEDLES

Only fruits wear earrings.
—Marge Schott, owner of the Cincinnati Reds

Stand by thyself, do not come near me, for I am holier than thou.

—Old Testament

You need it like a hole in your head.

—Mom

Much like tattooing, piercing has been around for millennia, but has only caught on for the mainstream in the last decade. Unlike the tattoo, which has a mainly aesthetic appeal, piercing has an additional element of sexual pleasure and ritual. Also unlike tattoos, a pierce can usually be removed situationally. There might be some scarring, but what's a few scars among friends?

The etiquette involved with piercing is much like that of tattoos (and most other things in life). This includes being polite, not copping a 'tude, asking good questions and showing up sober. The same hygiene issues also apply.

A more important difference between the piercing and the tat is the interpersonal communication issues that arise: *Do you need to tell your new lover about your genital piercing before they discover it on their own?* But that's just the tip of the needle.

MONEY

Most studios have a list of prices. Make sure you see it first. You should tip 10 to 15 percent of the cost of the piercing.

THE NEEDLE AND THE DAMAGE DONE

Well, it's not like going to the mall and getting your ears pierced, now is it? If the ear is just too damn pedestrian for your piercing needs, consider the following choices and their "Pain Factors." We think they give the phrase "being a stud" new meaning.

	SPECIFICS	PAIN FACTOR
M O U T H	**Labret** Just below the middle of the lower lip.	😮 😮
	Lip Anywhere else around the kisser. (Taffy and other sticky, chewy stuff can be hazardous.)	😮
	Madonna Either side of the upper lip. (Again, watch the taffy.)	😮
	Tongue Through the tongue, usually just behind the tip. (Might make you talk like Richard Simmons for a few days; infection guaranteed; but your girlfriend will love it!)	😮
N O S E	**Earl** Through the bridge of the nose. (Forget the glasses.)	😮 😮 😮 😮 😮
	Nostril Most popular site is low down on the side of the nose so a ring can hang from the nostril.	😮 😮
	Septum Through the ridge just below the cartilage between the nostrils (like a bull).	😮 😮 😮
B O D Y	**Navel** Usually pierced through a pinch of skin either at the top or the bottom. (Heals very slowly. Plus, how cool can it be if your little sister has one, too?)	😮
	Nipples Through the teets. (Close quickly if removed; can get caught on sweater; easily ripped.)	😮 😮 😮 😮

SPECIFICS	PAIN FACTOR
PRIVATES	
Clitoris Some women who have them claim to orgasm while they're walking down the street; can be torn off during rough sex.	😱 😱 😱 😱 😱
Inner Labia A piercing through either of the inner labia (or through both), enabling a ring or rings to pass through both piercings and close off the vagina. (If it comes loose, it can get buried in there; can tear condoms; can make things yeasty.)	😱 😱 😱 😱 😱
Outer Labia Through either of the outer labia.	😱 😱 😱 😱 😱
Prepuce Through the hood of the clitoris, sometimes arranged so that the ball of the ring used falls against the clitoris itself.	😱 😱 😱 😱

FOR THE DUDES

SPECIFICS	PAIN FACTOR
PRIVATES	
Ampallang Horizontally through the penis head, crossing the urethra. (Makes pissing a bitch for a while; can catch on undies.)	😱 😱 😱 😱 😱
Apadrayva Vertically through the head of your johnson, crossing the urethra. (See notes above.)	😱 😱 😱 😱
Dydo Through the ridge of the head, parallel to the shaft. (Can tear; can hurt your girlfriend, especially if she's small.)	😱 😱 😱 😱 😱
Frenum Through the web of the skin that attaches the foreskin to the head. (Watch out for the heavy jewelry; can hurt your girlfriend; can get lost during butt sex.)	😱 😱 😱 😱 😱
Quiche Through the base of the sack, between the legs.	😱 😱
Lorum Horizontally through the skin where the scrotum joins the base of the weenie, or through the skin on the underside.	😱 😱
Prince Albert Not named for Marv Albert, but for the royal member who liked to strap down his own member so he could fit into those tight pants. The piercing goes into the urethra from outside the head, most commonly beneath to allow for a cock ring. (The granddaddy of infections; no tighty-whities.)	😱 😱 😱 😱 😱 😱 😱 😱 😱 😱 😱 😱 **1/2**

C'MON BABY, MAKE IT HURT SO GOOD

Gen of the Genitorturers on Pierced Partners

You had to know that we'd hit up Florida's Genitorturers (the band's name is a term meaning the torture of the genitals for erotic pleasure) for an interview. Led by singer/piercer Gen, their music combines heavy guitar and industrial noise and a live stage show that features actual onstage body piercings! We dig it. If you get the chance, catch their live act. Just stay the hell away from Gen when she's getting wild on stage—you may wind up getting stuck with something sharp.

EFO: Should you tell a person about any intimate piercings before you go to bed with them?

GEN: In some instances it's probably a really good idea. Especially a man with—let's say—a very large genital piercing such as a O-gauge Prince Albert. I would think at that point they should probably mention something before any sort of contact takes place. That's something somebody should be prepared for. But I do think it's fun for people, sometimes, to just discover them.

EFO: Are there any types of piercings that could potentially hurt a partner?

GEN: There are some male genital piercings that if they're wearing very large jewelry with certain types of decorations or beads on them . . . the other person would have to be very aware of what's going on. The person who has the piercing must be sensitive to the fact that the person they are with might not be used to that. I've seen instances where it can cause some irritation . . . If someone had a Prince Albert piercing with a skull head and some diamond-cut eyes, anything with sharp edges, I'd be concerned about it. But your typical piece of jewelry that is made of surgical steel and rounded edges is fairly safe. There are people who might have different types of jewelry they may put in for sexual intercourse. They may have a showpiece of jewelry they wear around and then they may have another piece of jewelry that is functional jewelry. For example, a frenum is a male genital piercing. You can wear different types of jewelry in them. You can wear a straight barbell on it, or a ring with an oval head so it'll act like a cock ring. There are some people I've seen who will attach a cock ring to that, or who will change out that jewelry for sexual intercourse so that it's more of a functional piece . . . The only way there could really be any problems is if two people with jewelry got caught on each other.

THE PAIN FACTOR

How much will it hurt? Well, if we took a sharp needle and slammed it through your private parts, do you think it would hurt? Still, most piercings don't even come close to hurting as much as you think they would. Indeed, the phrase "That's it?" can be heard ringing though the halls of most piercing establishments.

However, as one piercer notes: "Pain is part of the process." Die-hards enjoy testing their pain threshold, and that's an integral part of the fun.

YOUR POSSE

As with tattoos, if you plan to bring in a posse to watch (which you shouldn't), get the piercer's permission beforehand. The studio may be a freak show, but you have to ask before the parade comes to town. One friend should do you. Also ask first if you want to take pictures. If they come out well, you can always hawk them on the Internet for extra cash.

SHOWING OFF YOUR HOLES

How you show off your jewelry is up to you . . . and your employer. Piercings can take weeks

JUST SAY AAAAHHHH!!

What to expect when someone sticks a needle through your tongue:

1. They sit your ass down and explain what the hell they're gonna do to you.

2. After washing their hands, the piercer puts on FRESH latex gloves.

3. Using sterilized forceps, the tongue is gently pulled out of the mouth and held firm.

4. Next, a fresh hollow needle is inserted through the tongue (bottom through the top), being careful not to pierce anything else. A cork is now placed in the sharp end of the needle to hold it in place.

5. Utilizing the hollow needle for guidance, jewelry is threaded through the end of the needle and then pushed through the new piercing.

6. The ends are placed on the jewelry and the piercee is free to go about his business.

7. Staff cleans up the blood.

or months to heal, during which time you can't remove them. If you think there might be a problem with a prospective piercing, consult your employer first (unless you're a true outlaw living on the lam). It'll save you money and pain in the long run, and it might save your job. Hell, who knows? Maybe your boss will recommend a good studio. It's also considered good form to wear simpler studs in the workplace. Ornamental and sexually stimulating jewelry can be more fun, but can cause distraction at the office.

wheels

HARLEYS AND OTHER "OUTLAW" TRANSPORTATION

Lots of people say they love Harleys. Lots of people say they can ride one. But it's easy to spot the people who really do ride and own one. There's usually seven-hundred pounds of Harley crankin' underneath them. And a long, winding road ahead of them.

—from the official Harley-Davidson website

Built American tough! Don't stand up while riding. Before performing "spin-outs," read instruction sheet. Always wear a helmet.

—box packaging for Big Wheel children's toy

It's not just about getting from point A to point B, but about how you look along the way. That's the fundamental premise for cool wheels. They're about status; they're about image; they can be a reflection of who you are or who you want to be. Want to appear upwardly mobile? Try a Benz. Care to make a style/status statement without looking like you're trying too hard? Buy a Saab.

Want to look cool? Hop on a motorcycle, the preferred mode of transportation for bad boys (and girls) worldwide. And if you want to look *really* cool, hop on a Harley.

There's something about that classic American look: those 650-plus pounds of quivering steel, aluminum-magnesium, and rubber, the chrome exhaust pipe bursting at the seams with the distinct Harley sound that comes from its patent V-twin motor—a direct descendant of the engine that William Harley and Walter Davidson connected to a carburator made from tomato paste cans at the turn of the century in a Milwaukee shed. For decades, Harleys have been an icon of rebellion, a symbol of free-spiritedness and a middle finger to the Establishment, holding a mystique for the suit-and-tie-wearing masses who make the nine-to-five commute on four wheels.

HIGHWAY

Not all rides are created equal. Here's a quick list of vehicles that do and do not meet with our approval.

Slick Wheels

1. Harleys (except AMC models).

2. Vintage Hot Rod: We're fond of the '32 Ford Roadster—a "deuce"—with stylized monster flames. But we'll settle for anything pre-1960 as long as it has two doors, no fenders and barely any windshield.

3. Primo Muscle Car: We like the Dodge Charger. A Pontiac GTO will suffice.

4. Vintage low-rider.

5. Lead Sled: We dig the '49–'50 Merc's. Make sure they're "shaved," (no door handles or insignias, all smooth), with a "chopped top" (top has had section removed and lowered). Go for Caddy hubcaps and "wide white" tires.

6. Big Wheel (outlaw ride for tykes).

Of course, you don't have to have thick forearms riddled with tattoos and a knife hanging off a bronze-buckled belt to ride a Harley. Riders come in all shapes and sizes, and from a wide variety of socioeconomic classes. This section outlines the ideal rules of the road as prescribed by Harley diehards, but the same protocol applies to weekend road warriors and "Rolex Riders," also known as "RUBs" (Rich Urban Bikers) and "DINKs" (Double Income, No Kids, spending all extra dough at the Harley shop).

In a few featured sidebars, we also touch on low-riding and other "outlaw" wheels of choice.

BIKER'S FIRST RULE OF CONDUCT

Here's the number one rule of conduct if you're just starting out on a bike. Do not profess to be an insider or an expert; do not intimate that you have more miles under your treads than you actually do. Bikers can smell a poseur a mile a way.

You cannot buy your way into the biker "brotherhood," so don't try with a shiny new $30,000 bike or a closet full of shiny new Harley motor gear. You earn your stripes by riding, by learning about your bike and by not taking shit.

Bow to the lessons of experience, grasshopper. Let older, more seasoned riders lead conversation and guide the way. It's a respect thing.

Other than that, most of the rules are semi-flexible. Part of being a biker is about individuality, about doing what you feel comfortable doing. A seasoned rider can do what he wants, as long as he doesn't infringe upon the rights of other riders.

CHOOSING A HOG

Your bike. The open road. Wind in your face. Fumes of gas tickling your nostrils. A pulsing monster between your legs (which may or may not be an unfamiliar sensation). Think of your bike as a wild stallion, waiting to be controlled. It's your job to tame it.

One biker we spoke with described the difference between driving four wheels versus two as the difference between "being asleep and screwing without a rubber." Extremists call a car a "cage." The point is that a motorcycle—any motorcycle—makes you an active participant rather than just a passenger. Once you decide to get on a bike, you're already halfway there.

The next step, obviously, is choosing a make and style.

With faster acceleration and more precise cornering, Suzuki and Kawasaki may dominate the sports class. But when it comes to big touring bikes, Harley is still king of the road. H-D diehards will tell you it's not how fast you get there that counts, but the quality of the ride. Their disdain for Japanese bikes is manifested by name-calling: "crotch rocket," "rice rocket" and "rice burner" are popular terms for Pac Rim rides.

If you've just got to go foreign, the bikes that hold the most respect of Harley riders are those from England, particularly Triumphs.

> ### Dick Wheels
>
> 1. Rice burner (unless you're a racer).
>
> 2. '70s 'Vette Stingray (unless you're Mark Hamill).
>
> 3. Camaro or Firebird (the bad muscle car).
>
> 4. Any tricked-out Honda, Nissan, Toyota, or other economy car with added tail fins, gold rims, or monochromatic, bumper-to-bumper paint jobs. No fuschia or turquoise custom paint jobs, either!
>
> 5. Rides with antenna balls or plastered with stickers.
>
> 6. Tricycle or Yugo (nerd rides for tykes).

As for Harleys, Sportsters—their smallest style—make good entry-level bikes. Don't let their "half-a-Harley" nickname concern you—beginners do not need huge, expensive, fully dressed "softails" with drag bars and all sorts of chromed-out, high performance crap. Keep a low profile, master your Sportster, then graduate to one of the fancier Big Twins.

RESPECT THE HOGS OF OTHERS

Don't touch someone else's bike . . . or get on it . . . or scratch it . . . or knock it over. Or someone might come over and pound your head. They don't have to ask you, "Do you mind if I pound your head?" They'll just do it.

If you notice a bike has a kick-start, don't park so close to it that the owner doesn't have room to start up.

Contrary to popular opinion, bikers are an honorable lot. At popular hog havens or gatherings, leaving helmets and saddlebags on your parked bike is generally okay. You can lock up your bike if it gives you a sense of security, but a bike alarm is overkill and says "new rider."

Don't diss another man's bike—unless you're ready to rumble.

If you steal a bike, all bets are off. Many riders feel that bike thieves should be hung, or drawn and quartered.

Show a rider the same respect you show his ride. Don't stare at him; don't stare at his woman. Specifically, don't take inventory of her nipples or crotch region, as that may be grounds for death. If you have to peek, be subtle.

BORN TO BE STYLED

Like we said before, style is in the eye of the rider. If you're into fringe, studs and big belt buckles, cool. If you want Harley logos on everything from your jacket to your undies, cool. A lot of first-time owners are so excited about their new toy that they want to broadcast it to the world: those are the folks with a Harley chain wallet, Harley hat, Harley tee, etc. That enthusiasm isn't necessarily bad—it just might brand you as a novice or a member of the Village People.

LOW-ROLLER

Mack 10 on Low-Riding

You've seen 'em—intricately designed, mechanically high-tech works of art-on-wheels, turning heads as they slide down the boulevard with their tails just inches from the pavement. And if you're lucky, you've had the pleasure of watching the driver hit the switch and make his ride bounce like fleas.

We're talking about low-rider cars, another mode of transportation that gets EFO's seal of approval . . . provided it's done correctly. We consulted multi-platinum rap star and devoted low-rider Mack 10 about some of the do's and don'ts of his favorite hobby.

EFO: What's the biggest rule of etiquette for low-riders?
Mack 10: You definitely can't drink and drive. If you've never driven a low-rider, it's hard to explain, but with those little bitty wheels on that big car, it's really easy to lose control. And you need a little experience.

EFO: Any other rules?
Mack 10: Don't bring your shit out if it ain't hot, 'cuz I'm going to serve your ass. Don't bring your low-rider out if it ain't ready, cuz it's about who can jump the highest, and if it ain't ready, you don't want to get outdone.

EFO: So your car has to be able to jump, right?
Mack 10: To me, that's the most important thing. But anything like a '58 on down, it don't really have to jump so high. But '59 to '98, it must jump. Any real low-rider would agree with that.

EFO: Are there certain times or locations when it's more acceptable to start jumping?
Mack 10: It don't matter, drive or stationary. Three-wheel driving. It's all about challenging . . .

EFO: How about color?
Mack 10: Color is a personal preference, but I kinda like original colors. Some people got custom interior, paint, whereas if I have [a vintage Chevy], I want the interior to look original.

EFO: Is it cool to have hood ornaments and things hanging from the mirror?
Mack 10: Low-riding is all about personal preference. Anything can look good if you do it right. I'm kinda like a plain dude—I don't really like overdoing stuff. I don't hang nothing from my mirror. Some people do.

The only absolute "don't" is improper gear: tank tops, tennis shoes and other garments that don't protect your hide from road rash.

Here's a solid, low-profile, but ever-stylish uniform for the seasoned rider: biker or cowboy boots, jeans, T-shirt, leather vest or jacket, chaps for wind and pavement protection on long rides. Other staples: leather, waterproof gloves (even in 110 degree weather—just get the fingerless ones) and curved or wraparound shades that won't blow off.

Some bikers wear scarves, but if you wear 'em, make damn sure they're tucked into your jacket securely, 'cuz scarf in wheel = danger! If you ride in the rain, spare no expense and get a top-of-the-line rain suit.

NO CAGES

Peter Fonda on the Call of the Road

30 years after he sported black leather and pork chop sideburns as Captain America in Easy Rider, *Peter Fonda reignited his career with his Oscar-nominated role in* Ulee's Gold, *proving he could do more than ride a Harley, smoke grass, and say things like "far out" and "that's beautiful, man."*

That doesn't mean there isn't still a part of Captain America inside him. He's always been a Harley rider, and even now, in is late 50s', he'll hop on his hog with with a mess of hooks and bait and put 3000-3500 miles on his treads.

Here's what Mr. Fonda had to say about his passion for the road. We think it pretty much nails the Zen-like, biker philosophy on the head.

Every year, I try to make a cruise down south to the Mexican border on the eastern side of the divide, then I turn around and cruise up the other side. I don't ride dusk or after, so if I'm not near a motel, up goes the tent, out comes the pad, I go to sleep hearing the burbling of the brook [thinking], "This is a heck of a good life."

I go on my own. If you take some people with you, they might not want to stop and fish that hole, you know what I mean [laughs]. I just drive along, I see a hole, I pull over to the side, roll up my leather pants, take off my shoes, put my hearty rod together, and cast away. It's idyllic.

I take the satellite phone with me, just in case I have to call [my wife] Becky to tell her I'm not making any motel that night and I'm camping out. Generally no one can hit me on the phone, because I'm out there on the roam. It's only me being able to call for help if I need it or being able to check in with my wife and say, "I'm fine, another good day has gone by, I caught eighteen fish," and so forth. It makes me feel wonderful.

[This kind of Easy Rider adventure] still happens, you see, because there are no fences on the highways. I stay off the freeways, I ride the side roads, the back roads, I take every great mountain pass I can find. I love this planet; it's such a wonderful place. I don't ride fast; I ride slowly and carefully. But I'm watching things, I'm looking at where I am, I'm feeling where I am. I'm not in a cage.

Some bikers wear pins from various riding destinations. Don't wear a pin from a place you haven't been, unless someone has given it to you or it has some special significance.

The overall look should say minimal effort—it's more about function than fashion.

Don't deck yourself out in fashionable Harley gear if you *don't* have a bike. Those who do are idiots and will be taunted by others.

Oh, and one last thing: Harley men generally don't wear lots of little hoop earrings or eyeliner, or carry pink keychains, or anything that puts them in pansy territory. Even "leather fags" wouldn't consider putting pink on their hog. Some things are sacred.

SKID LIDS

About half the U.S. states require helmets, much to the chagrin of Harley riders, who don't like being told what to do. The main argument against helmet laws is that it's bad precedent, opening the door for other state regulation.

No one will give you shit for wearing a skid lid where it is required by law. The half-helmet is the lid of choice, for two reasons: it looks a helluva lot cooler, and it provides more visibility. In addition to diminishing peripheral vision, full-faced helmets—it is argued by some—can be dangerous in the event of an accident. If someone has to pry that thing from your head, it can tweak you pretty bad.

A lot of anti-helmeters look down on those who wear 'em in states where it's not required. If you want to wear a helmet in a non-helmet state, go for it, but don't be shocked if you get a little stinkeye from other riders.

When not wearing a helmet on a bright day, consider sunblock.

ACCESSORIZE, BUT NOT EXCESSIVELY

Ideally, you get on your bike with a destination in mind, with no pager, no cell phone, no credit cards, and no maps. These modern items are antithetical to the Harley ethic, which is all about self-reliance. If you're not into taking chances, why get on the bike at all?

That doesn't mean you shouldn't be prepared for road trouble. Always have a bag of basic tools and spare parts with you. You

MACK 10'S LOW-RIDER RULES

Low-Rider Etiquette at a Glance . . .

1. No drinking and driving.

2. Don't lend your keys to a fellow low-rider unless they can afford to pay for it.

3. Don't stop in the middle of a crowded street and start hopping, burning rubber, three-wheeling, blocking traffic, or doing anything to piss off the police. One reckless driver might make the cops come down hard on everyone.

4. Hitting the switch while driving is fine as long as you're not endangering anyone.

5. Don't hit anybody else's switch.

6. Don't scratch someone else's car— that's a cardinal sin.

wouldn't hike in a desert without water, would you? And you don't ride without tools. Know how to fix your bike, lest you become a leather-clad pedestrian.

A girl makes a great accessory, hence the terms "bitch bars" (for the passenger backrest), or "bitch pegs" (for elevated passenger footholds). The best accessory of all is a girl with big hooters. Harley mantra: No hooters too big.

MOTORCYCLE MOMMAS

The road is the great equalizer. If a woman rider is still around, she must be good. While the typical H-D dude is far from liberal-minded, he recognizes this fundamental truth.

THE MOUNT

Mount your metallic steed on the left—that's the side with the kick-stand, so it's easier to support the bike. Put your right hand on throttle and brake lever, squeeze brake, lift your right leg over the seat. The bike should be in neutral as you straighten it up. Before dismounting, put down the kickstand. Keep your hand on the brake as you lift your leg back over the seat.

PLAYING IN TRAFFIC

There's nothing wrong with showing off your bike—stylin' and pro-filin' is part of the culture. But . . . you don't buy a bike to sit on it curbside at some hog haven or other trendy watering hole, hoping to bag chicks. Your scoot was made to be ridden, so don't let her sit idle. Rack up some mileage.

Which brings us to our next point. An experienced rider's biggest peeve is the green, unsafe "squid" who gets on a bike without knowing what he's doing. In other words, look and learn before you let loose on the open road. Here are a few tips.

Don't steer your bike. Just "lean" it. It's about gently shifting your weight. Your hog will follow your lead. If you're a passenger, lean into the turn slightly, taking care not to throw off the driver. A good way to do this is simply to look over the driver's shoulder—if the driver is turning left, look over his left shoulder, and vice versa. The subtle shift in your weight should be sufficient to facilitate turning.

Before turning left, go to the outside/opposite side of the road, then dive back in. Vice versa for turning right. The object is to give yourself more road to work with.

Ride in a staggered formation when cruising near another rider for maximum visibility and safety.

If someone wants to pass you, don't hang 'em up. Move to the right (so that they can't push you into oncoming traffic if they screw up); let 'em pass to the left. If someone lets you pass, it's not so important to wave "thank you" to them—staying in control of your bike is far more important.

Don't pass another bike too closely. This element of biker etiquette is particularly important for "rice rocketeers." Their bikes move so fast that when they pass a

Rules for a Low-Rider Battle . . .

1. Cars should be nose to nose.

2. No pushing on the trunk to get extra height.

3. No added weight in the trunk or in the bumper to get extra height.

4. What's important is how high the front tires get off the ground.

5. Highest wins.

6. If you jump high enough to break something on the car, you're doing something right.

slower-moving rider in close proximity, the effect is not unlike being buzzed by a plane.

In many states, bikers frequently wave to other bikers on the road. One exception is California, home to a number of rival biker clubs. While gang-style feuding between these clubs has calmed down quite a bit, the general rule in a state like Cali is to dispense with greetings on the road—you don't always know if he's friend or foe.

On the flip side, NEVER ever pass someone on the side of the road who needs help. Shit happens, and only a jerk would pass by a biker "bro" in need of assistance.

At the repair shop, a bike on the road in need of service takes priority over a "project" bike—a bike getting customized, etc. A mechanic faithful to the Harley code will abide by this unspoken law, and regular customers won't bitch about it.

Contrary to the image put forth by the media, bikes and booze don't mix. Ask any serious rider—it's cool to be smart, safe and sober on the road.

ROAD MAPS

A number of mags cater to the biker/Harley lifestyle. The bible is arguably the West Coast–based *Easyriders*, the largest-selling motorcycle publication in the world. Those looking for more of an East Coast slant might prefer *Outlaw Biker*.

As for flicks, *Easy Rider* is the quintessential biker flick, particularly in its portrayal of the spirit of adventure that has come to be synonymous with biking. For a solid depiction of the biker lifestyle, check out *Mask*, starring Cher. And while *Harley Davidson & the Marlboro Man* might seem like a lame big-screen product endorsement, it does feature bitchin' bikes.

What about Brando's *The Wild One*, you ask? Hey, he was riding a Triumph.

REAL OUTLAWS

Harley doesn't condone the outlaw image of their machines that is propagated by the media. They refused to back *Easy Rider*, and continue to refuse to donate bikes to such movies, despite the fact that

LOUD AND PROUD

Everyone knows a Harley when they hear it. Like a trumpet, that thundering, "potato potato potato" rumble announces a Harley rider's arrival from blocks away. Hell, Harley even trademarked their sound, suing Honda when they attempted to copy it. The actual loudness depends on the pipes you run on your bike, and for every decibel, you sacrifice horsepower. But who cares? What's a little performance in exchange for the sonic glee that's been proven to make chicks cream!

MOTOR SCOOTER
— RICHTER: 1.1

GAS-POWERED LAWN
MOWER FROM SEARS
— RICHTER: 2.5

DIRT BIKE
— RICHTER: 5.5

GENERIC RICE BURNER
— RICHTER: 6.5

HARLEY-DAVIDSON
DUAL EXHAUST TAILS
— RICHTER: 9.5

HARLEY-DAVIDSON
SUPERCHARGED PIPES
— RICHTER: 9.9

Peter Fonda's road romp launched thousands of bikers. In fact, the suits at H-D see Harley riding as the next American family sport. And for hundreds of thousands of riders around the globe, it is just a sport and nothing more.

There are, however, those who choose Harley riding as a lifestyle. Within this class of riders exists an even smaller subset, known as "outlaw bikers" or "one-percenters." Many belong to specific bike clubs such as the Banditos, the Vagos, Hell's Angels, the Outlaws—rival crews who used to war, but who are now generally at peace.

These "outlaws" are the most intense brand of biker. They don't like loose ends, and their shit is wired as tight as can be—on their bikes and in life.

Don't cross 'em, don't pose as one, don't talk shit about 'em. And be careful what you write about them, or you might get a knock on your door.

MOTORCYCLE MAMA

A Real Live Biker Chick on What She Likes in a Man

Loray Bartels is a long-term Harley chick. She grew up around Hell's Angels, and has dated a ton of bikers, whom she describes as "rogues or pirates with something powerful between their legs." She was kind enough to outline her fantasy in the flesh for us. Fellas, take note if this is the kind of gal you want to date.

He's got a long beard, long hair. I like big forearms, strong muscles, with lots of tattoos, Harley-Davidson written right on his arms. A very sexy, powerful image to me is a guy with tats on his hand holding his cock. Hidden tattoos are also fine. Doesn't matter if he's heavy. He's the kind of guy you feel perfectly safe with; you walk in the street and know that not a person in the world is going to mess with you. The chicks are looking at him. I can look tough on the back of his bike, and be tough by association.

He's wearing a tight T-shirt, probably black, and tight worn Levi's. You can't take a guy seriously if he's not wearing boots. Riding boots. Cowboy boots are also acceptable. Half-helmet, wearing a bandana underneath. Black leather vest or jacket. No studs or fringe on the jacket. Red leather doesn't cut it.

The chopper is the perfect bike for me, I like choppers. That bike's hard to ride, you have to be a man, got to be tough. He's got to have a couple of tools on the bike and know how to use them. A crotch rocket is a kind of a turnoff. If I hear a Yamaha clone of a Harley, it's like, at least buy a real one. That turns me off.

I want him to grab me, throw me down and fuck me hard. I want him to say "You fucking little whore I'm going to fuck you just like you know you wanna be fucked." I want to be manhandled. But then at the same time, if I say "stop," I want them to stop. "No" always means no. So I might steer clear of the heavy hardcore guys, because those guys will say, "Ha, fuck you, bitch," and keep going. But that's kind of a turn-on, too. They're nasty fucks—fast and furious, and that's how I like it. One of the most memorable things a biker boyfriend said to me was this: "Your ass is finer than most chicks' pussies." I don't know what it is about bikers, but they like to fuck girls in the behind.

I've never done it on a bike while being driven. But I know a lot of guys that have. She has to face him while he's riding, and she's got to do the "riding." A lot of women come while riding just from the vibrations, because your knees are high up on the "slut pegs." One of the tips I picked up [from a biker chick in the ladies restroom] was Ben Wa balls, because they jiggle inside while you ride.

BIKER PARKING ONLY

ALL OTHERS WILL BE TOWED

Guns

NUMBER ONE WITH A BULLET

The right of the people to keep and bear arms shall not be infringed.

—2nd Amendment, U.S. Constitution

Rat-a-tat-tat.

—Bonnie and Clyde

Nine out of ten outlaws agree that guns are cool, and as the NRA is so keen to point out, they're constitutional, too! Power to the people!!!

Consider that so many of the games we played as kids—cops and robbers, cowboys and Indians, war—all centered around carrying some sort of smoke wagon. Heck, even most of the better heroes carry guns: John Wayne, Clint Eastwood, Duke Nuk'em. Indeed, we are trained from birth, from plastic to BB to the real thing. We're strong believers that guns don't kill people, people kill people.

We must admit, however, that there are a *lot* of stupid people with guns. *Have you watched the news lately?* Hence, this section. In no other part of this book are etiquette and safety so closely connected.

GUN BASICS

There are four principal rules concerning proper gun etiquette:

1. It's not polite to point. Never point a gun at yourself, your body parts, or another person. Never point a gun at a person as a joke, a fake threat to make some sort of point, or to illustrate a movie scene. Every year some stupid M.F. kills their friend or is forced to explain to loved ones why the *unloaded* gun just "went off." Easy solution, Rambo: Assume all guns are loaded and ready to kill, and always point them in a safe direction.

2. No tricks, cowboy. Too many wannabe quick-draw artists have shot themselves and innocent bystanders by reaching for their weapon and pulling the trigger at the same time. Pull your gun, acquire your target, put your finger on the trigger . . . bang. Is that so hard? Premature firing is always bad social etiquette.

3. Unloaded is the best policy. Never keep a loaded gun unless you're going to use it. Many a kid has found Daddy's loaded rifle and killed themselves, or their little playmate.

4. Keep it out of your pants. Never carry an unholstered gun by your dick. 'Nuff said.

BUYING A GUN

As with most purchases, if you don't know what you're doing, feel free to ask the salesperson. He'll give you the information you need. That said, here are some basic pointers for the novice gun consumer:

1. Don't point a gun at anyone else in the store.
2. Don't mention even in jest that "this'll take care of my ex." Bad joke, bad form.
3. Never try to load ammo inside the shop.
4. Don't overarm yourself with the most expensive laser pointer or super bullets—it's like getting your kid a Benz as a first car.
5. Don't try to talk your way out of the waiting period to buy your gun; it won't work and it'll make you look suspicious.
6. Many states require you to pass a written gun safety test prior to purchasing a gun. It's about as hard as a written driver's test. If you pass the first time, great. If not, just take it again, Kojak.
7. Feel free to shop around. But don't skimp on quality. That could end up being far more costly.

HANDLING

In addition to making sure a gun is unloaded (barrel, clip, and chamber), make sure the safety is on before you pass it to someone. Pass it handle first, business end facing away from anyone. Make sure the person handles the gun in a safe manner and does not point it at themself or you.

TRANSPORTATION

Driving with an unregistered gun (loaded or not) is a felony. If you're traveling with a gun in the car (presumably off to a shooting range or to kill some deer), it's the law that your unloaded weapon be stored in the trunk and the ammo left inside the car. For you 'necks out there, substitute the gun rack in your pickup for the trunk.

Again, keep the ammo separate, folks.

AT THE RANGE

You know that whenever you have a room full of people with guns, there's going to be a few rules. Since the guy upholding these rules is also packing heat—probably a lot of it—we suggest you pay attention!

If you've never shot a gun before, the smart thing to do is call ahead and set up a gun safety class at the gun club or firing range you plan to attend. Generally, the price is a bit of a rip-off, but that's the breaks. You only have to take the class once, then you're locked and loaded. Feel free to ask all the questions you want.

Never show up at a gun range loaded: that goes for you and the gun. Firing a gun is a dangerous sport, and if you're wasted on drugs or booze, you will not get past the front door. Assuming you're sober, the attendant will either ask to see your weapon or make you pass your guns through a safe box prior to your entry into the shooting range. The attendant will then inspect your weapon (which should be empty) prior to assigning you a range spot.

You're generally required to bring earplugs and shooting goggles for your own safety at the range. If you don't have these, you can rent or buy them at the club.

The range master will show you to your spot. Load your weapon there (while keeping the gun pointed downrange). After you attach your target and move it into position, you're ready to rock 'n' roll. Now, simply aim and fire. Don't be a quick draw, don't practice your rapid firing technique, and never try to shoot at someone else's target. If you walk away from your gun, make sure it's unloaded and pointed downrange.

If someone is not following the rules—something that can put your safety and the safety of others at risk—go tell the range master. While you may feel like a rat, it's better to be a live rat than a dead person. Just watch your back when you leave the club.

And finally, a few words to the wise: Do not attach pictures of your boss, ex-wife or the president to your target, screaming, "Die muthafucka die," as you blast away. Again: bad form.

PULLING

Never pull a gun on a live human being unless it's a life-or-death situation. Someone flipping you off on the freeway does not qualify.

Never pull a gun out unless you're ready (and willing) to use it. When you pull out a gun, you've escalated the situation to a new level. You don't know how your enemy will react. Even if your intention is to simply scare them into retreat, you have no guarantee that they will not pull out a gun of their own and start blasting. In other words, if you're not ready to use it, keep it in your pants.

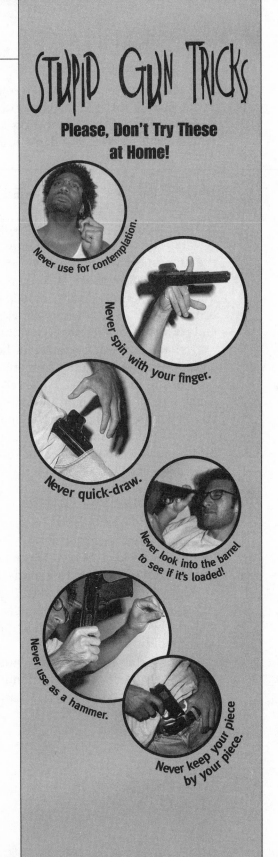

STUPID GUN TRICKS

Please, Don't Try These at Home!

Never use for contemplation.

Never spin with your finger.

Never quick-draw.

Never look into the barrel to see if it's loaded!

Never use as a hammer.

Never keep your piece by your piece.

And . . . never *ever* threaten someone with an unloaded weapon. In the eyes of the law, there's no difference; in the eyes of the street hood, their loaded weapon works better. It's like showing up with a condom and no erection—damn useless.

HOME DEFENSE

Proper etiquette dictates that you always take others into consideration...even when it comes to home protection purchases, the amount of weapon you get can have a *direct impact* on your neighbors. For instance, if you have no neighbors (perhaps you live on a farm or have a posh pad deep in the Appalachians), feel free to arm yourself with . . . whatever. Hell, go for it! May we recommend a nice Howitzer? If it goes "Blammo!" it'll work in the sticks.

However, if you're apartment-bound in the 'burbs, high-powered weapons such as Magnums or titanium-tipped ammo can be quite the nuisance, as they go through walls like butter. Killing an intruder is one thing, but blowing a hole through your next-door neighbor's kid is another! A 9mm, .38 or .380 will do the trick. If you're going the shotgun route, get birdshot for ammo. Sure, there's more potent stuff, but birdshot shoots more projectiles and covers a larger area, so you'll have a greater chance of stopping the sonofabitch without putting neighbors at risk.

Another point of etiquette is technically up to you: It's your house. Imagine an intruder has entered your house. You have your weapon cocked and locked, and your family is safely locked in the room behind you. Unless you're in a killing mood, feel free to warn the poor bastard of his fate: "Hey shithead! I've called the cops and they're on their way. I am also armed with a pretty menacing shotgun. I suggest that you leave now!" Generally speaking, nobody wants to ruin their rug by killing a sack of shit in their house. The warning could save you a lot of carpet cleaner.

When the cops show up hours later, put your gun on the ground, tell them you're the home owner, and explain what transpired. Keeping the gun in your hand could result in a messy case of mistaken identity.

KIDS AND GUNS

If you've got the gun around for hunting deer, make sure it's locked up and your kids don't have access to the keys. However, if your weapon is around for the purpose of self-defense, things get a little trickier. You want it accessible for emergencies, but out of little Timmy's curious reach.

Our suggestion is to have your gun locked up by your bed and have the only key on your key ring. It will slow your response time in the event of an intrusion, but having your kid accidentally off a friend will haunt you for the rest of your life.

In general, kids and guns just don't mix.

FEAR OF FLYING

If you plan to bring a gun with you on your vacation, there are some very specific rules about airplane transport.

Call your airline to make the arrangements. Most likely they'll ask you to bring your unloaded weapon stored in a locked box or case to a designated area at the airport. The airline will then check your weapon, give you a receipt, and store it in a locked cabinet on the plane (and no, we're not telling you where). You retrieve it when you land.

Needless to say, the airlines don't take kindly to those who try to bring weapons on planes. (See Part VII, "Travel") You will always get arrested and punished for this offense and, unless you're a rock star and can pay your dues with a Public Service Announcement, prepare for some jail time or a shitload of community service emptying bed pans at County.

Knives, etc.

A CALL TO ARMS

She cut off their tails with a carving knife...
—"Three Blind Mice"

Real tough guys don't *carry* weapons. They tend to be cumbersome as well as illegal (many carry a felony beef). However, "improvising" a weapon is an outlaw trademark. Classic street fight implements include the trash can, tire iron, baseball bat (you're in a softball league, right?), bar stool, and the always popular pool cue. But remember: picking up any kind of weapon in a fight automatically raises the stakes . . . and you never know if your opponent is packing heat! If you pull a weapon and your opponent kicks your ass or kills you dead, they can argue self-defense.

That said, here is the short list of weaponry for the adventurous.

KNIVES

Everybody's got to have a few knives: a Swiss Army knife, the "buck" knife you stole from your older brother. Laws vary about the size and kind of blade that you can carry on you, but some rules of thumb are that the blade can be no longer than four and a half inches long, can't be double-edged, and can't be spring-mounted (like a switchblade). Generally speaking, don't pull 'em on people: Knife robberies are way passé, and if you pull one out in a fight, someone might just bust a cap in your ass. On the other hand, it is always cool to have a nice pocket knife on you for utility cutting.

Knife rules include: keeping the blade toward you when passing it around, letting the cop know you have a knife before they frisk you, and not trying to sneak it past security at a concert or the airport. They'll almost invariably find it and confiscate it.

Never, ever keep your knife on your belt—fashion faux pas.

SWORDS

Schwing! We don't care how cool it looked in *Highlander*. Carrying a sword is way too eighteenth century for our tastes. If you must collect them, make sure they're actual swords and not that unsharpened fake Pier One crap.

MARTIAL ARTS WEAPONS

Grasshopper . . . if you're Bruce Lee or Jackie Chan, throwing stars, nunchucks and butterfly knives might serve you well. But the majority of the population should probably steer clear. Carrying such items on the street is illegal, and they will certainly amount to no good in inexperienced hands (especially if your opponent takes them from you and beats you senseless). However, if you practice some sort of karate shit, it's cool to use "found" weapons in a martial arts fashion—keeping the "waaaah" battle cries to a minimum.

WHIPS

Unless you're Indiana Jones, your whip is best kept in the bedroom (see "Alternative Sex" in Part II).

BOOMERANGS

Not unless you're an aborigine living in the bush.

BRASS KNUCKLES

Also illegal in fights, tough guy. Consider a roll of nickels, a ball from the pool table, or any small, heavy object as a substitute.

THE BROKEN BOTTLE

Ever try to break a bottle on the side of a bar? Never quite breaks off the way they do on TV. Odds are you'll end up gashing open your own hand. Please substitute a bar stool or pool cue whenever possible.

Meat

PLEASURES OF THE FLESH

Every moving thing that liveth shall be meat for you.

—The Bible

Nobody beats our meat.

—Culver City Meat Market slogan

Meat rules, whether it's a marbled fillet at Ruth's Chris, a 2:00 A.M. t-bone and eggs at the Pantry in Los Angeles, some greasy bacon or a big sloppy plate of baby-back pork ribs. Talk to most "outlaws" about cholesterol, food that "used to have a face," and the depletion of the ozone due to cow flatulence, and—like our pals in the meat industry— they'll shrug and tell you that *Nothing satisfies like beef.*

Of course, grubbing down on a juicy fillet around carni-phobic vegetarians can be a bit like barhopping with a recovering alcoholic or bumping into Mom on your way to a strip club. It can bum your high. It's like they've got something on you. You know in your heart of hearts that a bowl of steamed bok choi and a wedge of tofu is probably better for your health, but nonetheless you succumb to your primal urges: blood lust.

Well, we're here to confirm that there's no need to deny your intrinsic nature as an omnivore: Those pointy incisor teeth were made for shredding, those molars were built for chomping, those funky digestive enzymes swimming around in your tummy are tough enough to handle any porterhouse. For thousands of years, your ancestors hunted beasts with rocks and spears without an iota of guilt. History is on your side.

But hey, why preach to the choir? If you're a meat eater, you know tofu dogs and veggie burgers don't cut it. You know that soy steaks at a BBQ are a buzz-kill. You know that, bottom line, beef is super-tasty.

LET THEM EAT STEAK . . . THE RIGHT WAY

The code of the carnivore is simple: Eat meat, and eat lots of it. There is no inappropriate time to eat meat, and no amount is too much.

And eat it rare. None of that well-done nonsense. It should still be mooing on your plate.

For the real connoisseur, a plain-and-simple cube of butter is the only condiment needed on steak. Less choice pieces of meat can be enhanced with Heinz 57, A-1, BBQ sauce, etc. Ketchup will do in a pinch. Try tossing a shot of scotch on your dinner while it's grilling— adds a nice accent.

Definitely eat all the meat on your plate. The die-hard carnivore will clean the platter before him, gristle and all, gnawing at the bone for every last nibblet of muscle. We recommend you pick your teeth afterward. It's not so much that those little chunks between the teeth might gross folks out. Rather, we're concerned about those extra hidden morsels going to waste in there.

Finally, the ultimate carnivore hunts and kills his or her own dinner. He enjoys his meat with total cognizance of where it came from and how it got to his plate, rather than letting a butcher and a factory do his dirty work!

PORK FAT RULES

Like TV chef Emeril Lagasse says, "Pork fat rules." Same for lard and schmaltz. Vegetable oil may be better for you, but it never tastes as good. We endorse all rendered animal products.

BE TRUE TO THE CAUSE

As a carnivore who knows the joys of meat, it is your duty to attempt to persuade anyone who's on the fence—those people who insist they've kicked the habit, but who you know secretly crave it. Order meat in front of them and linger over every tantalizing bite.

THOSE PESKY VEGETARIANS

When it comes to being a carnivore in a too-PC world, here's the meat and potatoes of the matter—the first and most important rule of red meat–eating etiquette: Never apologize for following your basic instinct to grind into flesh. Whether your passion is bacon or baby-back ribs, tripe or tri-tip, lamb or Spam, your status as a flesh-eater needs no defense. If someone doesn't like meat, that's their choice, and it's not your problem. If they whine, tell 'em to piss off!

That said, we've come up with a few easy-to-follow guidelines that can help you interact with and even ingratiate yourself with those earthy-crunchy herbivores.

Socializing with the Enemy

If you're having a BBQ and plan to invite vegetarians, have a supply of veggie burgers or grilled vegetables on hand. Most vegetarians are used to being hungry and don't expect to be accommodated, so any gesture on your part goes a long way. Whip up a pasta salad for the fussy ones who won't touch stuff cooked on a meat-greasy grill.

As a rule, vegetarians, particularly half-assed ones who aren't super-committed, will generally find processed luncheon meat easier to stomach than a recognizable body part or carcass. That means that if you're dining in front of a vegetarian, Oscar Mayer might be less offensive than a turkey leg, and a hot dog might be more tolerable than a whole duck with the head still on. The bloodier the meat, the more of an impact you're likely to have on those squeamish lil' wimps.

Sleeping with the Enemy

If you attempt to date a vegetarian, don't take 'em to dinner at, say, a Sizzler, a rib joint, or a similar house of carnage, where the focus is on meat and where the non-meat options are extremely limited.

Many die-hard veg-heads won't screw meat eaters. They just can't hang with someone who perpetuates what they consider a cycle of cruelty, environmental waste, yada yada yada. Who cares. A lot of the veggie chicks don't shave their legs, and a lot of the guys are anemic pussies with low sperm counts due to lack of protein.

The Veggie Mind-set

A few questions and assumptions tend to tick vegetarians off. Feel free to avoid if you're in the mood to play nice:

"Oh, there's just a little bit of meat in it, just pick it out." Nope. A real vegetarian will insist that even a trace of meat will permeate the entire dish.

"This soup is vegetarian." Lots of vegetable soups are made with chicken stock, which makes them off limits to real veg-heads.

"You're a vegetarian? Oh, but you eat fish and chicken, right?" Nah-ah, not if they're really down for the cause. There are different degrees of abstinence, but "vegetarian" means no beast, fish or fowl. Vegans won't do eggs or dairy, either.

"You don't eat meat? What *do* you eat? How do you get protein?" Beans, peanut butter, soy, cheese—there are lots of ways, though most aren't fun and tasty like a burger.

"You're a vegan and you don't eat cheese? Is that because you're lactose-intolerant?" Often, those touchy tofu types resent any assumption that they're not making a personal choice, that their dietary restrictions are forced on them by some sort of food allergy. It's like you're not giving them credit for their self-discipline.

"When you eat a carrot or lettuce, you're killing the plant—isn't that cruel to the plant?" Probably not. Though there are over-the-top wackos called "fruitarians" who only eat stuff that falls off a shrub or tree naturally to avoid any sort of plant cruelty, the general consensus is that plants don't have consciousness. Besides, any veg worth his or her salt will tell you that a helluva lot more plants go into feeding the cow that becomes your burger.

"Are your cats vegetarian?" This really gets their goat. Cats and dogs know the joys of meat, and their digestive systems are built for it. Most vegetarian owners don't impose their views on them.

Meaty Issues

Vegetarians tend to be know-it-alls. Be armed and ready with comebacks to some of their silly arguments against meat.

If someone is really bugging you about your carnivorous diet, point to their leather belt or their Birkenstocks and expose them for the hypocritical scoundrels they are.

In the absence of leather goods, note that the sheep sheared for the wool in their sweater were less than psyched to have their hair hacked off. Frequently, their skin gets rather hacked up, too.

What, no wool? Tell 'em you pity the poor fowl plucked for their down jacket, or the worms killed to make that silk shirt. At the very least, they're bound to be wearing something with rubber or Gore-Tex or plastic, all of which are bad for the planet.

If the self-righteous vegetarian on your case is the artsy-fartsy type, remind them that their paintbrushes are probably made of sable, camel or squirrel.

Finally, if someone dares to comment that the methane produced by those gaseous, cud-chewing lil' doggies on the range contributes to the depletion of the ozone, laugh in their face at their absurdity. Their car and their fridge are far more detrimental than any cow fart.

EVERY TIME SOMEONE BITES INTO A TOFU BURGER,

a Soy Bean Screams Out in Pain

All right, so you tried to play nice, tried to be sensitive to their way of life, but they simply won't accept yours. Sometimes carnivore etiquette demands that you fight back. Here's a sampling of retorts to those annoying, self-righteous carni-phobes who try to sway you from the pleasures of the flesh.

VEG-HEAD SAYS . . .	CARNIVORE RESPONDS . . .
"Eating meat perpetuates a cycle of violence toward animals."	"Ever see the *National Geographic* where the lioness rips out a gazelle's rib cage while its heart is still beating? Now, that's violence!"
"Every time you bite into that, an animal screams out in pain."	. . . by putting his/her ear next to the steak and saying, "Talk to me, bitch."
"That thing once had a face."	"Yeah, and it probably had a name, a family, brothers and sisters and if they were here, I'd eat them, too!"
"Raising meat is bad for the environment, because it's a waste of natural resources."	"You want to talk about environmental waste? Go harass L. Ron Hubbard and Jackie Collins. Entire forests have been clear-cut for that rubbish."
"The grain used to feed cattle could feed millions of starving people in the Third World."	"Who wants to eat grain?"

Leather and Fur

BEAUTY IS SKIN DEEP

We feel that animals have the same rights as retarded children.

—Alex Pacheco, Director, PETA, 1989

This section is devoted to some of the etiquette issues surrounding the wonderful by-products of our four-legged friends, who so self-lessly sacrifice their lives so that we can look stylish.

HELL-BENT FOR LEATHER

If you eat meat, you should have no moral hang-up with other animal by-products such as leather. The cow's already slaughtered, and folks are already feasting on its innards. It would be a shame to let the rest of it go to waste.

Besides, leather looks cool. What would the Fonz or *Easy Rider*'s Captain America have been without their leathers?

Staples of hipness include the long leather coat and the bomber, preferably black or brown and looking a bit weathered. You can dress it up or dress it down. Goes nicely with faded jeans and a T-shirt.

Tight leather pants should be reserved for hot model chicks, fetish clubbers and eccentric rock stars ... unless you're an old and bloated eccentric rock star, in which case leave that shit at home (see "The Rock Star" in Part V).

AHH, THE SILKY LUXURIANCE OF FUR!

The next level of Carnivora—the pièce de résistance for vegetarians—is fur. Far greater are the masses who will sink their teeth into an animal than those who will sport its carcass around their necks for fashion.

Those who do take a fair amount of shit. And we salute their fortitude. Wearing fur in these politically correct times is as outlaw as anything else in this book.

NO APOLOGIES

The first rule of fur-wearing etiquette is quite simple: if you wear it, flaunt it, and never *ever* apologize for it.

Sure, it's a decadent luxury. But hey, if you eat meat and wear leather, fur's not that big a stretch. Plus it feels so good. If you've ever tried on a full-length mink or sable, you know that nothing quite compares. And nothing keeps you as warm—not wool, not polar fleece, not goose down.

Bear in mind that most fur doesn't come from endangered species. They have farms for those little critters. They're not trapped and left bleeding in the snow. They are raised specifically so that you can feel toasty and look glamorous. Shed a tear of remorse for them if you like, but remember that *you are worth it.*

Finally, bear in mind that minks are *not* cute. They are nasty, weasel-like rodents with webbed feet—oblong aquatic rats blessed with nice fur.

How to Wear It

Fur-wearers are a dying breed. It's not just about animal rights, either. In general, people today have a more casual approach to going out, which means you get less use out of your $5,000 investment. A lot of people just don't bother.

Those who do tend to steer away from the ostentatious stuff. In the '80s, it was hip to look like a movie star with a big poofy "look at me" coat. Sheared, less poofy furs don't last as long, but they're more in style these days.

WHEN ANIMALS ATTACK!

While organizations like People for the Ethical Treatment of Animals tend to poo-poo the idea of wearing fur and other animal pelts, citing cruelty toward animals, EFO dares to ask: Who are these animals, and why should we care?

Ratttlesnake: This venomous snake is always pissed off. Cross its path, and its strike can be lethal. Makes nice boots.

Mink: Known to eat their young, these carnivorous little creatures' only redeeming feature is their luxurious coats. They should be happy about their prized fur status: it's better than being written off as angry squirrels.

Cows: Big, dumb and lazy, cows have been known to sleep on their feet and not run from fire. Best used for jackets, shoes, belts and steaks.

Rabbit: An amoral creature whose concept of procreation without ramifications is abhorrent to most civilized countries. Use the fur for a fluffy jacket or keep the foot for a lucky charm!

Fox: Known as "The Trickster" throughout ancient mythology, this crafty little devil is considered vermin by many farmers. Makes a woman look foxy.

Here's a quick fur hierarchy: sable is at the top, followed by mink. Then you've got your fox, beaver, coyote, muskrat, weasel, and so on. Skip rabbit—it's déclassé.

Guys shouldn't wear fur coats. Unless they're a pimp. Or an Eskimo.

As far as fur accessories, keep in mind that a nice coat will upstage pretty much anything you wear. Nothing amazing is necessary underneath. Black is always a good bet. Diamond necklaces and pearls work well, too. Skip the tiara.

It's important that your fur doesn't clash with your 'do. No big, teased hair, please. Between you and the animal, it's just too much.

Wear furs at fancy places and special occasions: Christmas and New Year's, a wedding, the theater, the opera. Some are made for the slopes.

Fur is far more acceptable in cold, cosmopolitan places like New York or Chicago than in Southern California. And it's never appropriate in warm weather. Forty to fifty degrees is about the cutoff point. A fur coat is not glamorous when you're sweating.

Maintenance

If you're going to plunk down thousands of dollars on a coat, make sure you insure it. This is standard practice, like with a diamond. Unless you plan to be encumbered by a big, hot stuffed animal all evening, you want the option of leaving it at a coat check without stressing.

Fur coat maintenance is a bitch. It's almost like taking care of a pet. You have to pay to store furs every season or they will dry-rot. Sitting on them in the car, having a purse or shoulder bag across the chest, or using an armrest in a theater will wear it down in places. No matter how tempting, don't rub your mug into your coat or someone else's, as the face secretes oils that aren't good for the fur. And if your fur gets wet, you smell like a wet dog.

Watching Your Back . . . and the Pelts on It

Today, most fur fans think twice before sporting their coats. While the animal rights folks have chilled out a bit with their blood buckets, you can still expect dirty looks. A die-hard activist might even be down on fake stuff that looks real, since it promotes the image of fur.

Fuck 'em. Most of the complainers won't have the guts to confront you directly. They'll rant from across the street, or make offhanded anti-fur comments to a friend at a level you can hear. Wimps. Just ignore them. Besides, the people ranting at you generally have a leather wallet, or drive a car with fake leather upholstery with a half-life of a zillion years. Feel free to point that out to them. For more ammunition, see our chart on meat-eater retorts in the previous section.

Old ladies who bought their coats in less politically correct times are, generally, more exempt from anti-fur scorn.

Wearing fur to a Sierra Club meeting or the zoo is bad form. Wearing it to a vegetarian restaurant is on the fence. If you decide to go for it, be careful about hanging your fur on an unattended coat rack—we spoke to a number of fur-wearers who've come back to find nasty notes, among other surprises, in the pockets.

You will be most comfortable wearing your fur when and where others are wearing it. There's strength in numbers.

A woman should not wear a fur coat if she's by herself in a dark alley in a bad part of town. It's like a big giant neon sign that says, "MUG ME." In addition, don't wear your fur if you're trying to get a bargain on something.

If you spy an aggro-looking chick with unshaven armpits, attired in natural fibers, and carrying a bucket containing some sloshy, red viscous liquid, watch your back. If she starts heading toward you with a venomous glare, move out of her way . . . unless your coat is insured, in which case you should close your eyes and receive her with open arms, then dash off to buy a brand-spanking-new coat.

PART IV

The Lifestyle

Conduct is three-fourths of our life, and its largest concern.
—*Matthew Arnold*

There's more to being "outlaw" than just indulging in various sins and having the proper accessories.

It's also about attitude. It's about how you conduct yourself in daily life. You want to be street-savvy. You want to be a little rough around the edges. You want to be tough, or at least know how to hold your own in a brawl. You want to listen to the right music—something that echoes your edgy lifestyle. And you have to know how to have a good time, like appreciating a good laugh at someone else's expense.

As always, such deportment has do's and don'ts.

The following pages contain behavioral tips for the outlaw in the context of day-to-day life, from fighting to farting.

Basic Street Etiquette

WELCOME TO THE JUNGLE

The city is not a concrete jungle, it is a human zoo.
— Desmond Morris

New York makes one think of the collapse of civilization, about Sodom and Gomorrah, the end of the world.

— Saul Bellow

Once the mark of civilization, the city has become an urban jungle fraught with perils at every turn. Muggings. Carjackings. Gangs. Homeless. These terms send shivers down the spine of white mainstream America.

It's understandable. There are some badass people out there, and crime-filled headlines and over-the-top flicks about the 'hood have served to fuel our collective paranoia. But a little discretion and knowledge of urban etiquette can go a long way when it comes to survival on the mean streets.

So come take our hand, and take a little walk on the wild side.

WATCH YOUR BACK, JACK

The first rule of basic street etiquette is so simple, it's amazing so many people are too stupid to follow it: Use common sense.

For instance, if you go up to an ATM in a not-so-great part of town and see five scary punks loitering in the shadows, don't pull out $300 and count it. Just find another ATM.

Rule #2: Trust your instincts if you get a dangerous vibe. You might not want to jump to conclusions. You might not want to subscribe to stereotypes. But hey—if it walks like a duck and talks like a duck, duck for cover. If a black or Latino dresses like a gang-banger, or a white skinhead walks around huffing and puffing and glaring like he wants to fight, it's not your responsibility to give them the benefit of the doubt, regardless of whether they're badasses or just getting off on looking like badasses. A little bit of paranoia is okay—it's better to be accused of stereotyping than to be a victim.

ARMED AND DANGEROUS

Always assume an aggressor is armed.

It's difficult to tell ahead of time if someone is "strapped," AKA "packing heat," AKA "packing steel"—in this era of baggy clothes, cops have been known to pull sawed-off shotguns from the pockets of would-be criminals. But classic red flags include a) unusual bulges in pants or jackets, b) wearing a big ol' coat in summer, or c) a subject constantly touching a part of their clothing (to reassure themselves their weapon hasn't fallen out—they don't use holsters).

Keep your eyes on a would-be aggressor's hands. If his hands are in the open, he can't pull a weapon.

If someone sticks a gun in your face and demands your wallet or purse, politely hand it to them and tell them to have a good time at the mall.

CARJACKING

Carjacking is particularly big in areas with few cops and in areas with lots of tourists. The whole art of carjacking is to get a driver to stop. If you have a fender-bender with another car, particularly at night, feel free to keep driving until you find a well-lit, well-trafficked area to exchange insurance info. Carjackers have been known to deliberately get into an accident and wait for a potential target to get out of their car.

Keep a watchful eye in parking lots and in drive-throughs, two popular carjacking sites.

If someone sticks a gun in your face and demands that you get out of your car, oblige them graciously, leaving all valuables behind (small children excepted).

GANGLAND 101

A ttention, readers: you don't need to *automatically* piss in your pants when you see a group of black kids in blue jerseys, blue ball caps and sagging jeans strutting down the street. Gangs are largely an insular group. They become dangerous to outsiders only when certain rules are broken, when certain lines are crossed.

We've outlined a few of those boundaries. For more detailed information, see "The Gang-Banger" in Part V.

Deadly Detour

If you happen to take a wrong turn and find yourself driving in a not-so-nice, potentially gang-infested area after hours, you don't want to be mistaken for a carjacker or drive-by shooter.

When you pull up alongside another vehicle, make sure your face is visible, and don't make any sort of furtive movements. Don't drive up really slowly next to someone and roll down the window to ask for directions, especially at night. If you are in a known drug zone, be particularly careful: You might be in the crosshairs of gunmen stationed on both sides of the street.

On the other hand, if you're in gangland at night and you see a car driving slowly down the street, its headlights off, with three or four heads in the car, take cover. The other option is to take out your own gun and start dumping on the suspicious-looking vehicle, but we can't condone that sort of behavior.

Several years back, the media warned L.A. residents that a popular gang initiation ritual required prospective members to drive around with their headlights off. If another driver saw them and flashed their brights at them, the prospects were to get out of the car and shoot the driver. This has become a popular urban myth, but none of the cops or gang members we spoke with substantiated it. If you flash your brights at someone out of courtesy, you'll probably be fine.

Dress Code

If you plan to navigate through gangland, think twice about wearing blue or red. The notorious "Crip" gang sports blue, the notorious "Blood" gang digs red. These two vehement rivals control different turfs throughout the country, and take great joy in shooting each other.

If you show up in the wrong 'hood dressed for the wrong party, you could be shit out of luck. Be careful about ball caps and team logos, too, as they often signify various gang affiliations.

As we noted earlier, gangs are largely an insular group. The dress code is far more important for someone who could conceivably pass for a gang-banger due to their skin color or their street-oriented sense of fashion. If you're clearly a civilian without gang affiliation, don't stress too hard about it. An accountant wearing a blue double-breasted suit on Blood turf isn't going to be mistaken for a Crip. (He might get robbed, but it has nothing to do with the color of his duds.)

Signs of the Times

"Signing," the use of hand signals and movements, is a popular method of set identification and communication among gangs, not unlike sign language for the deaf or that secret Water Buffalo Lodge handshake. Gangland visitors should avoid random motions that involve twisting up or contorting the fingers, as the most harmless of gestures may have dangerous hidden meanings.

True story: A few years back in Los Angeles, an innocent couple was sitting and chatting inside their car. Gang members rolled up on them and shot them to death. Why? Because the couple was deaf, communicating via sign language, and the killers thought they were throwing up rival gang signs.

STREET PEOPLE

Okay, we don't want you to think we're going soft or politically correct on you. BUT . . . when you encounter those on the street less fortunate than yourself—the old lady pushing a shopping cart, the guy washing windows at the gas station for change, the teen with his bedroll in the store entryway, the residents of makeshift tents in the parks and on beaches, squatters under freeway overpasses and in abandoned buildings—we want you to show some compassion.

Sure, these people occupy the lowest rung of the ladder in our society. Many fish for food out of Dumpsters. Some can literally pull the crud off their unshowered bodies. Others drink all day. Most people automatically assume they are lazy and dirty and pathetic with no self-respect, lower on the totem pole than any minority, neck and neck with dogs and cats.

SIGN LANGUAGE

Many commonplace hand gestures—the "peace" sign, the Trekkie salute—are dangerously similar to popular gang signals. Here's a quickie guide, so that you don't end up sending mixed messages.

Blood Rolling 20s

Peace

Venice Shoreline Crips

"Live Long and Prosper" (Mr. Spock)

Harlem Crips

Siskel & Ebert

Harlem Crips + Extra Homie

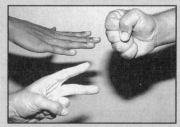

Paper, Rock, Scissors

Blood Handshake

Hey Man, Pull My Finger!

Please keep in mind that 1) they're probably hungrier than most dogs and cats, and 2) they are not animals, they are people. You don't have to shake their hands, chat with them, or have them over for dinner, but treat them with some dignity, asshole.

The next few pages prescribe rules of interaction between civilians (those with a roof over their heads) and street residents. Do your best to observe them. After all, someday you too could be down on your luck, and karmic payback is a motherfucker. (See "Homeless Etiquette" in Part VI)

Homeless vs. Street People

The term "street person" relegates an individual to gutter scum, and connotes a dirty, uncivilized creature who is somehow less than a person. "Homeless" is a more sympathetic reference to those residing on the streets.

Can You Spare Some Change?

Panhandling is the most common context in which civilians interact with the homeless. Getting asked for change is an experience shared by virtually every city dweller. Here are some common responses.

Response 1: Give them money. Quite popular among the homeless, this response will probably get you a smile and a "thank you." The more you give, the bigger the smile. But here's the crucial thing to remember: Once that money leaves your hands, you have no say where it goes. If they want to use it for a well-balanced meal, great. If they want to use it for Twinkies, smokes and booze, that's their choice (hey, if you were on the street on a cold winter night, you might want a little drinky-poo to take the edge off, too!). If you don't want to give, then don't. No one's forcing you. But if you opt to open your wallet, please do it unconditionally. You're not their parent.

Response 2: Ignore them. This is the rudest thing you can do to a panhandler. Every person on the street we spoke with cited this as their biggest gripe. Being forced to ask for handouts from strangers giving you stinkeye is a drag, and getting snubbed just adds insult to injury.

Don't turn your head and pretend they don't exist. They exist, so treat them like a human being and acknowledge them in some way—a smile or a nod will do. As one homeless man told us: "To be ignored is the absolute worst thing. Tell me 'no,' call me an asshole, but at least acknowledge my presence."

Response 3: Tell them to "get a job." No shit. This is the second most insulting response. Most of them can't, either because they're disturbed or because they have long gaps between jobs and no address or phone. Plus it's tough to look for gainful employment when your stomach is growling or you're stressed about your stuff getting stolen. It's also hard to get all spiffed up for an interview.

Response 4: Say "I'm sorry." This isn't bad, but it's not ideal, either. Someone hearing it hundreds of times a day may find it insincere. If you have the time, you might try to explain yourself (i.e., "I'm sorry, I don't have any spare change").

Response 5: Say "Not today." A good, solid answer. You're exercising your choice not to give while acknowledging them and being honest. Good for you! Just don't expect them to do somersaults of joy.

Response 6: Expose their sham. We've all seen folks at freeway off-ramps claiming stuff like, "Will work for food!" or "Please give to mother and hungry kids" or "Vietnam vet needs help." Then there's the person who lost their wallet and just needs bus fare. Sometimes it's legit, sometimes it's bullshit. Either way, don't probe for details to ascertain whether someone's bid for sympathy is true or false. That's how some privileged people deal with their guilt, and justify a decision to keep their wallet shut. No need to rationalize: Like we said, if you don't want to give, then don't. Just bear in mind that if a person is resorting to begging, he or she is probably *not* sitting on top of the world. Whether they're lying or exaggerating their story, they're still desperate—who cares why.

Response 7: Humor. Sharing a laugh with someone, or any piece of conversation, bestows on them a degree of dignity. A good-natured joke or banter is usually appreciated, though not as much as a fiver.

Response 8: Give them food instead. If someone outside a store asks you for money to buy food, don't say "no" and then go in and buy something for them. Some people do this in order to ensure that the money doesn't go for alcohol, and although their heart is in the right place, the effect can be quite condescending. It's like Mom telling you she'll spring for your new wardrobe, but she gets to choose the clothes. Ask them first: "Can I get you something to eat?" Give them the choice. If they say "yes," think twice before bringing them inside. Some shop owners or restaurants might take exception, and you run the risk of being refused service or making your newfound charity case feel uncomfortable.

Similarly, if you're approached after a meal out, you can offer your leftovers, but not every homeless person will accept. Beggars *can* be choosers. Don't cop a 'tude just because a person on the street doesn't want your half-chomped, saliva-laced roast beef sandwich.

Response 9: Suggest a shelter, homeless outreach agency, or soup kitchen. This extremely well-intentioned thought is actually annoying and insulting, since most homeless locals already know about services available to them.

Windows of Opportunity

All car-owning residents are familiar with the window-washers who attack with cloth, spritz bottle and zeal at gas stations and stop-lights. If you don't want your windshield cleaned, tell 'em so. If you don't have the customary buck or simply don't want to give it to them, let them know ASAP.

Caution Warranted

Most homeless people are not prone to violence, unless you steal their stuff, tip over their shopping cart, etc. But there are those pan-handlers who don't take kindly to "no." The public must remember that many homeless people aren't afraid of the law—jail, for many, is a res-cue. Hence, exercise commonsense rules of caution. If you sense aggression, leave quickly, or get loud and attract attention.

"Imaginary space"—that perceived radius around someone that constitutes his or her personal space—can be quite sacred to the homeless. Breaking their private bubble can be a serious breach, with potentially violent results.

When confronted by someone babbling to himself, to you or to anyone who will listen, just try to get out of their way.

Fighting

VICTORY OVER HONOR

The easiest period in a crisis is actually the battle itself. The most difficult is the period of indecision—whether to fight or run away. And the most dangerous period is the aftermath. It is then, with all his resources spent and his guard down, that an individual must watch out for dulled reactions and faulty judgment.

—Richard M. Nixon

This guy must be done. I'll stop him in one.

—Muhammad Ali

So let's say turning the other cheek just isn't an option. Some nasty dude shoves you at the bar, or squeezes your girl's tush, and it looks like things are going to come to blows, mano a mano. What are the rules of engagement?

The cornerstone of street fighting etiquette is this: There is no etiquette.

It all comes down to whether you win or lose, not how you play the game. You're not in a ring; there's no padded gloves, no referee, no bell. If a big ol' bully steps to you, you fight to survive, whether that means biting, scratching or hitting below the belt. Did you promise your opponent you wouldn't hit him with a trash can, a chair or a bottle? No. We say: It's better to be tried by twelve than carried by six—it's all about survival. (See "Guns," and "Knives, etc." in Part III)

Just remember that when you raise a chair over your head, it ups the stakes. The guy who was going to break your nose may now feel he has license to break your neck.

Also remember that the lack of rules goes both ways. If you're winning a fight, protect your 'nads and watch out for friends of the guy whose ass you're beating—they might jump in and take you by surprise. As we said, anything goes.

But while there are no real rules in a street fight, there is a methodology of sorts. We've taken our best shot at explaining it to you.

Quick disclaimer: We focused on fighting between guys because, well, guys are generally less evolved creatures and more prone to coming to blows. Apologies to any female bruisers who might feel left out.

CHOOSE YOUR BATTLES WISELY

If you frequent places where potential brawlers congregate (i.e., a rough-and-tumble bar), identify ahead of time what your boundaries are, what your priority issues are, what will get you swinging—whether it's getting nudged without an apology, being cursed at, being the victim of a racial slur, or having someone act rudely toward your date.

Don't confront people who cut you off on the freeway or cut in a line—you look like an idiot if you kick someone's ass for that. The only reason to confront someone is for an offense worthy of an ass-kicking. If they apologize, accept it.

If possible, always try to defuse a fight rather than escalate it. If an aggressor outweighs you by 100 pounds, point out the ridiculousness of his kicking your ass. You can also try to put off the fight, giving someone time to simmer down. Tell him: "I'll fight you in an hour, but right now, let me buy you a drink." That $5 gesture could save you both a lot of pain. Adding a little good-natured levity can be helpful as well.

Discretion is always the better part of valor, which means don't be afraid to run. That can be difficult for a guy out with his friends, or worse, out with a date. If a guy backs down, he certainly runs the risk of losing a girl's respect. But consider this: Do you really want to be with a chick who gets pissed because you won't take an ass-kicking in front of her? Moreover, if you fight a gorilla-sized killer, you might emerge with your pride intact, but something far more valuable to both you and your date might be incapacitated.

If you're in a potentially volatile bar or club situation, make friends with the bouncer and tip the bartender and waiters well. A fuming bully might well have pissed off everyone in the joint with his aggressive behavior, and the bouncer and/or waiters can be your best friends in the event of a fight. If you anticipate a problem with said bully, mention it to the bouncer ahead of time.

If you are a person who won't win a fight but likes to stand up for yourself, be prepared to lose and experience some degree of pain.

Alcohol + testosterone = beer muscles. Don't mistake your beer muscles for actual fighting prowess. Likewise, don't confuse shadow-boxing or karate chops in a mirror with applicable fisticuffs skills.

SIZING UP YOUR OPPONENT

Always assume that an aggressor is serious and dangerous. The wimpiest-looking fellow could be a killer. According to many pugilists we spoke with, it's a myth that someone who doesn't look you in the eyes isn't a serious contender.

There are, however, a number of clues as to whether someone is ready to throw down, or is just blowing off steam.

A real fighter doesn't do a lot of cock-talking and chest-pounding before he takes a swing. He won't tell you he's a black belt in karate. He won't tell you he's got mob connections. He won't tell you he's got a gun. Instead, he might look for elbow room—space needed to square off and launch into attack. His body might be tense, but without physical symptoms of fright. Wide eyes and quivering lips suggest that someone hasn't had a lot of fighting experience. A calm and ready fighter is far more intimidating than a boisterous showoff.

Standing your ground with a would-be aggressor goes a long way.

BEAT 'EM TO THE PUNCH

If walking away simply isn't an option for you, but you know you're outmatched, never be afraid to throw the first punch. Don't hesitate. When it comes to fighting, training is good, experience is better, but the best weapon of all is willingness. If you're willing to go there without pause, you have a great advantage.

And make sure the first one counts. A shot to the face hurts a lot and bleeds a lot, which might be enough to end a fight. On the other hand, the head and face are also quite hard, and can severely damage your hand. Consider going for the legs—a swift kick to the front of the knee can be very effective.

Never give your back to an opponent, before or during a fight.

BACKUP

Backup is a privilege, not a right.

If you are with a friend who is acting like a belligerent asshole, it's not required that you step in and help if he gets into a fight. Ideally, inform said asshole ahead of time that if his bad attitude causes some static or strife, you're not going to have his back.

However, if your friend or date gets into a scuffle, it *is* your responsibility to get in a neutral position so that the fighter doesn't have to worry about your safety. Get out of the way, and be prepared to go for help if necessary.

If you're with someone who doesn't care to fight, or a child, or anyone who can't defend themselves, do not compromise their safety just to defend your honor. It's very selfish.

Attention, ladies: Please use discretion. A bully probably isn't going to swing at you. But in the event of a confrontation, bear in mind that your boyfriend might pay the price for any bile that comes out of your mouth.

THE FEMININE TOUCH

Speaking of confrontations between guys and the fairer sex, the overriding rule is this: Boys don't hit girls. If you're unlucky enough to find yourself in this situation, you can restrain her to protect yourself from injury, though you should have witnesses to corroborate that restraint was absolutely necessary. But don't ever *ever* throw a punch or shove. You might win the fight, but you'll lose with the judge.

R O U N D   O V E R

If you see the cops or a fleet of bouncers coming to break up your fight, go limp, drop to the ground, act like a victim, and start screaming, "Stop hitting me!"

Never fight the bouncers—they're bigger, greater in number, and usually more experienced. Never fight the cops—they've got clubs and guns and dogs and stuff.

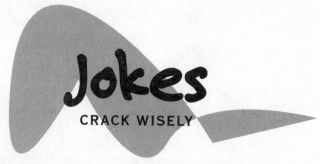

Jokes

CRACK WISELY

A dirty joke is a sort of mental rebellion.

—George Orwell

Fuck 'em if they can't take a joke.

—Anonymous

A good joke should make people laugh. Whether you're cracking wise with friends at a bar, making a crank call, or sticking a snoozing buddy's hand in warm water, a joke ceases to be funny when it demeans someone to the point that they feel like shit, or when it causes someone bodily injury.

JUST REMEMBER:

- It's always funny until someone loses an eye.

- Screaming "fire" in a crowded theater is never a big applause-getter.

- Racist jokes are fine (sticks and stones, right?!). Just take stock of your audience and those within earshot. If you offend anyone, apologize.

THE BUTT OF A GOOD GAG

Pat Boone on Wisecracking

It's important for any jokester to know his bounds. Singer Pat Boone certainly does. Here, the American icon of Wonder white–bread wholesomeness manages to show his cheeky side, while still coming out smelling like roses . . . or gardenias. We're sure the story is true, since Pat never lies.

I went in for a routine prostate examination, and knowing the nature of that exam, I made sure I was hygienically acceptable. I then picked a fresh gardenia from our garden, and put this gardenia where I knew [my proctologist] would encounter it. In walks the doctor—I thought his sense of humor was a little dry, so I thought he'd have fun with this. So he's putting on his rubber gloves, and he says, "Bend over, put your elbows on the cot," and I say, "Okay, I know the drill." So I lean over, and feel his hands on my cheeks, and then I hear, "Wh . . . wh . . . wh . . ." He couldn't even get the word "What?!" out of his mouth! So I said, "Oh, do you see it? It's a gardenia—I wanted to enhance the environment." He ran out of the room quickly, and returned a few minutes later with tears in his eyes from laughter. A few days later, he called to tell me everything was fine [with the exam], and said to me: "I've put your gardenia in a vase." I said: "I bet it's flourishing, too!"

Crapping, Farting, Burping, and Masturbating

HOW DO YOU SPELL RELIEF?

Hey, don't knock masturbation. It's sex with someone I love.

—Woody Allen

Hey, did somebody step on a duck?

—Rodney Dangerfield

Pull my finger!

—Dad

Even on their best behavior, Emily Post and Martha Stewart still have to visit the crapper sooner or later. Then what do they do?

Hell, we all fart, burp and poop, and until someone comes up with a way to make our shit smell like rose petals, we have to abide by certain rules of common courtesy, listed herein. And while we were on the subject of relieving oneself, we threw in a few lines about masturbation, too.

POTTY PROTOCOL

We don't care if it's only a number one or some piece of lint, always flush.

If you loose a load, light a match. If you leave skid marks, flush twice. If that doesn't eliminate the problem, hold your head high, grab a nearby scrub brush or tissue, and take responsibility.

It's always a good idea to keep some odor-eliminating agent in your bathroom for yourself or guests.

If you've got to take a dump in a private home where the downstairs bathroom is by the kitchen, dining room, living room or other audible location, we suggest taking it upstairs. Tinkle and poop noises can be very unsavory amidst a cocktail party. If upstairs isn't an option, use discretion—try not to blow your cargo out your colon at full speed. Again, use a match or some air freshener, and open a window to help dissipate any green clouds of death.

Shit Happens

If you clog up your friend's crapper, you must try to fix it! If there's a plunger, plunge away. If no plunger is available, ask. Simply leaving the stuffed bowl for the shit-fairies to tidy up is the poorest of form. Don't do the crime if you can't do the time.

It's always common courtesy to replace toilet paper when you finish the roll. Don't wait for the next person to scream out or clinch-cheek it out of the bathroom foraging for TP. Bad form. If you're all out, get some Kleenex in there for emergency use.

Venus and Mars in the Bathroom

Men, if you live with a woman, make sure to put the seat up before you pee (thus avoiding peeing on the seat), and put the seat down after you go. Unless they have a helluva aim, women have to sit down on the throne to go number one or two. If the seat's up and the woman's not paying attention, it's cold hard porcelain and a wet ass for her. This especially comes into play late at night when it's dark and the senses are diminished. Putting the seat down signifies to your sig-o that you understand her needs and will accommodate them.

Women, any and all feminine hygiene products (FHP) need to be flushed or buried in the trash (preferably wrapped in something else). No matter what any guy says, he wants nothing to do with it, even if it's just a wrapper. The worst sin of all is to leave a used FHP unflushed where your man can find it. If you're guilty of this ultimate bathroom faux pas, be prepared for him to pack his bags.

The Public Restroom

When using a public restroom, feel free to fart and shit your head off without any sense of embarrassment. Hey, that's what they're there for. Farting while you pee is also acceptable.

Please refrain from the "potty play-by-play," whereby you verbally document your bowel movement. In other words, a few short, low-profile guttural sounds are fine, but don't moan or scream with glee. That's called crossing the line.

It's not your job to fix a public toilet (even if you went through a roll of paper with only one flush). If possible, try to inform a maintenance person or manager.

In a crowded bar or restaurant, it's okay to use a single-stall bathroom designated for the opposite sex if your own sex's bathroom is occupied. Things get questionable when, say, a guy tries to take a leak in a multi-stall female bathroom filled with nice old ladies.

Fellas, stay off the cell phone while you're at the urinal. No call is that important.

A Matter of Personal Enjoyment

No one cares about the size and regularity of your bowel movement (or lack thereof) except for you and your doctor. Keep it to yourself.

FARTING:
IT'S A GAS GAS GAS

Everyone does it. It feels great when you do it in private. And when little foul-mouthed cartoon tykes like Cartman do it, it can elicit big TV ratings.

But farting in public can range from hilarious to humiliating. Personally, we think farts are always funny. It's just that you can't count on other people to find them funny (they're in denial). Here are a few tips on passing gas politely.

Vapor Trails

If you're feeling gaseous, you might want to excuse yourself to the bathroom and let out a test fart prior to letting loose in a public forum. A tester helps you determine whether you can control the volume, and whether the stench is minimal (they vary). If this is indeed the case, feel free to let 'em fly.

While it's technically bad form to fart at weddings, funerals, etc., use the test fart for risk analysis. If the volume and smell are within an acceptable range, go for it. But remember that many people are hip to the one-cheek sneak, so keep it discreet. Be extra careful if you've got the liquid drizzles—a Hershey squirt always leaves a trail of evidence.

Never fart in an elevator, unless you're leaving a present for somebody.

The bottom line on farting is that if the fart can be traced back to you, roll down the window, go outside or withhold. A good rule of thumb is that it's okay in a moving crowd where you have some plausible deniability; always exercise due caution when you're stationary.

"Whoever Smelt It, Dealt It"

If you let fly an SBD (Silent but Deadly) in a group of people, say nothing. There are plenty of suspects, and silent farts are difficult to trace. And whatever you do, don't try to pass the buck, screaming "Who cut the cheese? Gross!" and pointing fingers. As we know from grade school, that's practically an admission of guilt.

If you break wind audibly, do your best to laugh it off, especially when you're having sex (it happens). A good-natured, smile-faced "Whoops!" or "Excuse me" will suffice.

Danger!

When you're on a date (particularly one that might lead to some nocturnal activities), it's best to avoid any dish loaded down with garlic. Your breath might be the initial victim, but within a few hours the

GAS GAUGE

Goin' on a date with your new squeeze? **EFO** offers this handy chart to make sure that the food you eat doesn't come back to bite you in the ass later that night.

ASPARAGUS
Makes your pee and other bodily fluids smell funny.

BROCCOLI
Good for the heart, bad for the nose. Make sure your lover doesn't squeeze you!

CABBAGE
Makes you and your house smell like old gym socks.

BEANS
Beans, beans, the musical fruit, the more you eat . . .

GARLIC
DANGER!! Will make your pee, sweat and farts stink to all hell!

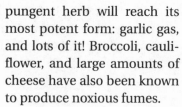

pungent herb will reach its most potent form: garlic gas, and lots of it! Broccoli, cauliflower, and large amounts of cheese have also been known to produce noxious fumes.

If you are a gaseous sleeper or "widow maker," it's best to alert any guests to that fact before they find out themselves. Perhaps a warning for the morning to lift the covers carefully. Perhaps a second warning about avoiding spontaneous morning hugs—they can backfire.

Tooting High Jinks

It's still considered juvenile to light your farts on fire. Trying to convince others to do so is another story. Never offer to light someone else's farts.

The "red-eye" (whereby you drop trou, spread your cheeks, and fart in someone's direction) and the "clown face" (cupping your fart, then placing your hand on someone's mouth and nose) are *always* in bad taste—but still funny when they happen to someone else.

Fart contests with your friends get our stamp of approval, just not in public.

BURPING: THE OTHER GAS

A second gaseous anomaly is the burp. While many cultures see the burp in a positive light (it shows that you liked the meal, for example), ours doesn't.

Cute little champagne burps are always more permissible than long, protracted belches à la John Belushi in *Animal House*.

Burps are generally accepted among friends and families. Deliberately blowing a burp in someone's direction is not acceptable, unless the target is your little brother or sister. If you've been able to develop the burp/talking technique or can belch the alphabet, your special talent should, again, be reserved for those closest to you.

If you burp in front of less intimate acquaintances, just say "excuse me" and society will forgive you. No big deal, unless you've been eating bologna, in which case get the hell away from us!

PUKING (AKA YAKKING, AKA BLOWING CHUNKS, AKA THE TECHNICOLOR YAWN)

See "Vomiting" in the "Booze" section in Part I.

MASTURBATION

Lock the damn door.

Best done in private, or in the company of a lover.

No pocket pool when you're wearing shorts or super-tight pants.

Don't do it at camp when you're sleeping in a communal cabin, particularly if you've got the top of a squeaky bunk bed. Don't do it in the public shower at the gym, or a public bathroom when cops might be around.

When participating in a "circle jerk," don't fall for the old "Let's close our eyes and see who wins" routine. Make sure everyone's pulling their own weight before you get caught with your pants down, much to the amusement of your unexposed peers. And keep an eye out for camcorders—it might hinder future political aspirations.

Always clean up after yourself.

And guys, don't leave that crunchy sock or towel under the bed for mom, the housekeeper or your latest romantic interest to find. It's a real turnoff.

Also see "Battery-Operated" in the "Basic Sex" section in Part II and "Jail" in Part VI.

Music Scene Etiquette

LISTEN AND LEARN

No change in musical style will survive unless it is accompanied by a change in clothing style. Rock is to dress up.

—Frank Zappa

If it's too loud, you're too old.

—Rock 'n' roll adage

Every outlaw has his or her own soundtrack—that anti-establishment type of drumbeat to which they march, rebel and party. And whether its swing, death metal or Swedish clog dancing, every genre of music seems to spawn its own subculture, with its own do's, don'ts and dress code.

This section outlines the basics for any concert or live music event, and then focuses on the three scenes we believe to be the most vital, relevant and interesting: punk, hip-hop and rave/electronica.

We've also thrown in our two cents about Deadheads, just for kicks.

CONCERT 101: THE BASICS

When attending a live music event, rules vary between venues. Call ahead of time about dress codes, age limits, and so forth. It sucks to drive all the way down there and pay for parking only to be denied entrance.

Clothes and Accoutrement

Big shows often search at the door. Leave that little knife attached to your key chain in the car. Stricter door men might disallow nail clippers or pens. FYI: When security pats you down, they skip the shoes—a good place to stash contraband. Another hint: Quite frequently, they won't pat down women.

Wearing a vintage shirt of the band you're seeing is cool—it suggests dedication, that you're a true fan. But don't buy one of those super-pricey new shirts at the show and put it on in the bathroom—it's like a big neon sign that says "DORK." And don't buy a bargain shirt from the guys hawking them on the street—one washing and you'll know why.

Earplugs are condoned and advised if you're a regular at live music events, but go for the flesh-colored ones so you won't be outed as a wuss.

Musical Chairs

In the event of festival seating, feel free to move down to those unclaimed seats at the front. But bear in mind that big venues have become a lot more strict about such liberties—keep an eye out for Nazi-like security in the yellow jackets checking ticket stubs. And if the actual owners of said seats do show up, vacate immediately without causing static.

When you're the only person in the section standing up, sit down.

Sitting on someone's shoulders or on a chair is part of the fun, but is often not permitted.

When wading through the crowd at a show with festival seating, or a show with standing room only, be considerate. Don't shove your way to the front in the middle of a song. If you move in front of someone, make sure they can still see. Exception: if you encounter a hippie, feel free to push them aside or step on them—they will invariably apologize to you.

Applause Meter

If you're into the band, you can cheer and clap and bang your head. If you're at a big show and the band truly sucks—particularly an opening band tagged onto the bill—feel free to boo. Might be less appropriate in intimate club settings. Also gauge the sentiment of the rest of the crowd. If everyone's digging it except you, refrain from boo- ing or risk getting clocked by a die-hard fan.

No matter how hard they suck, please refrain from throwing bot- tles, keys, heavy chains or wrenches. It's rude and dangerous. However, if you really dig the band, it's generally acceptable to toss up flowers, Baggies of weed, bras and panties (usually women's only). Just make sure there's enough of a party vibe for such antics. Never throw panties at Sting.

Shouting out requests in between songs is always acceptable. Just make sure it's part of the band's repertoire.

Torching Up

Holding up your lighter during a torch ballad went out with Blue Oyster Cult. Please refrain, unless it's done with a wink for ironic effect.

Watch your lighter if the metalhead dude or dudette in front of you has very big metalhead hair—it's a potential fire hazard.

Weed is a concert staple. Again, keep an eye out for the yellow jackets. If they see you sparking up, they'll probably just shine a very bright flashlight at you and request that you extinguish.

If someone asks you for a toke, oblige, but you don't have to get the whole arena high.

Drinking

It's cool to drink in the parking lot, especially at a stadium show where beers cost $5. Just watch for the ever-vigilant cops and security.

Generally, it's also cool to piss in the parking lot behind a car— just don't pee *on* the car.

If you knock over someone's beer inside, offer to buy 'em a new one. And don't leave bottles or glasses on the dance floor or near the stage where someone might step on them.

Dancing

When dancing, let loose, go nuts, but don't hit the people around you unless you're down in the pit.

The Backstage Pass

If you're lucky enough to get backstage, or get invited to some exclusive postconcert party, be grateful you're there, and be cool. Don't chase an artist down with a camera or pen and ask him to sign a T-shirt, your arm, or some other body part. (Utter babes have more leeway in this department.)

Don't save your backstage pass and then wear it at your next concert as some sort of badge of honor.

Last but Not Least . . .

Don't go to a Billy Squire or Journey concert. Ever. Just don't.

PUNK PROTOCOL

Now that the basics are out of the way, it's time for the rules of specific music subcultures, starting with punk.

When it kicked off in England in the late '70s, punk was about anarchy and nonconformity. Punk as a whole is far less political these days. It's also a younger movement, which means that some of the debauchery once associated with it is less tolerable. But the diehards still preach nonconformity, "D.I.Y.," and a healthy disrespect for authority to the tune of three chords.

Do It Yourself

The mantra for punk is "do it yourself," also known as the D.I.Y. ethic. That means you take matters into your own hands and circumvent corporate America whenever possible.

Here are two easy-to-follow punk models of behavior: Start a fanzine, and attempt to record an EP in your garage. Both are very D.I.Y.

Buy your records at a mom-and-pop store rather than at Sam Goody!

Know Your Punk Past

Buying a Green Day album or wearing an Offspring tee does not classify you as punk. Expand your listening beyond the mainstream stuff and check out some vintage X, Descendents, Black Flag, Dead Kennedys, Crass or Circle Jerks. Good to be up on new indie underground bands, too.

GROUPIE ETIQUETTE

Do's and Don'ts of Doing the Band

If you feel the need to live vicariously through the loins of your favorite rock star, then the groupie life is for you. Here are some basic tips to get you through the velvet rope.

1. Be a hottie. We can't stress this enough: If you're not hot, expect to have sex only with the roadies or local club security. You will not get past the front door. Be stacked, scantily dressed, and ready to party if you want go backstage.

2. Befriend security. While you don't have to bone the security guard to get backstage, a little friendly graze of their nether regions should get you the laminated backstage pass. Flirt, laugh, and do what you feel comfortable doing to get backstage.

3. Bring your own protection. In this case we do not mean firearms! If you want to make it with a rock star, make sure to bring your own condoms. Remember, if they're fucking you, odds are they've fucked many others like you.

4. Be prepared for company. Don't be surprised if your one-on-one becomes a two-on-one or something else entirely. You may not get the lead singer . . . do you like the bassist? Rock stars are known for band fucks and groupie orgies. Be prepared for these scenarios as well as lots of alcohol and the possibility of being involved in things you didn't plan on (like fucking the entire band). If you want a one-on-one, ask first and be prepared to leave.

5. Have a ride home. If you showed up with your friends but stayed to fuck Joey the guitarist, make sure you have cab money to get home. Your transportation back to suburbia is not the band's responsibility.

6. It's just sex. Just because you bone 'em doesn't mean you own 'em. Groupie sex does not constitute a relationship with the band. You can give them your number, but don't be hurt if they don't offer you theirs or if you call and they don't remember you. Consider it a fun one-night stand.

Looking the Part

If you want to be punk, you don't have to be all surly and look pissed off. Being punk and smiling are not mutually exclusive.

On the other hand, punk is not pretty. It's about nonconformity, so feel free to go out of your way to look ratty and ugly with multiple face piercings, tats, dark makeup and torn clothes, either from a thrift store or stolen. Don't shop at Neiman Marcus, don't wear Calvins. Steel-toed boots are a must.

Dyed mohawks and spiky bracelets, once the calling cards of the punk, are both still legit, though many older punks ultimately outgrow them.

Don't confuse a punk rocker with a skinhead. Unlike the latter, punks are racially tolerant (their only beef is with hippies). Don't confuse a punk rocker with a death metalhead. The long black stringy hair is an instant giveaway.

The Mosh Pit

Though it has migrated into the realms of death metal and hip-hop, the slam pit or mosh pit is a distinctly punk invention. The crowd parts in an area near the stage to make room for enthusiastic listeners swinging their elbows high and menacingly and ramming into one another to the music. When the music stops, so does the bashing—sort of like musical chairs, but without the chairs. Unfortunately, what started out as a relatively good-natured way to get out energy and aggression (like wrestling with your buddies) has turned into a vortex of testosterone more akin to a cockfight. We've outlined model moshing behavior, but don't assume that everyone moshes by the rules.

First and foremost, gauge your pit. According to our friend and longtime punk Bill Stevenson (the Descendents, Black Flag), the key to being a good "mosher" or "pitter" is being able to evaluate each pit on a case-by-case basis: "There's a time and a place for different amounts of aggression. Sometimes it's appropriate to be extremely aggressive, other times not. There's an unspoken etiquette parallel to fucking—knowing how to fit in with [the prevailing mood] makes you a better or worse pitter or fuck respectively."

Like sex, the mosh pit is, above all else, supposed to be fun. It's not an excuse to start a brawl. The idea is to make as much contact as possible without really hurting someone, with an aim to bruise but not to break anything (although getting a broken nose can be a source of pride). Don't deliberately knock a guy who's down. In fact, give a fallen mosher a hand up, as long as it doesn't put you in harm's way.

If there's a hippie in sight, knock him down and kick the shit out of him. No mercy.

The audience members on the periphery of the pit have implicitly agreed to act as a buffer or "human wall" for the moshers. If you don't want to get bumped or bounced against, then move. Shoving back is part of the fun, but don't get pissed off, don't take a swing. At the same time, if someone has accidentally been sucked into the pit and wants out, do not push him or her back in. Back up and allow them to exit.

Should a female mosher get slammed less hard? Hell no! If she's in there by choice, she ought to be ready for anything that hits her. She clearly wants to play hard. And while it's not "cool" for male moshers to cop a feel, it's certainly not uncommon. Ms. Mosh should be prepared to deal with it.

Surf's Up!

It's quite common at shows for an audience member to "surf" the crowd, swimming across fellow fans as they support his or her weight with their hands. The lighter and more attractive you are, the more receptive an audience will be to holding you up. If you're ugly and fat, you might hit the floor.

It's kind of like a mirror of life.

Same goes for stage-diving. Light, good-looking, charismatic stage-divers always get caught. If you have marginal charisma, think twice. And if you're really obese, please refrain altogether. It puts your fellow patrons at risk.

Knowing exactly when to stage-dive—the peak of the band's and crowd's adrenaline level, when you have the eye of the entire crowd—is what will make you the coolest person at the show. If you stage-dive at an inappropriate moment, your peers may reprimand you by not catching you. Inappropriate times: during a ballad or between bands. If a band truly sucks, not stage-diving is an implicit form of protest.

What's Your Poison?

Drugs are bad, kill brain cells, and make you an unproductive human being. We don't advocate them; we're just stating the facts when we say they're quite standard in punk culture.

Basically, all drugs are game; none are particularly frowned upon. Speed and assorted pill-popping are popular.

Still, alcohol is the biggest party agent. Once the hard liquor and beer are gone, go for Thunderbird, Ripple, wine-in-a-box, Robitussin, and NyQuil, in that order.

Pro Tips

If you're in a band, don't spit on the audience, unless they're doing something really vile. The moment for that has kind of faded.

No complex chord progressions! Abide by the three-chord rule.

Last but Not Least . . .

Don't listen to Journey, Billy Squire or Asia. Ever. Just don't.

And never mind the bollocks.

HELPFUL HINTS FOR THE HIP-HOPPER

So maybe spiked bracelets and loud guitars aren't your thing. Maybe you're more into rhythm, high-end athletic gear, baggy pants and ball caps.

Once considered a fly-by-night trend, the street-savvy movement known as hip-hop has exploded into mainstream culture. Traces of its sonic fragments can be found in everything from soda pop and fast food ads to Hollywood blockbusters and high fashion. The hip-hop nation's music of choice is rap—a mix of infectious party music and social commentary, all based around two turntables and a microphone.

Know Your Hip-Hop History

Always show respect for the genre's pioneers. Hip-hop is a whole lot more than Puff Daddy, and true fans have a great regard for the art form's roots, AKA "the old school," AKA all the acts who came before Run-D.M.C. Buy a book and bone up.

Know your Ice-T from your Ice Cube from your Vanilla Ice.

If you're in the presence of hip-hoppers, and feel compelled to drop a few artists' names but really have no fuckin' clue, cite Rakim, A Tribe Called Quest before their breakup, or Wu-Tang Clan. All are failsafes. (Note: if you mention Wu-Tang, make sure you have a favorite member in mind.)

Be down with the underground. This is fundamental in the cred of any hip-hopper. Support local, up-and-coming indie groups. Support vinyl. Support mom-and-pop record shops.

Pledging Allegiance

Pledging allegiance to one coast (East or West) is a somewhat dated practice, but feel free, based on the type of music you like.

Do not, however, succumb to the notorious East Coast versus West Coast rivalry. While the question of coastal supremacy in the rap game has inspired many a heated debate, it's never worth coming to blows. In fact, the core hip-hop head judges a group on its individual merit, regardless of their zip code. In the words of mic poet extraordinaire Rakim: "It ain't where you from, it's where you at."

Be Freshly Dipped

Do your best to be "fresh dressed like a million bucks."

Baggy clothes and athletic gear are usually cool, though some clubs have stricter dress codes. "No ball caps" is a popular rule at snootier clubs trying to cater to a more upscale or "Hollywood" crowd.

Ice (diamonds), Rolex watches and other flashy jewelry are cool *if* you can afford it. Don't floss unless you've got the cash.

No Van Halen T-shirts, please.

Live Hip-Hop

Be fashionably tardy to any and all live hip-hop shows, as rappers, rap promoters, and rap fans are almost always on "hip-hop time." The conversion formula is simple: Take the official showtime for the opening act, add two hours, and then add another hour for every subsequent act on the bill.

In the case of underground hip-hop events such as a warehouse party, add three to four hours, but still show up early, as the event will invariably be oversold way beyond capacity.

When attending a show, leave your gang colors at home. In addition, leave behind the gun or any bad attitude. Because of the stigma of violence attached to hip-hop, venues are often reticent about booking rap acts, making live shows few and far between. Starting static of any kind is always bad form: It means less live hip-hop for everyone. In addition, it fuels media hype and law enforcement stereotypes that the only good hip-hop is no hip-hop. Be cool. Have fun. Don't shoot anyone. Of course, not everyone abides by these rules. Hence . . .

Don't step on someone's nice new squeaky-clean sneakers.

Hip-hop shows are frequently a sausage fest, with females in minority. Men should protect their dates from predators. Conversely, don't mack on already claimed women or men. You run the risk of getting bitch-slapped.

As you exit, be polite to the rows and rows of cops in riot gear waiting outside.

Dancing

Hip-hop is, first and foremost, dance music, so if you're at a show and you feel the urge, by all means get jiggy with it. If dancing's not your thing, just nod your head, wave ya' hands in the air, and wave 'em like you just don't care.

Slamming and stage-diving are more and more acceptable these days at rap shows. Feel out each show case by case.

What's Your Poison?

No heroin, no blow. Chronic AKA buddah AKA indo AKA weed AKA marijuana is the drug of choice for the hip-hop nation. At shows, security tends to be lenient about pot smoking. Popular technique for smoking in public: Split open a Phillys' Blunt cigar, dig out the tobacco, stuff with sticky green herb, and reseal. (See "Cigars" in Part I)

Your booze should always be top-shelf. Cristal, Hennessy, and imported beers only.

Greetings

Handshakes come and go quickly, but a current fave is the pound-pound. Just make a fist and let it drop on your homie's fist. Said homie will return the pound.

DANCEFLOOR DECORUM:

Annabella on Club Cool

British "new wave" act Bow Wow Wow is best known for their 1980s mega-hit, "I Want Candy." Their super-sexy lead singer, Annabella, who became the masturbatory fantasy of teen boys worldwide (EFO's authors included) when she posed naked on the band's album cover at age fifteen.

These days, Annabella lives Stateside. When she's not on the road performing, she enjoys getting her swerve on at a good nightclub. What she doesn't necessarily enjoy is the unsolicited male attention she sometimes receives. If you're out clubbing and happen to bump into her, here are some tips on how to conduct yourself on the dance floor or at the bar.

EFO: When you're at a club, what kind of things piss you off?

ANNABELLA: I find that guys will check me out—they will just watch me. I have a thing about being watched all the time. It's like when you are eating your breakfast and someone is just staring at you. Guys will just stand in little groups and just check. What the fuck are you doing here, let's get down and dance. Even if they wanted to pick up a girl, how are they supposed to when they just stand at the bar, just staring?! It's best to get onto the floor and get into the action. When we have trouble with the guys [on the dance floor], and they think they have a chance or whatever, we'll then start dancing with each other, the girls, like in *Basic Instinct*. Then you start getting all over your friend. You start dancing with each other like just really getting down. So it looks like we are lesbians or something. It's a really good trick. It is quite funny to see how well it works.

EFO: Ever dance by yourself, and have guys come up and join you?

ANNABELLA: Yeah, that's happened to me.

EFO: Do you like that or not?

ANNABELLA: Sometimes. If they are good dancers. I don't like it when they start getting tactile. It happens rarely, but it has happened a couple of times. I stop dead on the dance floor and just say, "Who the fuck do you think you are?" Then they say, "I'm sorry. I didn't mean to touch you." Then I go, "Don't you know you should get to know a person before you start doing things like that?"

EFO: So on the dance floor, guys should respect a girl's space?

ANNABELLA: Yeah, they should always respect your space whether you are dancing by yourself or with a group. Sometimes when you are dancing away you can join them as long as you respect their space. Sometimes you can get into their space, sometimes you can't. It's how you do it. Some people can be very open. You can start little dances with people. That's really good fun when you do that. You meet new groups of people. You all start doing the same dance and it is kind of like *Saturday Night Fever* or something. When everyone is getting into each other's step. It's quite nice when that happens.

EFO: What could a man do to really annoy you?

ANNABELLA: If they approached a friend of mine just to get close to me. My friend kind of thinks that he is interested in her, and then of course we find out he's not. That's happened a couple of times.

EFO: Anything else?

ANNABELLA: If you were to spit in my drink. Scratch your balls in front of me. If you had a tic while you were talking to me or you eat your boogers. Things like that would really repel me.

A handshake followed by quick shoulder-to-opposing-shoulder hug is also a good standby, though it's generally reserved for closer acquaintances.

The "Wigger" Syndrome

Hip-hop is a nonexclusive club, as evidenced by the multi-culti turnout for national hip-hop tours like Smokin' Grooves and the massive crossover appeal of acts like Cypress Hill, Ice Cube, and Puff Daddy. In other words, you do not have to be black to enjoy hip-hop music, or to wear hip-hop clothes. Pasty white suburbanites can be down, too.

That said, those with less melanin in their skin are subject to a number of rules of their own. They are as follows . . .

Please refrain from the "White Overbite," commonly practiced by overzealous, rhythmically challenged Caucasians who bite their lip while dancing as an expression of how much they're grooving to the beat.

Don't toss around street vernacular you don't understand. You run a high risk of looking like an idiot. Example: Vanilla Ice made a famous faux pas when, in one of his songs, he used the word "jimmy" (cock) instead of "jammy" (gun), inadvertently rapping that he wore a strap-on dick for protection.

As a rule, don't fake the funk. Instead, always do your best to keep it real and stay "trizue" to the "gzame." (In other words, don't be a poseur, and don't sell out.)

Pro Tips

Aspiring rappers should keep the following in mind.

Don't be a sucker MC. In other words, don't get on the mic if you ain't got the skillz to pay the billz.

Don't hog the mic at open-mic freestyle sessions, particularly if you ain't got the skillz to pay the billz.

Don't bite (steal) someone else's rhymes.

The rap stage is one of the few public places where it's perfectly okay to fondle yourself. The more hard-core you are, the more times you should grab your nutsack.

Last but Not Least . . .

Always pump up the volume, turn up the bass, test the limits of those woofers, and let 'em know you're coming from two blocks away.

RAVE RULES

*O*kay, so aggression and dick-grabbing aren't your cup of tea, but you still dig baggy clothes. Raves might be the move.

Focused around techno-based dance music (dubbed "electronica" in recent years), the rave scene is less about noncomformity and more about the worldwide tribal community. A hybrid of '60s Flower Power and technology, it's all about peace, love and high BPMs. The official rave mantra is "PLUR" (Peace, Love, Unity and Respect); the *unofficial* mantra is GWADAN (Getting Wasted and Dancing All Night).

Beat Basics

Know your "house" from your "techno" from your "ambient" from your "big beat" from your "drum-n-bass." Don't feel like you must be loyal to one type of music or one kind of club. Most fans have a few faves.

No Wallflowers

The spirit—the core—of rave culture is dancing. Hence, the most important rule at any rave is to get out there and shake your moneymaker. You can dance alone, with a partner, with a group of friends or with complete strangers. Don't stress if you're terminally off-beat. Most of the people around you are either too involved in the music or too fucked up to care.

Hey, Mr. DJ

Leave the DJs alone. No song requests, no jocking or flirting—they're working, so let them do their job.

What's Your Poison?

Drugs are illegal and dangerous. They kill brain cells and make you do stupid things. Just say "no." That said, here are a few facts about substance use at raves.

First and foremost, it's not a place to preach abstinence. Even though we don't (can't) endorse them, drugs are a part of the scene. The raver's drugs of choice are ecstacy (or "E") and amphetamines such as crystal meth. Ecstasy and its touchy-feely-friendly effects fit in nicely with the culture's peace-and-love ideals; meth keeps you dancing through the night until the break of dawn, which can be quite helpful at all-night affairs. Special K (cat tranquilizer) and weed are also popular. No shooting up, please. Traditionally, raves are "pills, powder and pot only" affairs. LSD is popular at big outdoor or desert events.

The media and the mainstream often characterize raves as pill-popping frenzies, losing sight of the other positive aspects. A rave is more than just a late-night pharmacy. It's about the music, the scene, the tribal dancing thing. Hence, going to a rave just to score choice drugs isn't cool.

In fact, in rave culture, it's always considered good form to be self-sufficient with your drugs, even within your own clique. It's like carrying your own food when you go backpacking. Don't expect your friends to bring enough to share, unless you've worked it out ahead of time. After all, psychedelics don't grow on trees—they're expensive and can be difficult to obtain. The exception is weed: if you've got it, don't be stingy, and if you need it, feel free to ask for a hit.

Buying drugs at an event is always a crapshoot. *Obviously*, we don't recommend it. The law of supply and demand (or desperation) means that quality control goes out the window. Epsom salt can be passed off as crystal meth; breath mints can look a lot like "E" to the untrained, unsober eye. Moreover, undercover cops love to entrap drug-hungry ravers.

Also watch out for GHB (the date rape drug), which is sometimes used by ravers coming down from "E." It looks like water, tastes like shit, and is a helluva lot more potent than people realize.

If you do succumb to the evil temptation of illegal substances, know your limits. Avoid falling, vomiting, or convulsing uncontrollably in the middle of the dance floor. If a friend or someone next to you is having a bad moment, be attentive and supportive. Don't hesitate to go for help; many raves have some sort of medic or EMT attendant on-site.

Clothes

Wear baggy clothes for comfort. Gals, wear a sports bra. This is an athletic event—dress accordingly. Tight jeans, double-breasted suits and cowboy boots are a no-no.

Fuzzy, shiny, colorful hats, shoes and outfits add to the carnival-like atmosphere at many raves. Dressing in a way that is fun for others to look at is always encouraged. Just be careful of the clichés: Those big Dr. Seuss hats coupled with big Mickey Mouse gloves might brand you as a novice, while tons of necklaces, a neon pacificier, and a whistle dangling from your neck are often the calling card of younger "candy ravers."

If you do opt to wear a whistle around your neck, feel free to blow it intermittently while dancing as a celebratory gesture. It's quite common. Just don't be obnoxious. Excessive blowing is another novice raver hallmark. And please . . . don't do it by the DJ.

Travel light. Pack a backpack with a sweater or extra clothes for warmth. A pup tent can come in handy for an all-night event. Bring ID, cash (bottled water and other concessions can be expensive), perhaps a piece of fruit. Having a stash of candy will endear you to any raver. We recommend watermelon Jolly Ranchers or Blow Pops.

Bring shades for the next morning.

Water, Water, Everywhere and Not a Drop to Drink

Drink lots of the ol' H_20, as sweaty dancing, among other "ravey" activities, tends to drain fluids. Generally, it is not acceptable to bring in your own—as we mentioned before, they sell it inside at exorbitant prices.

Be a sport and share your water with anyone who asks, unless they have visible mouth sores.

Touchy-Feely

Ideally, a rave is not a meat market. It's a nonthreatening environment where guys and gals can party together freely without the pressures or harassment often encountered at bars or more mainstream dance clubs. Honor this fundamental premise.

It's cool to get caught up in the music and start dancing with strangers. Public back rubs are standard. It's acceptable to pet someone sporting a furry or otherwise tactile outfit, as long as it's in a nonlecherous way. But . . . if you're a creepy old dude, keep your hands off the teenage chick in the bright fuzzy top.

If you do hook up at an all-night, outdoor affair, or are with a sig-o, humping at daybreak is often acceptable, though it's best to evaluate each rave on a case-by-case basis.

Last but Not Least...

Despite the peaceful, hippie-like, "collective consciousness" ideals of rave culture, there are those who are simply waiting to steal, scam and take advantage of you. Watch your backpack and your wallet, and keep tabs on your friends, particularly if they're looking rather spacey and glassy-eyed.

AND DEADHEADS . . .

Just stop. The party is over. He's dead and cremated. Quit clinging to bands like Phish. People are laughing at you. Retire the tie-dye, nix the patchouli oil and, for god's sake, take a shower.

PART V

The Professionals

Nihilism is best done by professionals.

—Iggy Pop

We do not need to be shoemakers to know if our shoes fit, and just as little have we any need to be professionals to acquire knowledge of matters of universal interest.

—Georg Hegel

The following section provides an insider's peek into some very exclusive clubs and subcultures, outlining codes of conduct for them . . . the people you fear, the people you aspire to be, the people whom you may have little or no personal contact with in day-to-day living.

Most of it will have little applicable use in your own life . . . unless of course you plan to quit your day job. But so-the-fuck what?! It's fun to play armchair outlaw.

The Porn Star

NAUGHTY BY NATURE

"Adult entertainer" means a person who is engaged in or participates in the production of live or recorded entertainment performances featuring the display of specified anatomical areas. "Specified anatomical areas" include: (i) human genitals or pubic region; (ii) buttocks; (iii) female breasts; and (iv) human male genitals in a turgid state.

—Sacramento city ordinance

ACTORS WANTED. Must be young, hung and full of cum.

—Classified ad

Just because someone fucks total strangers with abandon in front of a potential audience of millions doesn't mean he or she doesn't have morals. Or rules of conduct.

In fact, the porn industry is governed by a plethora of both legal and internal codes. Though smaller, sleazier, renegade outfits might choose to ignore laws, safety hazards, and other porn protocol, we've focused on the industry standards that most of the bigger production companies and most of the savvy stars adhere to closely.

True, most of us don't have the acting ability or appendages to be an XXX movie star, and much of our porn protocol will find little application in the day-to-day life of the average reader. Just think of yourself as a Peeping Tom, and enjoy the show.

WHO ARE YOU CALLING DIRTY?

Despite the stigma of filth generally attached to it, the adult film industry prides itself on professionalism. Much of its etiquette revolves around its struggle for legitimacy in a hypocritical society that refuses to admit its own lascivious, voyeuristic tendencies. Millions of consumers get off on porn, whether it's by themselves or with a close friend. Porn stars, directors and producers simply see themselves as pros supplying a demand.

Hence, descriptives like "smut," "dirty movies," "pornography," and other terms with negative connotations are frowned upon. Instead, porn stars and starlets refer to themselves as adult film "actors" and "actresses," while those who pose in the buff for print are "models." Others see themselves as "dancers," using porn shoots to enhance their cachet among strip club owners and patrons. If a woman gets her picture on a magazine or video box cover, she can use it to market herself and gain a following as a "feature dancer" on the road, which can be more lucrative for her than the photo spread or the movie itself.

THE POWER OF THE "P" AND PAYING DUES

A porn set is one of the few workplaces where women hold the power. Guys have the harder jobs, but chicks are considered more valuable. Actresses generally command a much higher salary than their male counterparts, and have more say in whom they work with and the type of sex to be filmed. They often submit a list of potential "co-stars" ahead of time.

Contrary to popular opinion, the director doesn't automatically get to test out the merchandise. Many naive women who are just breaking into porn think that's the only way to get a job, and they'll willingly submit. But the ironic truth is, if you've got talent, there's no need to sacrifice your integrity by sleeping your way in.

Aside from the name-brand actors, men need to be willing to work with anyone. A man gets into porn because a) he's got an elephant cock, b) he can keep going like Energizer, or c) a female star wants to work with him.

Most fledgling performers of both sexes are expected to pay dues. Your "veto" power about when, what position, and with whom is directly proportional to your established star power.

Performers are paid either per day, per movie, per scene, or per partner.

HOMEMADE PORN

Adult Film Star "Summer Knight" on Homemade Porn

When making your own home porn video, the object is to create something erotic, not embarrassing. This adult film actress and sex therapist was gracious enough to give us her personal tips.

1. **CONSULT THE PROS.** Watch a real porno first for help and ideas. I recommend the following: Ed Power's *Dirty Debutantes, Uncle Roy's Amateur Adventures* and *Bikini Beach, Parts I & II.*

2. **PRACTICE MAKES PERFECT.** Even professional actors don't always get a scene right on the first take. You might want to practice in front of the mirror, trying various positions, practicing your "lines," et cetera, before you start the camera rolling. Furthermore, don't try things for the first time on film. For example, your first experience with anal penetration can be rather awkward, and you probably don't want it recorded. Most importantly, don't stress too much about anything—you can always tape over mistakes.

3. **LIGHTING IS KEY.** Keep things soft, dim, and indirect—candlelight, for example. Hard, bright light shows every stretch mark. The look you're going for is fantasy, not harsh reality.

4. **PLAY MUSIC IN THE BACKGROUND.** Silence adds to the stark, glaring reality of it all—it's just not as sexy as some pulsing background rhythms, which always lends an erotic flair.

5. **TAKE YOUR TIME.** While it's fun to hump quickly like bunnies, you'll be disappointed at how silly it looks on screen. Do it slower than usual, and, if possible, film it or watch it in slow motion.

6. **TALK IS CHEAP.** Keep the smutty, over-the-top "give-it-to-me-baby" talk to a minimum. A little bit is cool, but too much usually comes off sounding corny, and will simply cheapen your erotic epic.

7. **DRESS UP.** Costumes and lingerie are part of the fun. Besides, you can use them to cover up marks or blemishes you don't want captured on film.

8. **CHOOSE ANY THIRD-PARTY CAMERAMEN WISELY.** For more ambitious angling, get a friend. I suggest someone you've already had sex with, or wouldn't mind having sex with, so that you feel comfortable in front of them. It also leaves the option open for you to have him or her join in.

9. **ALWAYS BE THE BEARER OF THE TAPE.** You just never know what a bitter ex-lover might do with your smutty memoir. Don't be caught with your pants down like skater Tonya Harding!

10. **KEEP YOUR EROTIC MASTERPIECE IN A SAFE PLACE.** Don't leave it where it can be found or stolen, particularly if you are a celebrity. Rob Lowe, Pammy and Tommy all know what I'm talking about!

BE FLEXIBLE

A performer should never walk onto a set without knowing who he or she is working with. They must be up on who's who in the biz, who's hung down to their knees, who's got an extra nipple, and so forth, so that there are no surprises. If you get to the set and suddenly decide that your co-star just isn't for you, tough shit. You've been hired to do a job, so do it, even if it means getting your hands (or other appendages) a little dirty.

In addition to spreading her legs and giving head, a female performer should also be comfortable getting down with another chick. These things are considered "normal," par for the course. A willingness to do "A" (anal), "DP" (double penetration), and three-ways will enhance a gal's résumé and marketability, but they are not a job requirement. You get paid extra for them.

As we noted, men must be more flexible than women. They should be adept at working in all orifices. The exception is gay porn—a straight male may opt to do another guy on camera just for the money, but it is never required or expected that he swing both ways.

Performers generally aren't forced to do bondage. That's a specialty. Bondage flicks generally make use of "character" actors and actresses and by law cannot show intercourse.

BE CLEAN, BE SAFE

Hygiene is key, not only for the sake of your partner, but because that zoom lens gets into every nasty little nook and cranny. A porn star should always shower/douche before a scene.

If a performer has a cold or the flu, he or she should call in sick rather than spreading the germs to all his or her co-workers. A girl shouldn't schedule a shoot if she's on the rag, unless she can hide it well with a sponge.

An actor or actress should always show up to the set with proof that he or she is HIV-negative. The slip should be current within thirty days; a polymerase chain reaction test is the industry standard. More stringent production companies require that tests be taken at specifically approved clinics.

If a performer has symptoms of any type of transmittable disease, he or she shouldn't show up to work. If someone suspects a co-worker is ill in any way that could jeopardize others, he or she *must* disclose. There is no anonymity code in the adult film industry; finger-pointing is condoned and expected.

Pretty much the norm in gay porn, condoms have become more and more acceptable in hetero flicks. Some of the bigger porn companies—Vivid, Wicked, VCA—even insist that all their actors wear condoms. Bigger stars might demand them, too. Still, some filmmakers believe a condom detracts from the fantasy, arguing that protected porn sex is the equivalent of heavyweight shadow boxing or a game of pro flag football. A director or producer can say "no" to a glove, in which case an actor or actress has the right to walk off the set.

Guys choose their own condoms. They frequently bring their own, unless the company doing the shoot has a condom-only policy, in which case they'll provide the jimmy hats. If a guy prefers a certain brand to what's available on set, he can ask a production assistant to go get him a pack. Rainbow colors excepted, the guy can usually use whatever type works best for him, even if it's a brand deemed less reliable—lambskin, ultra-thin, etc.

No open drug use on set. And intravenous drug use by performers on or off the set is a definite no-no. If you suspect that an actor or actress has a needle habit, you go public. Again, porn is one of the few subcultures where there is no shame in tattling.

"NICE TO MEET YOU"

Before their scene, a male and female might shake hands, hug, or even make out a little bit. But it is not unusual for a couple to be cold as ice until the camera starts rolling.

The guy must be ready, willing and able to perform without a warm-up, or he won't work too long in the industry.

HARD WORK

When the director says "Action!," a male performer must rise to attention immediately. A limp dick is an unemployed dick.

One of the biggest faux pas a male actor can make is to come too quickly. The director needs a lot of footage to make a scene, and if an actor shoots his wad before the director is done shooting, he's going to be pissed. He might pay Mr. Quick only half his money; he might not pay him at all. And that poor performance can impact future work.

A woman with rigorous, back-to-back workouts might request a breather, but complaining about soreness mid-scene generally won't fly.

THE MONEY SHOT

No internal come shots! The guy must squirt outside the girl. Viewers want proof of the orgasm. That's what they're paying to see, hence the term "money shot."

In addition, any movie should have a minimum of five sex scenes, with at least one anal sex scene, in part because the film won't sell overseas in Europe without the inclusion of some "A."

BE PROFESSIONAL

An actor/actress can bring a friend to a shoot, but they should get permission first. Bringing more than one friend, though, is pushing your luck.

If you are one such lucky spectator, taking snapshots to remember your XXX field trip is acceptable with permission. Just don't do it during filming. And do it in a dressing room—directors can get touchy about photographs taken on their set.

Don't whack off. Nonperformers—directors, producers, production assistants, cameramen, spectators—are supposed to conduct themselves in a professional manner. If you can't help touching yourself, be discreet, don't whip it out, don't be a distraction. And definitely don't point it in the direction of the lens.

UNWANTED PREGNANCY

A working female actress should be on the pill. If she gets pregnant, she generally has an abortion.

Those who decide to have the baby generally do not ask the father/co-star for financial help, as pregnancy is considered an occupational hazard. But, conceivably, a pregnant actress could point her finger at a male co-star, make him take a blood test, and sue him for child support. In fact, she could film a gang-bang scene, discover she's pregnant, and legally make fifteen different men take blood tests in search of the father. (Might make a great episode on TV's *Law & Order*.) Of course, such behavior won't win big points with directors or potential future co-stars.

LEGALITIES OF CONTENT

If you're a porn filmmaker or vendor, you've got to know what you can shoot and where you can distribute it.

The often random and inconsistent laws governing porn films and magazines are very strict, and vary by zip code. Send certain printed or taped materials (home porn included) across the wrong municipal or state lines, and you could be charged with the shipment of "contraband," punishable by hefty fines or imprisonment. *Hustler* publisher Larry Flynt—still embroiled in legal battles to this day—is a textbook example of why you need to keep current on the do's and don'ts. We've jotted a few down. Consult local, state and federal penal codes for the rest.

- Some municipalities are very tough on any photo spreads that display or *imply* bondage.

- In the United States, you can't film bondage and penetration together.

- Bestiality is a hairy subject, so much so that in a bondage film, you can't have any animals in front of the camera. A person's cat can't accidentally walk across the frame. Some bondage film companies are careful to take down any pictures of animals on the walls of the set.

- Urination scenes are considered too obscene for public viewing by many local governments.

- It's illegal to film "fisting" in the United States. Filmmakers generally stick to the "three-finger" rule.

- You can't film a sex scene in which there's a "Peeping Tom" watching an unsuspecting couple. The couple must acknowledge Tom's presence in some way.

- A female performer can't pretend to be asleep while her male co-star penetrates her. Nor can she be blindfolded so that it appears that she doesn't know who her partner is. Both are deemed too close to a rape fantasy.

- A female star can't dress up like a little girl in PJs and pigtails, doing little girl things like carrying a teddy bear. The theory is that such antics posit nasty ideas in the heads of pedophiles.

PORN STAR—CIVILIAN RELATIONSHIPS

A porn star need not immediately disclose his or her career to a civilian romantic interest. One actress we spoke with usually dips

THE LUCKIEST BLACK MAN ALIVE

Adult film star Mr. Marcus is best known for his role in The World's Luckiest Black Man, *in which he has sex with 101 women. (FYI: Though he prefers not to wear condoms, he did suit up properly with each of his 101 co-stars, going through 300 Trojan Magnums during the course of a 2 1/2-day shoot.) We asked him a few questions about his job.*

EFO: Have you ever gotten to a set, saw the woman you were supposed to hump, and changed your mind?

MM: I've gotten to a set and said, "Nah, I really don't feel well." I'll make a phone call and say, "Something came up, but I got a replacement—a guy who can do it for you."

EFO: But generally you should do the scene?

MM: Yeah. You just need to know who you can [make excuses] to, who you can't. Sometimes I know the director or producer well enough to get away with not doing it.

EFO: Do you ever have to do stuff you don't want to do?

MM: Usually when I show up, I pretty much know what I'm going to be doing. I've been doing this for five years. I'm one of the few guys, the luckiest guys, in that I can pretty much call the shots when I'm on the set. That's an exception. If you come into the business, just expect not to enjoy all of the women you're with. And don't expect 'em all to be really excited about fucking you. Half the girls won't want you to touch them until

you're about to have sex. If you're lucky and the girl likes you, maybe she'll do a little more for you. But be prepared to get your shit hard by yourself.

EFO: How can a guy break into the game?

MM: You know what guys got to stop doing? Coming up to me and saying, "Hey, how can I get into this business?" It pisses me off. They have to do their own homework. Know what companies to solicit, how to set up "chance" meetings that turn into work. Get in shape. Bring a girl with you. A woman can bring her boyfriend in. I would rather help women get into the business, because it benefits me. If you really want to get in this business, do your homework, go to the parties, mingle with the producers, directors, actors and actresses.

EFO: Do actresses have to have sex with a director to get a job?

MM: Most girls got it in their heads that that's what they gotta do. Bullshit. [Laughs] They don't have to. There are producers, agents, directors who do that, and say they her toes in gingerly, first talking about men's magazines and adult movies in general to gauge a new lover, before she drops the bomb on him.

After three or four dates, though, an actor or actress should let the cat out of the bag. After all, it's in print or on film. Best to say something *before* your new boyfriend or girlfriend accidentally sees you in the buff in a magazine spread, or on a tape they rented with their buddies.

If you're a porn star and your mate is outside the industry, it's not uncommon to pull your partner into a "swinging" situation or other

have to do it. I've done it, I've taken advantage of girls. But they really don't have to.

EFO: Any pet peeves with actresses?

MM: When they fake it. All that moaning and groaning and I haven't even put my dick in them yet. Every so often I get these girls who are just total actresses, and they've done it too many times, or watched too many movies. Usually it happens after they've watched one of their own movies. They think they have to overexaggerate.

EFO: So they have to come for real?

MM: Nah, but I do expect them to give themselves a chance to enjoy it. And don't overact.

EFO: What's the nastiest thing you had to do when you were coming up in the biz, paying dues?

MM: Anal with a girl who was really messy.

EFO: What was the worst thing you've had to do recently?

MM: The 101 girls. Even though that was a great shoot, to go through 30 girls, and know you got two more . . . I love women so much, so for me to do 30, and know there's nothing left in me and I got two girls to go . . . to muster up the erection, to muster up the performance and then come . . . that was the hardest thing.

EFO: How many times did you come during that shoot?

MM: 20. Someone counted.

creative sexual scenarios, so that everything feels kind of even between the two of you. (See "Swinging" in Part II).

An actress or actor is not "cheating" on her mate by going to work every day, but sleeping around off the set is not allowed.

If you choose to date an actor/actress, you can't demand that they stop unless you can afford to make up for the income that will be lost. On the other hand, civilians must be mindful that their porn star mate is not necessarily going to be a sex-o-matic fantasy in the flesh. After screwing eight different partners for eight hours straight, he or she might not want to get all freaky-deaky at home.

HAVEN'T I SEEN YOU SOMEWHERE BEFORE?

Most actresses stay somewhat insulated from the public. She might use her real name, but she never lists her phone number. Guys have more leeway, but should still exercise caution—there are a lot of sick motherfuckers out there.

If you recognize a porn star in public, use discretion. It's not that they're shy. But they might be with a family member, a new love interest, and so on, who isn't aware of their on-camera persona. And always be tactful: Asking something like "Haven't I seen you before?" or "Are you an actress?" gives the performer an easy way out of the conversation.

Don't assume a porn star will just fuck you on the first date, or that they prostitute themselves. Civilian: "So, how much do you make for a movie?" Porn star: "$500." Civilian: "What if I give you $500 for an hour?" They get that all the time, and they usually don't like it.

Just because a porn star discloses their profession doesn't give you license to act like a sex-craved, salivating pig. Porn stars, particularly women, will really appreciate it if you treat them like a person rather than a fuck fantasy. Asking a question like "What's your best movie?" is fine, but don't hit them with a bunch of trashy, graphic sex talk unless they initiate it. They're not on the clock.

A good way to meet porn stars is to tell them you're writing a book. They generally love attention.

The Rock Star

SEX, DRUGS, AND ROCK 'N' ROLL

If I were a girl, I'd rather fuck a rock star than a plumber.

—Gene Simmons, Kiss

Rock music should be gross. That's the fun of it. It gets up and drops its trousers.

—Bruce Dickinson, Iron Maiden

Long, sweaty flopping hair. Ripped-up jeans. A middle finger to the establishment. Groupies in every town. These are some of the trademarks of the rock star. But how to get there, and how to maintain that life of glamour and debauchery once you arrive?

If panties are flying in your direction, and phrases like, "Nah, that's on the house," "Wanna party with me and my roommate?" and "Just don't do it again" are all too familiar, you've already made it, and we're jealous. Cashing in on your rock star status is not only a perk of the job, it's your God-given duty. You're expected to indulge in every vice in this book, and can probably get away with anything you want, as long as you go about it in the right way.

The following pages outline the basic etiquette for rock stars in all their glory, but the aspiring local rocker can certainly profit from the career-building wisdom we've put forth. One of the best things about being a professional rocker is that you don't necessarily need any talent—someday it could be you biting off rats' heads on stage and inviting screaming fans up to your room for the "after party." Don't forget us when we call you for backstage passes.

WHEN THEY WANT MORE THAN YOUR AUTOGRAPH

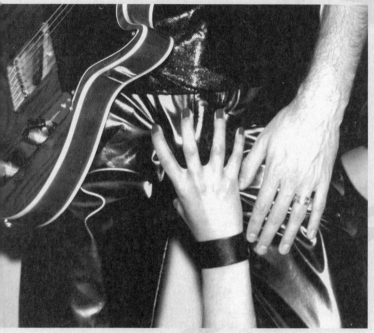

Dave Navarro on Groupie Etiquette, Hookers, Etc.

Dave Navarro, former guitarist for Jane's Addiction and the Red Hot Chill Peppers, is quite familiar with groupies. He has his own special way of dealing with starstruck female fans who have a tendency to get a little too attached. He also has a few suggestions for overeager fans who spot their favorite rock star in public.

EFO: Have you ever employed the services of a prostitute?

Dave: Yes, I used to be a regular patron of the, uh, the late-night services. Let's put it that way.

EFO: Why would someone in the public eye like yourself, who doesn't need to pay for sex, enlist the services of an escort?

Dave: That falls into groupie etiquette. For traveling musicians, or at least myself—I can only speak for myself—traveling around the world playing shows becomes incredibly lonely. And so naturally female companionship and sometimes a sexual exchange seems like some sort of prescription for that ailment. In my early days of touring, I'd slept with young female audience members. What ends up happening is this: As rock musicians, we risk hurting our admirers. These women become emotionally attached for a moment, and some of them begin to think there's more to it. And my thinking is, I would rather pay for an escort than hurt some young girl's feelings. I've had women move to L.A. with their bags and they don't know anybody here, and they're like, "I'm here, remember me, I'm Nancy from Virginia." It's like, "Nancy from Virginia, you gotta go." And so I decided that it was in my best interest and the interest of mankind to sleep with a woman who's made the conscious decision to sell her body for the evening, by the hour.

EFO: Are most musicians as considerate as you?

Dave: I don't think so. It's not for me to speak for them. But I will tell you that the irony here is that because I would rather sleep with the escort than with the fan, I'm the one who gets looked upon as the sick bastard. I feel I'm a really sensitive person. Not to sound arrogant, but it's hard for me to leave a city knowing that I might have broken a heart, or affected a girl who doesn't have any intention of that kind of vice, and somehow gets herself wrapped up in it because she's [starstruck].

EFO: Did you tip your escorts?

Dave: I would overtip. It would just be ridiculous in terms of what the fee was. The reasoning behind it was, if I ever got into this situation in the future, where I needed to hire these services at the drop of a hat, they would remember the tip and blow off whatever other client they have lined up for the evening.

EFO: Kind of like throwing down a $20 to a bartender, and having his undivided attention for rest of the evening?

Dave: Right. But then these services become yours any evening in the future.

EFO: Is there any other etiquette you observe with a hooker that's different from the etiquette you observe with, say, your hairstylist? Do you treat them with the same respect?

Dave: Essentially. I mean, you know, the service in question is the only difference. These are human beings just as a hairstylist is or a doctor is. They should be treated with the same respect in accordance with the way they're treating you. If a doctor is an asshole I treat him like a jerk. Same thing with the prostitute or any other service provider.

WHEN APPROACHING A ROCK STAR IN PUBLIC . . .

1. Wait until the musician is not eating. Unless you know them, never approach anybody in public while they're eating a meal. I hate when a guy comes up to shake your hand and you've got a sandwich in it.

2. Don't approach them if they're in the middle of an intimate conversation. If he or she is sitting on a bench with their significant other, and they're talking deeply, holding hands, and looking into each other's eyes, back off.

3. If the artist is with someone, their voices are raised and it appears that they're in an argument, back off.

4. If they're enjoying a movie, back off.

5. If the artist doesn't have his mouth full, isn't enjoying an intimate moment or a flick, and isn't in the middle of a fight, approach them calmly and politely. Say something like: "Hello Mr. or Ms. So-And-So, I am a fan of yours, do you have 30 seconds to a minute?" It gives them the opportunity to say yes or no.

6. If they say no, respond with: "Thanks anyway, I like your work" or "I understand, have a nice day."

7. If they say yes, it's okay to ask for their autograph or ask them a few questions.

IT'S GOOD TO BE BAD

Rock stars should not be role models. Their job is to rock hard and live the life that others can only fantasize about. Their responsibilities are as follows: to consistently say the wrong thing, drink hard liquor straight out of the bottle, and taste the forbidden fruit of nubile groupies whenever possible.

As a rock star, (almost) everything will be either forgiven or understood, so cry havoc and let slip the dogs of war. Get drunk and throw up all over a restaurant? That's what rock stars do. Trash a hotel room and go skinny-dipping with the maid at 2:56 in the morning? Hey, that's what rock stars do. Do drugs, get arrested, get community service? You're a goddamned rock star. If you haven't been arrested, you're not doing your job.

Just the Sex, Ma'am

Integral to rock starness is copious amounts of sexual activity. Whatever you want, wherever you want it, it's there for you. Be as weird as you like. Bang every groupie in sight. Let her take pictures, let her tell the tabloids, it's all good, you know what we mean? It builds the reputation. What would rock 'n' roll be without sex? Yep, easy listening. We rest our case.

The one caveat to the sex-all-the-time thing is that the rocker should always have safe sex. We know we've been hitting you over the head with all that safe sex stuff, but rock stars need to be especially mindful. If they're begging to bang one rock star, odds are they've done half the other rock stars touring through their crummy town.

It's not just about leaving Boise without an STD, either. A smart rocker will refrain from planting his seed all over the Midwest. That way he doesn't have to fork over huge amounts of his royalties to three different moms when little Billy, little Sally and little Peter are born.

DON'T BE SHY

The rock star should publicly rail on all publicity and music journalists, proclaiming them opportunistic gossip-mongers, the scum of the earth, et cetera, and then grant as many interviews and pose for as many pictures as possible. He should say outlandish things to the press to ensure getting quoted, and he should find a great ghostwriter to help him write his autobiography, complete with graphic, hyperbolic details of all sexcapades and substance abuse. Option your life story to the highest bidder. Don't worry about overexposure—they probably won't make the movie until after you're dead and buried, anyway.

No ridiculously trite poetry books, please.

BE THE BAND

While a rocker should always have his bandmates' backs, it's not necessary that he like them, hang out with them, or be their best friend. Strife can make for some explosive onstage chemistry.

Even if things are really bad—name-calling to the press, brawls, lawsuits—a member of a successful band should think twice before cutting loose in search of the solo spotlight. Witness the solo careers of Vince Neil, David Lee Roth and Mick Taylor. That move should generally be reserved for those singer/songwriters who in fact are responsible for the band's greatness, à la Ozzy.

DON'T BE A DINOSAUR

Certain bands have long, fruitful careers, endure the test of time, and go on to become legend. Others go on to become retro dinosaurs or just plane lame. Here are some basic tips for rockers wishing to avoid the "Where are they now?" syndrome.

Along with partying, it is the job of every rock star to "keep it real." What that translates to is simply this: Don't let the fans down. Bands like Metallica have kept pretty true to the music that got them there in the first place. A band that makes its mark with loud should keep it loud. Branching off into the occasional ballad is acceptable, as long as the band is ready when it comes time to rock.

Some bands will grow and naturally develop into new areas. Old fans might prefer the old stuff from "back in the day," but the band's rep is still respectable. The flip side to this natural progression of talent is the concept of "selling out": overtly changing a sound and style just to keep current with trends, watering down songs for mainstream pop airplay, et cetera. Being labeled by fans as a "sellout" can be hard for any die-hard rocker to take, but if Soundscan keeps racking sales for said commercial sellout album, it can certainly ease the pain.

Instead, a rock star or band who's dated and no longer relevant might consider a temporary breakup until their sound comes back into style. Or the band can wait to reach "retro" status, breaking out the old spandex or fringe garments or bizarre circus-style makeup, and attempt to reignite their career. Or they can just skip it all and become web programmers, bitterly dreaming of their faded stardom.

A rock star who can make a living touring off his past hits has reached "dinosaur" status. Though no one cares about his new records, he should feel free to make them, as long as he doesn't play too many of the new songs live. In concert, he should give the fans what they want and stick to the hits they came to hear. If a rock star ceases to get gigs at even the smallest of clubs and is instead playing the Garlic Festival circuit, he should pack it up or be prepared to be mocked by the likes of us!

Finally, if a rocker had a hit at some time or another, VH1 will probably do a *Where Are They Now?* segment featuring his rise and fall. Tip: The star of years past who thinks that such exposure might push sales of old records or renew interest in his career should do the show. But proper faded rock star decorum suggests that the fat pig playing shitty old songs at the local county fair—the lead singer of, say, Loverboy—should get his huge red-leather-wearing ass off our TV screens!

COMMERCIAL FAME

It's cool for a rock star or band to be in it only for the money (and the chicks and the drugs), but try not to hit us over the head with it by selling out too soon.

There are the two basic rules of thumb. First, a rocker should never sell his songs for use as ad jingles until after he's past his prime. If he jumps the gun, he risks alienating his core fans. Second, if he's built his career on flipping the bird to the corporate establishment, he should blow off Madison Avenue altogether.

DEATH

Any rock star needs to remember that the more miles he puts on his body, the less likely he is to last all that long. Heart failure? Cirrhosis of the liver? Depression-induced suicide? Every rock star should carefully consider his options. Die correctly, become a legend; die incorrectly, become a footnote.

Classic ways to meet the reaper, apart from old age, include: car crash, plane wreck, or the always popular accidental drug overdose. Once the rage, drowning in a swimming pool, getting shot by an ex-lover, and choking on one's own vomit are considered passé. Finally, bearing in mind that how you go can reflect how you lived, we recommend that all rock stars steer clear of autoerotic asphyxiation.

One of the best ways to become immortalized is by suicide. While we don't advocate it—unless you're Barbra Streisand or a member of Yes—it's a reality among rock gods. Sometimes all that sex, drugs, fame, fortune and unconditional love by millions of fans is just too unbearable. Popular, legend-making suicide tactics include overdosing or jumping out a window. The highly dramatic self-inflicted gunshot wound is also a great way to go out with a bang. Just make sure you're a megastar first—unknown musicians cannot be assured immortality.

Do your best to time your demise with the release of a new album. It will invariably result in a huge spike in posthumous sales—always a nice thing to do for any kids or spouses you leave behind. Works particularly well if you go out in a mysterious blaze of gunfire, and the crime is never solved.

If possible, try to drop some clever death references in the album title, cover art or song lyrics, ensuring speculation that you in fact faked your own death and are alive and well in South America. Again, this will fuel album sales as well as keep your legend burning bright in the annals of rock history.

The Gang-Banger

MEMBERSHIP HAS ITS PRIVILEGES

The town is divided into various groups, which form so many little states, each with its own laws and customs, its jargon and its jokes.

—Jean de La Bruyère

Where you from?

—Gang-banger, Anyhood, USA

Gangs are everywhere, populating every city across the country and representing a wide range of ethnicities: Chinese, Korean, Armenian, Samoan, white, black, Hispanic, etc. They all have their own quirks, rules, initiation rites, etc.—enough to fill up several books.

So we've focused on the most renowned of the lot: black gangs, which, in turn, are divided into the Crips and their historical rivals, the Bloods, and Hispanic gangs. It's important to remember that each of these broad groups is further subdivided into thousands upon thousands of "sets"—mini-cliques that represent neighborhoods across the country. Most of our research was conducted in Los Angeles. As the birthplace of modern gang culture, L.A. has established a blueprint for gang trends nationwide, and can provide a reasonable national model. Ironically, many L.A. gang members are the ones least likely to adhere rigidly to the rules, perhaps because they feel they have less to prove. In fact, it's important to remember that etiquette can vary greatly for each individual clique and by region. Gang etiquette is also ever-evolving: protocol set forth in the following pages could very well be dated by the time you finish this section.

While there are plenty of female gangs, they're certainly in the minority, and our male gang–skewed coverage reflects that. We apologize to any "gangster bitches" who might feel left out.

Much of the etiquette set forth herein won't apply to the average citizen. While most gang-bangers aren't nice, law-abiding citizens, and might victimize innocent people for gain, they generally don't go around blasting "civilians" for fun. We have, however, thrown in some tips for the unfortunate laymen caught in the wrong neighborhood at the wrong time. (Additional info can be found in "Basic Street Etiquette" in Part IV)

THE GANG-BANGER PROFILE

Before we get into gang-banger etiquette, it's important to define who we're talking about.

A gang member or "gang-banger" is an active member of a gang, generally of lower economic class, often a minority. They dress a certain way, walk a certain way and talk a certain way.

Using the term "gang-banger" to describe any old street punk causing trouble is incorrect. Assuming that a kid in saggy, baggy pants and a ball cap is in a gang is also incorrect. In fact, millions of rich suburban white kids have adopted hard-core "gangsta" rap as their music of choice, and now emulate the stereotypical speech, dress, and overall demeanor of gang members as depicted in flicks like *Colors, South Central, American Me,* and *Menace II Society.*

Gangland style is trendy. In other words, don't judge a book by its cover, and don't use the term "gang-banger" as an all-encompassing term for youthful criminals. Stealing a candy bar doesn't make someone a career criminal; committing a murder doesn't make someone a serial killer. Hell, plenty of young delinquents are just independent contractors.

This knowledge is a double-edged sword. Any twelve-year-old can carry a gun and shoot you, whether he's in a gang or not. You might know he's a fake, but bear in mind that a wannabe is just as dangerous, if not more dangerous, than the real deal.

BLACK VERSUS BROWN

Now that introductions are out of the way, let's get into specifics.

There are a number of key differences between black and Hispanic gangs. The biggest disparity is the fact that black gangs are alliances based on money, whether that means doing robberies or selling crack. Hispanic gangs, by contrast, are centered more on pride, loyalty and territory. Members often view themselves as barrio warriors or protectors of the 'hood.

This fundamental difference permeates many aspects of their respective sets of etiquette.

INITIATION

Many gangs require prospective members to undergo some sort of initiation ritual. The most common is getting "jumped in," whereby one or more members of the gang beat the shit out of you. When getting jumped in, the pledge is expected to grin and bear the pummeling in silence.

Other rites of passage include committing some sort of crime for profit.

When you join a Hispanic gang, it's generally "*por vida,*" for life. Even if you graduate from active membership when you get older and get a respectable job, etc., you never publicly disavow your set.

Blood and Crip affiliations can be lifelong, but they don't generally run as deep. In fact, inner clique feuds are common and deadly. Those who leave the 'hood or gang life to pursue more noble career goals might not find open arms and a welcome banner waiting if they return for a visit. They may find that their gangland pass has been revoked by the same kids they used to bang with. As one reformed gang member told us: "I'm more worried about my own kind than [members of rival sets]."

Some gangs demand that a member be "jumped out" before he leaves voluntarily or is ousted. Once again, they beat the shit out of you. Or they just kill you.

ALL IN THE FAMILY

Don't attend a gang meeting unless you want to be part of that gang. If you're a gang member attending a gang-related meeting, think carefully before bringing a buddy. If your fellow members are suspicious, they might not want to talk about the good stuff in front of a stranger. Or they might whoop your ass for bringing an outsider into the cipher.

If a member brings in a new guy, he is responsible for that newbie—he is sponsoring him. If the new guy behaves inappropriately, the sponsor must make it right, whether that means slapping him on the wrist or shooting him in the head.

FLYING THE FLAG

Gang-bangers are tired of getting hassled by cops, who have become quite savvy in detecting gang colors and insignia. And they are sick of getting picked off by rival gangies. Accordingly, more and more members are keeping a lower profile these days.

Still, part of being a gang member is letting folks know, and getting off on the power that comes with people knowing. While you can't judge a book by its cover, a number of characteristic trappings for gang-bangers remain.

Should I Wear Red, or Blue?

The biggest gang fashion statement has to be the colors associated with Crips and Bloods. Crips like blue; Bloods like red. Color-coding is less prominent now than it used to be, particularly in Los Angeles, but allegiance can still be denoted by anything from the color of a cap to the air freshener trees in a car. Color-coding can go from head to toe (a Crip in a blue cap, blue Dickies pants, a blue shirt and blue Converse), or can be subtly signified by one article of clothing, or even a telling emblem on one article of clothing (a Blood sporting a Boston Red Sox cap, or a Cleveland Indians cap with the red-faced Native American).

Ball Caps and Jerseys

Athletic team logos are also quite big with black gangs, with team initials representing a specific set. A Montreal Expos hat might signify Marvin Gangsta Crips, Menio Gangsta Crips or Mansfield Hustlers. A jersey with a University of North Carolina team emblem is a welcome addition to a Neighborhood Crip's wardrobe; San Diego Padres gear might be found in the closet of a 6-Deuce Blood.

Sometimes jerseys will have Old English–style numbers custom-ironed on like football numbers, representing a gang's block number. These days, that practice is more common among Hispanic sets.

Are You a Righty, or a Lefty?

Bloods usually hold stuff in their right back pocket, and keep their belt buckle turned to the right side. Crips are lefties. Adjust accordingly. The practice is more in force in places outside L.A.

Real Men Don't Wear Pink

The standard uniform for a Hispanic gang member consists of immaculate black Nike Cortez shoes, a well-ironed T-shirt or jersey, and well-ironed size 52 khakis. A belt buckle might sport the gang's initials. Shorts are long, with white socks pulled up high so that the legs are never exposed. The color palette is simple: brown, black, khaki or gray. Bright red, lavender or pink is a no-no.

A bald head, or "bullet head," and a goatee or mustache is all the rage among Hispanic gang-bangers.

War Paint

For Bloods and Crips, tattoo subject matter echoes their color-coding (for instance, a popular Blood tat is a Red Dog beer logo). But since black skin doesn't always ink so well, tats are more common among Hispanic gang members.

An aspiring Hispanic gang-banger might start with three dots on the web of the hand (it suggests "gang-banger-in-training"), and later blaze their hood or gang name across their stomachs in Old English–style lettering. Stylized low-rider art is also popular among Hispanic bangers. A teardrop inked below the eye, once a popular and proud symbol of jail time served, is somewhat dated.

If you encounter someone with lots of visible gang-related tats on places like the neck and eyelids, keep your distance. Like we said, today's gangies are less likely to advertise their affiliation so blatantly. Hence, a guy wearing a big neon sign on his face advertising his gang status may well have adopted an "F the world" attitude. He doesn't care who knows where he's from, whether it's cops or rivals. His tats are like war paint. (See "Tattoos" in Part III)

THE PROPER TOOLS

If a group of gang members is out in public, it's standard practice for the majority to be "strapped" (carrying a gun). At the very least, proper protocol dictates that they have a firearm within easy reach.

WALKING THE WALK

Want to walk like a gang-banger? It's easy!
You can either adopt a rhythmic swagger and put a little dip in your step, more common among black gang members.

Or you can puff out your chest and do your best peacock imitation, popular among Hispanic gang members.

TALKING THE TALK

When in the company of gang members other than your own, two basic rules apply.

First, don't ask questions. In particular, don't ask about business (drugs, killings)—it's like asking a hit man to tell you about his day at work. Ask a lot of suspicious questions, and they might take you for a cop.

Second, don't try to be too hip. Where you come from, addressing a fellow Crip as "cuz" might be standard protocol, but it might be the wrong thing to say in some other area. Best to sit back, observe, and take mental notes.

Don't Disrespect Someone's Hood

Never say anything to a die-hard Hispanic gang member to disrespect his 'hood and his gang. Dissing his mother or his race won't win you big points, but insult the barrio he claims, and it's war.

For instance, in East L.A., The Mob Crew, known as TMC, and the gangs from Primera Flats simply do not get along at all. TMC refer to their Primera Flats rivals as the Papas Fritas. A Primera Flats gangie might bait his TMC rival by calling him a Tamale. Might sound cute, but such exchanges can end in bloodshed.

213

Don't Question Someone's Manhood

Another no-no is to question a Hispanic gang member's manhood in any way. You don't call him a "punk," "bitch," "punk bitch" or "*leva*" (translates to any of the aforementioned). Accordingly, calling him a "homo" will probably get an angry reaction as well. This sense of machismo is so strong that at one point Hispanic gangies refused to eat creamed foods because of the sexual connotations.

Any insult to a Hispanic gang member is ten times worse if made in the company of his girl or his homeboys. He will be obliged to throw down to defend his honor and pride.

Four-Letter Words That Start with "C"

When in the company of Bloods, do your best not to use words that start with the letter "C." C-words are simply too close to the word "Crips" for Blood ears. Some years back, if a Blood wanted a cookie, he might ask for a "bookie" to avoid uttering that dreaded "C." Or he might describe the color of a car as "boo boo" or "flue" rather than let the word "blue" pass over his lips. The practice is a bit dated, particularly among older Bloods who just felt too damn clownish (oops, *blownish*) about it all. One word that definitely continues to hurt Blood ears is "slob" (Etymology: *blood < blob < sloop < slob*.) Crips commonly use it to taunt their crimson-clothed rivals.

Crips don't have the same hangups with "B" words, but they won't take kindly to the following terms of derogation: "crab," "cricket" or "e-ricket."

Among themselves, Crips generally address one another as "loc" or "cuz." Bloods prefer to call each other "dog." Don't mix 'em up.

Hand Jive

"Signing," the use of hand signals and movements, is a popular method of set identification and communication among gangs, not unlike sign language for the deaf. Gang members and their visitors must avoid random gesticulations that involve twisting up or contorting the fingers, as the most harmless of gestures may have dangerous hidden meanings.

For example, a good-natured "peace sign" thrown up in the wrong crowd could mean war: It's quite similar to the sign for L.A.'s Rollin' 60s. Meanwhile, if Mr. Spock flashed that dorky Star Trek sign at a surly group of Crips, he might have some problems: that "V"-like gesture is used as an identifier by Blood subset the Villains. (See "Basic Street Etiquette" in Part IV)

Once popular among various Watts gangs, a "W"—two middle fingers twisted up, thumb across the palm—has been appropriated by West Coast hip-hop fans as an expression of coastal loyalty. Throwing up a "W" in the company of die-hard East Coast hip-hop fans might cause some static, but it's hardly an appropriate cue for violence. (See "Helpful Hints for the Hip-Hopper" in "Music Scene Etiquette" in Part IV)

Generally, hand signs are far more elaborate among black gangs than among Hispanic sets, who use very rudimentary gestures to represent their barrio. "A" might stand for "Avenue." A "P" and an "R" might stand for "Pico Rivera."

At the same time, these simplified gestures pack more of a wallop. While Crips and Bloods might flash their signs back and forth as part of a long, dramatic, pro-wrestling-esque prelude before a real altercation, a Hispanic gang sign is an immediate declaration of war—like a rattler poised to strike. When a Hispanic gang member flashes his sign, run for cover.

THE DRIVE-BY: HONOR AMONG KILLERS

If there is one crime automatically associated with gang members, it's the drive-by shooting. The act entails members driving by an enemy on the street, or by his home, sticking a gun(s) out the window, and pumping said target full of lead as the driver hits the gas.

Once a cornerstone of gangland activity and a major cause of civilian casualties, the much-ballyhooed "drive-by shooting" has become less popular in recent years. Sure it still happens, but it's definitely on the wane.

Whether you are in a Hispanic gang or a black gang, it is, for the most part, no longer permissible to cruise down the block and spray a street corner or house with bullets, risking innocent lives just to nail one enemy. Likewise, if a gang member sees an enemy strolling with his mom, girlfriend, baby or parole officer, he generally holds off.

There are a few reasons for this. First, it's bad for business. You shoot up a drug-vending spot, it scares customers away, and everybody loses. Second, cops don't take kindly to the deaths of innocent bystanders. If a stray bullet nicks the wrong person, the city gang task force is likely to call out the cavalry, turn up the heat, sweat everyone in the area and kick some ass of their own.

Once again, it's bad for business, everybody loses.

In California, the Mexican Mafia, an organization that exerts a strong influence on street gangs largely from the inside of prisons, has issued an edict that there are to be no more drive-bys. Likewise, elders from both the Crips and Bloods—known as O.G.'s or "original gangstas"—have called for an end to this statistic-raising form of execution. Consequently, civilian gang murders have dropped significantly.

"Walk-ups," or target homicides, are, however, still perfectly acceptable and very much in vogue. Gangs generally know not to bang in affluent suburban neighborhoods with low crime rates where hordes of cops are just waiting to bust any minority for spitting on the sidewalk.

WHERE YOU FROM?

"Where you from?" is what a gang member or members might ask a stranger in their 'hood. It roughly translates: "What gang are you in?" It's a challenge that can be fatal if the stranger responds incorrectly—i.e., with the name of a rival set.

If you are not in a gang and don't want trouble, an appropriate response is: "I ain't from nowhere." Nearly every 'hood in every city has a gang, so simply naming your place of residence could be misinterpreted, with deadly consequences.

If you are in a gang, and those doing the interrogating are your rivals, you have two choices: 1) lie, or 2) risk getting shot.

If you are in a Hispanic gang, you never "front" on your status— with pride, you tell the rivals which gang you represent, even if you know they've got a loaded barrel pointed at you.

If you are in a Hispanic gang and a cop asks you if you're in a gang, you happily admit it. And if you're in court and you are asked if you are in a gang, you 'fess up.

To lie or disavow your membership, known as "ranking out," would be a disgrace under any circumstance, even under the threat of arrest, jail or death. It's just not acceptable.

For a Crip or a Blood, lying and denying to save your ass is often perfectly acceptable.

NO FRONTIN'

Never claim a 'hood or gang set that isn't your own. That will get your ass whooped or shot off real fast. A "transformer" is someone who says "wassup cuz" in one hood and "wassup dog" in another, shifting gang alliances out of convenience. A "buster" is someone who fronts on street status altogether, making out like he's down with a gang when he's not. Both "busters" and "transformers" are severely frowned upon.

SNITCHING: THE CARDINAL SIN

If there is one thing a Hispanic gang will not tolerate among their ranks, it's a "snitch," also known as a "rata," "cheese-eater" or "queso-eater." You don't snitch or "cheese out" on guys in your crew. You don't snitch on guys in rival crews. If it's a choice between snitching and jail, you do the time. If a rival blows a hole in your chest and you miraculously live to be questioned by cops, you tell 'em, "I fell down the stairs."

In recent years, penalties for gang-related crimes have gotten tougher. If a kid faces twenty-five years for a shooting he didn't commit, he might receive permission from his gang brethren to give up the shooter. Or the cops might receive an anonymous phone call. But generally, cheesing out—on your homies *or* enemies—is the worst thing a Hispanic gang member can do. It carries a sanction of death.

Amongst Crips and Bloods, loyalty is ephemeral. Members often rat on rivals and on each other.

RESPECTING THY ELDERS

A common misconception is that an O.G. with a long-term history with and devotion to a gang set automatically commands respect from younger members. Battle scars only go so far. Older or more seasoned members are frequently defied and challenged.

In recent years, the Mexican Mafia has tried to reassert control over Southern California Hispanic street gangs with strong sanctions for those who defy things like the drive-by edict mentioned earlier.

Again, obedience is spotty. But a Hispanic gang member disrespecting laws laid down by "La M" had better keep his ass out of prison. The Mexican Mafia exerts a powerful influence behind bars, and will deal swiftly with insubordinates once they're trapped inside.

SWEET REVENGE

Want to piss off a rival gang member—you know, really get his goat? Simply screw his girlfriend. They hate that.

TUNES

Many 'hoods or gang sets have a theme song or party song.

For black gangs, hard-core or "gangsta" rap is the music of choice. Many rappers have their gang affiliations, and in years past, it wasn't acceptable for, say, a Blood to listen to a rapper who had a Crip history. These days, though, it's acceptable, as long as that artist is low-key about it.

DJ Quik, an extremely popular multiplatinum rapper with a Blood affiliation, started blatantly making fun of Crips in his lyrics. In such an instance, it is no longer acceptable for a Crip to buy and listen to his music.

At one point, Crips came up with their own dance, the "Crip Walk," which is something like the Charleston-meets-Stomping-on-a-Roach, spelling out "Crip" or your street number with your toes and bouncing on your heels. To perform this dance at a party attended by Bloods would be very inappropriate.

Hispanic gang members' tastes run the gamut. Ethnic pride dictates that traditional Mexican music like banda, mariachi, or cumbia is cool at things like family functions, but generally not with the homeboys. In a gang environment, they might listen to hip-hop, funk or oldies.

The Graffiti Artist

THE WRITING'S ON THE WALL

Graffiti ain't canvasses; it's on the trains and the walls... taking the risk.

—Zoro in Wildstyle

*O*ften confused with the gang-banger, the graffiti writer is, in fact, a different animal entirely.

True, some graf writers are in gangs. True, they often run in packs, or crews, "battling" rival crews. And true, these tagger rivalries can turn violent.

But ideologically speaking, graf writing isn't about fighting or selling drugs or ethnic pride. It's about leaving one's mark, not unlike a dog spraying a fire hydrant. It's also about beating one's rivals down with artistic skills rather than with baseball bats.

Graf developed as a movement in New York in the 1970s alongside rap music, break dancing, and deejaying—collectively known as "hip-hop" culture. Like the other three branches of hip-hop, graf started as a creative outlet for urban youth, a way to create something beautiful out of limited resources. Forget pricey art schools, easels and stretched canvasses; for graf writers, Krylon's collection of exotic colors became the palette, while public walls, buildings, trains, buses, et cetera became the canvas.

We mention these roots because they're so clearly reflected in graf etiquette—in the unwritten rules of writing on the wall, so to speak. Keep them in mind if you ever decide to pick up a spray can.

ONE PERSON'S TRASH IS ANOTHER'S TREASURE

You might call it defacement of public property; graf writers call it art. There is far more to the art of graffiti than just a bunch of random scrawls and scribbles. It can take hours of work, often under difficult (illegal) conditions, and the results can be dazzling.

Hence, think twice before referring to street art as "graffiti," particularly in the presence of serious graf artists. Not PC. The term denigrates their elaborate and time-consuming works. For many, "aerosol art" is the preferred nomenclature, while participants think of themselves as "writers," "taggers" and "bombers."

Not unlike more traditional painters, graf writers refer to their significant works as "pieces."

INHERENTLY "OUTLAW"

Forget the canvas.

Graf art is renegade art, inherently and implicitly rebellious. Graf artists are spray can outlaws, and their work is site-specific, done illegally where the general public can see it. Once you place the work on a canvas, in a frame or on a pedestal, it loses something. It's out of context.

As recognized bomber Slick puts it: "Once you put it in a gallery environment, it's no longer graffiti. Call it something else. Now, say I stroll into the Louvre with my spray can and do my shit all over the masterpieces—then that's graffiti."

LEVELS

A "tag" is essentially a signature—a nickname often followed by a number representing a block of residence. For instance, famed writer Mare would sign his name "Mare 139" because he grew up on 139th Street in the South Bronx. The practice started in New York in the late '60s as a way to say, "So-and-so was here." For tagging, a fat marker is often the writing implement of choice.

Hitting the streets, subways, buildings, etc. with spray cans is referred to as "bombing" or "hitting up." Bombing can be as rudimentary as a signature, or more complex, like a "throw-up"—usually a two-color image composed mostly of bubble-style lettering.

The highest level of bombing is the "burner," comprised of many colors and the elaborate, abstract hyper-calligraphy known as "wild-style"—often difficult to read for the untrained eye.

Writers might add some cartoonish characters next to their wild-style lettering to supplement their piece, but the pinnacle of great graf art is a mastery of the lettering. The truly great writer's letters stand alone as works of art unto themselves.

A graf writer should get the lettering down first.

TOOLS OF THE TRADE

Any writing implement is acceptable for graf—a can of spray paint, fat markers, pencils, even chalk—making Keith Haring one of the most successful graf artists in history.

There is no shame in using special tips or nozzles on spray cans for different kinds of coverage and line thickness, though some old-school writers think that using really fine, eyelash-thin, airbrush-quality nozzles is cheating.

Graf is generally not a brush medium, though writers will sometimes use rollers for large-scale pieces. Stencils are always considered bad form.

Any style of spray paint is acceptable, the best known being Krylon, which clearly has a love-hate relationship with graf artists. Creating crazy colors seemingly tailor-made for bombers—Icy Green, Metallic Periwinkle—Krylon nevertheless refuses to sponsor graf-oriented competitions and won't affiliate themselves with the culture in *any* way. It's a bone of contention with writers, who contribute millions to the company's annual bottom line. So even if you use their paint, feel free to rag on them.

The best paint is stolen paint. The best tips or nozzles are stolen tips or nozzles.

SLICK STYLE

Slick is a "fame" grafitti writer who was born in Hawaii and transplanted to Los Angeles. His résumé includes trains, houses, cop cars and the Hawaii State Capitol building. He currently co-owns Shaolin, a hip line of clothing and skate-boards. Though most of his graf is now done on a computer, he is still a devout spray can junkie, and goes out bombing every now and again for the rush—and to smell the sweet scent of the fumes.

EFO: How can you justify marking up public property with your work, subjecting people who might not share your aesthetic?

SLICK: From my visual perspective, billboards are litter on the freeway. Same with sky writers. They paid. I can't pay, but I've got the resources to make something out of nothing—something beautiful, positive. I see a wall as a blank canvas.

EFO: You bombed the State Capitol building—is there anything you wouldn't tag?

SLICK: [By the state capitol], there's a statue of Father Damian, who helped all the lepers. I got my respect for Father Damian—I didn't write on him. I don't write on churches, syna-gogues. I don't fuck with trees. I have my own codes.

EFO: When I go hiking, I sometimes see a rock all tagged up, and it bothers me.

SLICK: It's no different from cavemen or Indians doing their hieroglyphics, leaving a record of history.

EFO: Back then, pristine nature wasn't such a scarce commodity.

SLICK: The first airbrush was a caveman with his hand against the wall, with a tube with some pigment and some spit and boom—the first stencil, leaving his mark. When an ani-mal finds his mate, he pisses all over it, leaving his mark. But if I did some graffiti in a nature setting, it wouldn't be spray paint on a tree or rock. I'd probably take the rocks and make a formation into my name.

EFO: How seriously do artists take it when someone goes over their work?

SLICK: I just did a mural inside the office of *Giant Robot* (a cutting-edge pop culture pub-lication). [The owner] says he wants to get another writer to go over my piece. I told him he has to buff my piece first, 'cuz if that kid goes over my piece, that's like war. I just let him know, 'cuz he didn't know the codes. It's not like a written rule, it's just respect.

EFO: Anything worse than discovering that someone has gone over an elaborate piece of your work?

SLICK: One time, we had just finished a piece—we went over some simple silver block let-ters with a color outline [done] by a local gang. Gangsters got their own codes. Whatever codes we go by in the graffiti scene, they don't give a fuck. And they rolled up on us, jacked all our paint—like forty cans—and crossed out our piece right in front of us. That's worse.

IF A TREE FALLS IN THE FOREST . . .

If a graf artist creates the most brilliant piece in history but a sudden rainstorm hits before it dries and washes the work away, was it still the most brilliant piece in history?

No. Audience viewership is intrinsic to the art form. It's about notoriety. Hence, the aspiring graf artist needs to paint where he can be seen by the public, or at least by other writers. The goal is to become a "fame" (famous) writer.

Take pictures of all your work. A good writer knows his piece is ephemeral, subject to the elements and city cleanup task forces. He will always document his big pieces with photographs.

THE WORLD IS YOUR CANVAS

As a general rule, nothing is sacred for the graf writer. Buildings, police cars, airplanes, houses, churches, schools, buses, trains, trees, hallways—it's all one big canvas.

The only problems arise when certain neighborhoods are considered gang turf. Under such circumstances, writers must be extra careful—hitting up claimed gang turf might irk the locals. Use of red or blue may not be appropriate colors in some areas. (See the preceding section, "The Gang-Banger")

Writers often bomb under the cloak of night, but any time is acceptable.

Racist slogans or imagery is frowned on in the graf community, but otherwise there are no rules governing content.

Hitting up a place once doesn't preclude you from going back. In fact, in most cities there are "yards"—areas where writers congregate and bomb over and over again.

The inaccessibility of a location, and the greater the danger of being caught for hitting it up, are directly proportional to the status achieved among one's peers. For example, a freeway off-ramp sign or several stories up the side of a building is referred to as the "heavens." Requiring a mix of balls and skill, hitting up the heavens is generally worthy of respect.

In big cities, a prime target has always been the subway. A train car painted top to bottom in wildstyle lettering, rolling through a part of the city where everyone is bound to see it, is the ultimate conquest for many writers. If a writer can do this, and do it well, you owe him respect. In an effort to combat aerosol art on subways, some cities now have stainless-steel "swipe-clean" train cars. In such instances, subway tunnels, buses, freight trains, storefront grates, and the pavement of well-trafficked streets are reasonable substitutes.

"BURNER" WORK ETHIC

When doing a collaborative burner with your crew, teamwork is the name of the game. If you're working on a burner, you know your role—different members work on different portions of the piece—and each individual must work hard and fast. For instance, each person might be responsible for one entire car on a subway.

The experienced writer will be attuned to his environment, able to paint while keeping an eye open for cops, rival crews, or work bums (those responsible for subway maintenance). He will also know the work bums' schedule and the window of time he has to complete his piece.

THIS IS MY WALL, BABY!

Perhaps the biggest faux pas in graf is going over someone else's work. In graf's infancy, going over a writer's hard-wrought piece was a declaration of war that could result in fatal violence. This has calmed through the years. Now, bombed-up trains and buses get cleaned so quickly by the city that writers take the short life span of a masterpiece for granted. Still, going over someone's piece is taboo.

"Toy" writers—new, inexperienced artists—are expected to make compromises. If a toy tags a subway car and a fame writer later decides he needs that space to do a top-to-bottom wildstyle burner, the toy should be willing to sacrifice his tag. It's a matter of respect. Fame writers have more clout.

It's okay to go over someone's piece if it's already crossed out.

BITING

In the ever-evolving, derivative world of graf, "biting," or copying someone else's style, is acceptable. It is particularly acceptable for a toy to emulate a fame writer's style. It's flattering to the originator.

But if you want to bite, you should put your own twist on it—give it your own stamp, or, in graf vernacular, "flip it and take it to the next level." The rule is to bite and add. That's what keeps the art form in motion.

BATTLING

Grafitti battling goes on between crews and individuals. As we've noted, rivalries can turn violent, but the aim is to attain supremacy by spraying Krylon, not bullets.

Sometimes, rivals will pick adjacent walls or buildings and try to "out-paint" one another. In such cases, the warring parties should be evenly armed—it's not a fair match if one guy pulls out a special air-brush tip that the other doesn't have.

Other times, one artist or crew will put something up, and then another will respond, almost like a dialogue. In one famous battle between L.A. writers Hex and Slick, Hex painted a rat running into a castle. Slick responded with a scorpion on a throne, with a rat tail coming out of the poison monarch's mouth. Hex, in turn, responded by mimicking Slick's scorpion, and depicting the creature being killed by a Medusa-like character. This exchange of "insults" went on for about a week.

When battling, the key is to be witty as well as technically proficient. No guns. No knives. That's the rule.

GEAR

In the pioneering days of graf, artists wore custom-painted Lee jackets, bell-bottoms and Pro-Keds. But these days, there is no standard uniform. Some wear baggy shorts with Converse sneakers, others wear commando garb with night vision glasses. The key is maximum mobility, minimum visibility. No loafers. No high heels. No reflective shoes. A flashy dress code might get you or someone else caught.

Some former graf stars now own and run hip-hop and graf-inspired clothing companies: Third Rail and Subwear are two highly successful lines run by fame writers. It's considered good form for bombers to support such companies by sporting their hats and tees.

PAINTER'S PROFILE

The graf subculture intersects with a number of other subcultures: many rap music junkies, gang members, skate rats, and low-riders are also into bombing. The art form crosses all ethnic boundaries. And today, the graf community is more supportive of female writers than ever before. The subculture is predominantly made up of ghetto youth.

There is no specific, universally accepted rule about excluding white, affluent writers from the graf community, but many believe that if you're driving a Porsche, you shouldn't be carrying a Krylon can. Why strive to master an art form predicated on limited financial resources when you can afford an artist loft, custom-stretched canvasses and expensive painting classes?

If a privileged suburbanite has his heart set on bombing, at the very least he should do it in his own neighborhood, rather than leaving his gated community and hitting up the 'hood. Moreover, he should express his own reality—manicured lawns, tract housing and a Community Watch person shaking an ominous finger—rather than misrepresent himself with ghetto-inspired imagery. Only poseurs paint what they don't know.

Ultimately, a trust fund isn't an insurmountable obstacle to an aspiring writer. If you prove yourself through a combination of skill, risk and commitment, you will ultimately be accepted by the most die-hard writers no matter how much dough your folks have.

The Dominatrix

SMACK TACT

S/M is the use of a strategic relationship as a source of pleasure.

—Michel Foucault

Q: What did the sadist say to the masochist?
A: I'm not telling.

—popular S/M joke

High patent-leather boots with six-inch stiletto heels. A black leather corset. Matching black gloves. One hand grasping a riding crop, menacingly tapping the other palm. Foreboding questions like "Have you been a bad boy?" echoing through the hallways. These are the images most often associated with the dominatrix.

But there's another side to it. The real-life hired dom is a man or woman versed in the art of punishment, and highly attuned to the pain thresholds of his or her clients. The dom is to your pleasure–pain principle what the shrink is to your mental health and the chiropractor is to your spine. They know their shit, and follow a stringent set of rules designed to keep things safe and effective. After all, you wouldn't fork over $200–$300 dollars an hour to have the tar beaten out of you by just anyone, right?!

We've already provided general information on beginner's S/M play in "Alternative Sex" in Part II. This section outlines the most basic rules for the professional dom.

Warning: S/M is risky business, and we don't recommend you try this stuff at home without the supervision of an expert, or without inviting us over to watch.

WHIPPING ANXIETY

The difference between horsing around with whips and masks at home and hiring a "professional" dom is the same as the difference between confiding in a close friend and seeing a shrink. In both instances, you're hiring a pro, and it's all about you . . . as long as you're on the clock. We came up with a few other similarities (and differences) between these two professionals.

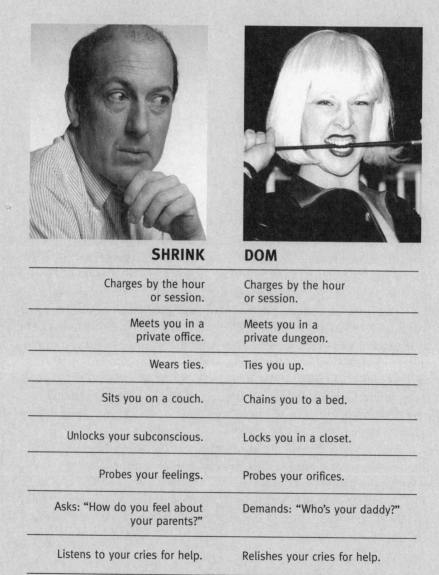

SHRINK	DOM
Charges by the hour or session.	Charges by the hour or session.
Meets you in a private office.	Meets you in a private dungeon.
Wears ties.	Ties you up.
Sits you on a couch.	Chains you to a bed.
Unlocks your subconscious.	Locks you in a closet.
Probes your feelings.	Probes your orifices.
Asks: "How do you feel about your parents?"	Demands: "Who's your daddy?"
Listens to your cries for help.	Relishes your cries for help.
Allows patient to go after appointment.	May allow patient to cum after appointment.

BUT FIRST . . .

It must be noted that there is a difference between tying your honey up to the bedposts at home versus seeking the services of a professional Dom or Sub (they have those, too!). Having S/M with a civilian (your sig-o, or sig-o for the night) is about the two of you getting off on some sort of fantasy and adding some color to your sex life. Seeking the help of a pro is about filling a void in your life, going where your sig-o ain't prepared to go, and dealing with some personal psychosexual issues.

PROFESSIONALISM, NOT JISM

The most surprising thing to many folks about hired S/M help is their professionalism. Just as a doctor asks for past medical history and gives exams prior to treatment, the professional Dom will survey a new client about likes, dislikes, fantasies, etc. If your fantasy is missing some specifics, the Dom will fill in the blanks. What's that? An Irish business mogul wants to be punished for his greed by a leprechaun? The Dom will sport green leather and demand to know where he hid his pot o' gold. Once the Dom ascertains a client's tastes and needs, they are better qualified to make a client grovel.

It's important for the Dom to establish boundaries up front—fantasies they won't indulge, et cetera. The most common boundary regards sex.

Doms are not prostitutes. While they may or may not allow a client to reach orgasm, few pros will have actual sex with them. It is considered unprofessional, and most Doms will frown on one of their own who compromises the standards and respectability of their trade.

SETTING THE STAGE

The practice of S/M is the creation of a scenario and a strict collection of rules, starting with how partners address one another. A dominatrix will usually come up with a title of respect and formality that precedes their name—Mistress, Sir, Mighty Sovereign of the Universe, whatever works—and *insist* that their subs never address them without it. Failure to do so is met with the whip.

Establishing a safety word is key. As we noted earlier in the book, the safety word gives the Sub an instant out if things get too hot once S/M "play" begins.

It's also crucial that a professional Dom, particularly one with a busy schedule, carefully gauge the duration of a client's fantasy. It's always bad form to leave someone hanging, unfulfilled, by their ankles while you scurry off to your next appointment.

Billing—how much, cash or credit card—should always be taken care of before S/M play begins. You don't want money issues to distract your client while he's being flogged.

THE TOOLS OF THE TRADE

Doms are expected to be the master of their tools—whips, paddles, cages, a rack, whatever. A professional will never try out a device on a new client that they haven't practiced with or tried on themselves. It's also important that they stay on top of trends and current information about the scene.

When applying restraints, the Dom must make sure they don't cut off circulation or cause skin abrasions (it's like a nasty rug burn).

Many Doms like leather restraints—a good thick leather strap is cheap and effective. Padded leather cuffs and shackles are comfortable, practical, and won't mark up furniture. Many avoid silk scarves and sash cords, which can both tighten and slim up like wire. Likewise for slip knots, which can tighten without warning. As for rope, a pro knows enough to go for the "all-cotton" designated bondage rope found at an erotic specialty store, rather than the cheap stuff at Ace Hardware.

Skimping on handcuffs is also a no-no. The pro wants a good pair that won't tighten as the wearer wriggles. A diligent Dom will always make sure that they have the key (or keys) before play begins.

BOUND AND READY

Once a Sub is bound and at their mercy, the Dom must exercise due caution and care.

A pro knows how to pace and escalate. He or she knows that when someone is experiencing erotic pain, it takes their body about twenty minutes to start producing endorphins, the natural body chemical that causes pleasure. Thus, that first half-hour of play is crucial. If they go overboard with the hitting, they run the risk of losing their Sub before they're in shape for the good stuff. Proper etiquette is to start slowly and work your way up the pain threshold, surrounding a good thwack with milder blows.

Popular implements include the paddle ("slappers") or a riding crop. The paddle is larger, so the pain will be spread out over a wider area, and there's less chance of injury. The riding crop, however, is easy to control and makes a very pleasant cracking sound. The Dom may start with these basic instruments and move up to heavier stuff.

A good Dom will vary their whipping sites (so as not to irritate just one location), interspersing caresses or scratches over punished skin (to maintain tissue stimulation without overloading pain). They will do their best to get the whipping room to room temperature (a cold room heightens the sting and can lead to greater injury).

The Dom should avoid hitting the face, head, kidneys, or knees. When skin is accidentally broken, wounds are dressed immediately. The professional should be prepared for such first-aid needs. In case of emergency, a cell phone and knowledge of local hospitals can't hurt, either.

CRIME AND PUNISHMENT

The Dom makes sure that the punishment fits the crime (this helps the Sub gauge the beating).

Any Dom worth their salt will never lose sight of the fact that the Sub's safety is their personal responsibility. Any punishment that might do permanent damage is off-limits. The Dom must be sober and alert at all times, keeping an ear open for the Sub's issuance of the safety word. The slightest lack of attentiveness on the part of the Dom can have tragic consequences, and that's just no fun at all.

NEVER GO TO THE OFFICE IN A BAD MOOD

Check your emotions at the door!

The professional Dom never, *ever* disciplines a Sub in anger. If he or she is having a rotten day, proper protocol dictates that they take a "time out," cool off . . . and *then* proceed to tan their client's hide.

PART VI

The Aftermath

Don't do the crime if you can't do the time.

—time-honored saying

So say you didn't follow our advice. You didn't play by the rules, you sinfully indulged to the point of excess. You knocked back one too many shots of tequila, smashed a chair over the wrong guy's head, brawled with the wrong bouncer, and pulled out your firearm at the wrong time. You gambled away most of your life's savings, blew the rest of it at strip clubs, lost your house and family, and opened up a chop shop in order to get those much-needed parts for your Harley or low-rider vehicle, which you then drove with reckless abandon under the influence of copious amounts of marijuana. You joined a gang and proceeded to spray-paint your initials on your neighbor's SUV. You imprudently solicited a hooker, or bought a copy of *Barnyard Follies* in the wrong county.

And you got caught.

Any outlaw recognizes that you shouldn't do the crime if you can't do the time. (Just ask Tommy Lee, Charlie Sheen or Robert Downey Jr.) Whatever dirty deeds you did, it's now time to pay the piper, whether than means a twelve-step program, a day in court, a few months in the joint or a year in a homeless shelter. The following sections are intended to make your road to rehabilitation and respectability as pleasant and painless as possible.

Of course, if you're beyond salvation or are *dead set* on a highway to hell, we've got a few suggestions for you as well.

Rehab

THE ABC'S OF AA

Betcha you can't eat just one!

—Lay's Potato Chip slogan

Just say "No!"

—Nancy Reagan

If you're sick of bad trips, debilitating hangovers or interventions from friends, and ready to travel the clean and narrow path of sobriety, Alcoholics Anonymous can give you a shot at freedom from the sauce.

The only prerequisite for attending AA meetings is a desire to quit using booze or drugs (no sober looky-loos, AKA "normies," allowed; authors of etiquette books should keep a low profile). Once you embark on the oft-cited "twelve-step program," there are plenty of rules to follow. Disregarding these rules won't get you kicked out, but, according to AA, it will hinder your quest for sobriety. Many AA members swear by the twelve-step; others opt for the meetings but come up with their own program.

This section deals specifically with the etiquette of Alcoholics Anonymous, but because AA is used as a model for many other recovery programs (Gamblers Anonymous, Overeaters Anonymous, Crack Smokers Anonymous), the rules included herein should be applied to rehab in general.

S H H H H H H !

The stigma of being a drunk is bad enough. Hence, what you or anyone else says within the confines of an AA meeting stays there (ergo, Alcoholics *Anonymous*). Kicking the habit is hard enough without folks blabbing about it.

Meeting etiquette is as follows: Use your first name only; don't talk to your friends about who else you saw there; and if you meet or see any celebrities (AA is always a popular star hangout on the coasts), don't call the *National Enquirer* or ask for autographs.

As an exclamation point to this basic rule, meetings often feature a pledge such as, "Who you see here, what you hear here, let it stay here," to which the audience replies, "Here! Here!"

Try not to laugh when you're there for the first time; it'll grow on you.

MEETING BASICS

There is no dress code for AA, but leave the Jack Daniels cap at home. If you show up drunk to your first AA meeting you will not be kicked out. Indeed, many a drunk has ended a "Lost Weekend" (years, perhaps) by sobering up at their first meeting. If you're planning on becoming sober in the near future, testing the meetings while under the influence is fine; it's like a baby step.

If you're buzzed, don't be loud—disrupting the meeting can be grounds for expulsion—and try to refrain from any impromptu speeches.

While meetings are free, AA attendees are encouraged to give donations. Newcomers are not expected to pay, but they can bring food or help clean up. The idea is that by contributing and helping out, you are taking an active role in your journey to sobriety. Any commitment you make to the organization is considered a commitment to recovery.

Drink all the coffee you want during meetings, and unless you're in California, feel free to chain-smoke. Most meetings will also have something to nosh on.

SPEAKING OUT

As a newcomer, you're expected to be seen and not heard. You're there to listen to people who have more experience than you do. It's sort of like going to church, complete with a sermon. Some meetings have an inspirational speech, followed by a thirty-minute "sharing" round-robin event (open mic for the audience members). If you're a newcomer, that's your time to shine.

If you're going around a circle sharing war stories, you can always opt to "pass."

In addition, you can share your trials and tribulations with others before and after meetings. Just remember to bring enough smokes.

COLD TURKEY

Even though sobriety is "one day at a time," the first ninety days are the most important. Early rules are the most stringent. Don't drink or use drugs under any circumstances (that means most over-the-counter pain pills). Stay away from nonalcoholic beer. With AA, it's all or nothing.

Other ninety-day rules include not making any other big changes in your life that might distract you from your pursuit of sobriety. No new jobs, new relationships or moving. The only change you're expected to make is the termination of any relationships with addicts, whether they be lovers, housemates or co-workers. One other suggestion (not mandatory) is that you take three months off from work, but no one will sweat you if the nature of your job or your financial situation precludes this possibility.

A SIDE OF CHIPS

For the first thirty days of sobriety, you are encouraged to come up to the front and get a "sobriety chip" and a big "Welcome" from the other attendees. It's like a gold star. Don't feel awkward about going up and getting it, unless you're drunk and afraid you might trip on the way to the podium.

At thirty days, you get a special "thirty-day chip," followed by a sixty and a ninety then six months and nine months. You don't have to keep the chips with you, but if it helps, cool.

Every year you get a cake, or other treat, to celebrate the "birthday" of your sobriety. Be prepared to share your cake with others who have the same sobriety birthday. Don't expect a rum cake.

GET WITH THE PROGRAM

Following the AA lifestyle is like joining a religion. And if you desire salvation, you bow down to AA's twelve-step program. Etiquette in this department is simple: Just abide by the rules. Here are the Cliff Notes to the whole enchilada. We skipped all the "higher power" bullshit.

To go "AA" you must:

- Admit that you are powerless over alcohol and drugs.

- Abstain from drugs and alcohol (even when used in cooking).

- Attend meetings regularly (90 meetings in 90 days, then depending on your needs).

- Make amends to the people you hurt, whether they're aware of what you did to them or not. Be forthright and apologize, unless your honesty will do them more harm than good (i.e., telling your wife you "strayed" versus telling her you had "anal" with her sister). More importantly, remember that just because you're ready to apologize doesn't mean that they're ready to accept and forgive. If you did some really rank shit to a loved one, don't expect all hugs and kisses. Give them time.

- Make a personal inventory by identifying and emptying any skeletons in your closet, which you must disclose to another person (usually your sponsor).

- Help other pathetic drunks get their shit together without being preachy.

A DRUNK FOR A DRUNK

AA suggests that all newcomers get a sponsor, someone to talk to in times of crisis. You can ask any recovering or recovered alcoholic to be your sponsor. Maybe you heard them speak at a meeting, or maybe they just look like someone you can relate to.

Men should have male sponsors and women, female sponsors. Your sponsor should have at least one year of sobriety. It should not be your mother!

The strings attached to a sponsor vary from person to person. Basically, they'll lay down the rules; you follow the rules.

Call your sponsor any time you need to talk, day or night, 24-7. It's their duty to be available.

If someone asks you to be a sponsor, it's your duty, as a recovering alcoholic, to accept, unless you're overtaxed with other twelve-step work.

FALLING OFF THE WAGON

Don't fret. Not everyone gets dry on the first try—in fact, few do. If you fall off the wagon (going "out"), you can always climb back up.

At AA there's no stigma attached to coming back after a relapse, though you have to start with a newcomer chip. And no cake until next year.

THE SOCIAL IMPLICATIONS

It's neither encouraged nor discouraged for drunks to date drunks, and thus AA is a good place to meet potential mates (hey, they already know what you've done, right?). Feel free to go for it. Just don't ask them out for cocktails. Also remember that, as we said, new relationships that could distract you from your recovery within the first few months of AA are frowned upon. While there are no real AA cops, be prepared to take some shit if you're a seasoned AA vet who's banging some vulnerable, easily manipulated neophyte. It's called "taking the thirteenth step," and it's bad bad bad (unless she's like really hot, in which case it's still bad, but we understand).

It's cool to network. AA is kind of like a tight-knit fraternity or sorority of recovery, with brothers and sisters professionally hooking up fellow graduates of their alma mater. Just wait 'til the break before you bust out the business cards, and be mindful of the fact that some of the folks in attendance may want to keep a low profile. Don't "flyer" your band, and never ever ask that recovering rock star for an autograph.

PARTY POOPERS

Don't intervene with someone's drug or alcohol addiction unless you're positive that you know what you're doing, or you could do more damage than good. Call the rehab center or a local AA chapter for proper steps and protocol.

IT'S NOT OUR PROBLEM

Finally, while we're glad you're in recovery, please don't be a nuisance to those of us who want to continue our (recreational) consumption of mind-altering substances. Just because you wake up and smell the coffee doesn't give you the right to rouse everyone else from their drunken stupor. Some of us are quite content with our vices.

The most important piece of etiquette advice to the recovering addict is this: DON'T BE A BORE. Don't preach to and try to convert everyone you meet. We don't want your Psych 101 analysis about why we're not happy; we don't want you to point out without cessation that we're in denial.

Furthermore, we don't need to know the twelve different things you're addicted to (what we call a "144-stepper"), or hear all your war stories. Suffice it to say, save it for the meetings. We don't care. If you find yourself talking like Stuart Smalley, then it's time to shut yer yap hole.

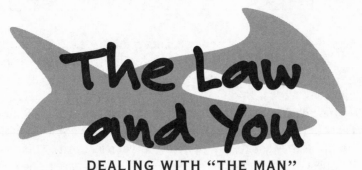

The Law and You

DEALING WITH "THE MAN"

I'm not against the police; I'm just afraid of them.
—Alfred Hitchcock

It's late, and you've been out and about on private business. Then you spy them in the rearview. Quick, what to do? Hit the gas and high-speed it across the state lines to Mexico? Maybe head north to Canada? Shit, there's no time and you don't have the gas or the desire to have your parents watch you in *Cops* reruns. When the red light hits, it's too late to hide.

Time to buckle up, pull over and meet THE MAN.

No rules of etiquette are more acute and important than those for dealing with the law. Sure, Rodney King got a huge cash settlement, but getting pummeled by a feeding frenzy of cops ain't nobody's idea of a good time. *Maybe next time he should just pull the hell over and do what they say.*

Sure, any outlaw or rebel wants to kick ass rather than kiss it, but sometimes prudence is the proper course of action. Johnny Cash said it best: "I walk the line." Accordingly, this section is here to help you delineate the behavioral boundaries when it comes to law enforcement.

BASIC RULES

While most cops don't expect you to like them, they do expect you to respect them. The two things that will get you the furthest with law enforcement are compliance and politeness. Since most of the time you get pulled over for a reason, just try to be cool: It won't kill you. If you're not guilty, generally this tactic will make them go away faster. If you are guilty, it might help your situation; indeed, rudeness will only exacerbate your problems (and perhaps get you tagged with some additional citations for abuse). Warning: The total jerk gets a full cavity search!

Behind their back, you may refer to the police in any number of ways—pigs, 5-0, One-Time, Cagney & Lacey, Johnny Law. But to their face, we suggest "Officer," "Sir" or "Ma'am." If they're sporting a sheriff's badge, try "Sheriff" or "Deputy." And never call a Highway Patrol officer "John" or "Ponch."

Do what an officer asks you to do, but don't be afraid to ask for your lawyer. Feel out the situation, and hey, you know if you've got something to hide, right?! If they ask to, say, search your vehicle, clarify whether or not it's a request or a demand. If it's a request, you don't have to let 'em. If they demand it, you're fucked. It used to be that an officer would need a search warrant to look through your shit, but the Supreme Court has watered that down to having "probable cause," which means just a hunch that you're up to no good. Universal rule: if Joe Friday can see it, smell it, taste it, hear it or feel it, it's probable cause.

If that's the case . . . you're fucked.

There's a fine line between not giving up any information and outright lying. Lying to officers is sort of like lying to your mom. When it works, you're off the hook; if you're caught, things will undoubtedly get worse. They'll probe more. "What else are they lying about?" will be the probable cause to ransack through everything. A simple rule of thumb: If you know they're going to look, just try the honest approach. For example, you're pretty sure they're going to frisk you and find a joint or a pocketknife. Just let them know before they go through your pockets, and maybe they'll let you off with a warning (generally the small shit ain't worth the paperwork). Lie to them, and they'll take you downtown. On the other hand, if you have a gun in the trunk and it's a felony either way (cop to it, and you're still going to jail), keep quiet and hope they don't find it. (See "Guns" in Part III)

Finally, ever since the Rodney King beating, many police departments have equipped their patrol cars with videotape surveillance units (for the officers' protection and yours). Remember this: If you don't resist, you generally won't get abused. But any resistance to the officers and all bets are off. Don't think they won't beat the tar out of you if you give them the opportunity. With the videotape unit, your resistance will be recorded and probably shown on FOX, so you'll be humiliated as well as bludgeoned.

THE TRAFFIC STOP

So you've been pulled over. Unless you want to find yourself on the curb with your hands behind your back, a few simple rules will help you get through this trying time. Most important, when you see the red lights behind you, pull the hell over. Maybe you've got a taillight out and you don't know it. But the longer you take to pull your car over, the more cause the police will have to fuck with you.

When pulling over, the proper etiquette is to pull your car over to the right (cops hate when you pull into the emergency lane), roll down your window, turn the inside car light on, and put both of your hands on the top of the steering wheel. If there's visibility in your car and the cop can see you're not holding a gun, he or she feels a whole lot safer (a traffic stop is one of the more dangerous tasks an officer can do). If you're on the phone, get the hell off! Immediately!!! Please do not start looking for your registration when you get pulled over. When the officer sees someone scrambling for something in the glove box, it puts them on edge.

Next, greet the officer. Try "Good afternoon, Officer," or some similar salutation. If the officer wants to see your license and car registration, they'll ask for it.

The preferred question of most law enforcement is, "Do you know why I pulled you over?" To this, the correct response is "No, why *did* you pull me over?" Whatever you do, don't admit to a crime until you know that you've been caught. You'll feel really stupid if you admit to running a red light if the cop's pulling you over for a busted turn signal.

Moreover, admitting the crime usually means you've lost all chances of disputing it later. Generally, when an officer writes up a citation, there are three copies made. One copy goes to you, one to the cop, and one to the courts. There's also a space for notes from the field. If the cop writes, "Admitted to crime," you'll look like a jackass trying to get out of it with the judge.

The only thing dumber than admitting to a crime is joking about a crime. Somewhere deep in the police academy is a special team of scientists that surgically removes all sense of humor from police officers. Please, never grin and say, "Was it the bloody hand coming out of the trunk?" Not funny.

When you know you're guilty, and it's clear the cop knows it, the conventional wisdom varies. Some say that an honest apology is the best bet. Sometimes the officer will take pity and think justice is served by a warning.

If you think you're innocent, just take the ticket politely and compliantly so they don't remember you, and try to fight it in court. It is always bad form to try to argue with an officer about your innocence or guilt. Even worse is to call an officer a nasty name or rip up the ticket in disgust. It will simply strengthen their resolve to show up in court

ROAD TRIPS FOR THE BUZZED

A little DUI knowledge Can Go a Long Way.

So you've knocked a couple back: the tunes are blasting; you're feeling groovy as you drive home for the night. Then it happens: that dreaded flash of red lights in your rearview. Most partygoing, alcohol-consuming folks will, at one point in their lives encounter this scenario. To make sure you're prepared, we've come up with a quick list of do's and don'ts. Laws and practices vary from state to state, but our list can usually be applied to some degree across the board. A quick disclaimer: if you are dumb enough to drive wasted, thereby putting your life and the lives of others in peril, and you get pulled over, these tips aren't going to help for shit. In fact, we don't particularly want to meet you on the road ourselves, so we hope those bad boys in blue nail your ass.

Here's the deal. A cop who suspects that you are driving under the influence will pull you over and ask for you to take a test to determine if your BAC (blood alcohol content) is above the legal limit. You've got to do it, or risk immediate suspension of your license (it's called implied consent). But you are generally allowed to choose how you want to be tested. The choices, in order of accuracy, are blood, urine and breath. If these options aren't offered, feel free to ask why—there's no harm in asking.

Your choice should depend on how accurate you want the results. Accuracy is important because if your case ever goes to trial, you want to give your attorney the leeway to argue that the test was bogus. If you are sober, with nothing to hide save a little beer breath, you might want to go with the blood or urine test. Blood tests must be conducted in a hospital, urine tests at the station, so it's a hassle, but it's hands-down proof of innocence.

Now, if there's been a goodly amount of time since your last cocktail, and you know that you are drying up, you want to wait as long as possible to get tested. Obviously, a request for a blood or urine test can buy you some time.

Let's say you opt for the breath test, but need a little time: right before you blow into that little plastic thingy-bobby with the tube and ball, give a burp. Not a meek, dainty burp, mind you—we're talking a loud, visible belch that the cops can see or hear. Don't be shy! See, when you let that gas fly, the thingy-bobby misreads your "mouth alcohol," which isn't cool at all for the cops. They've got to then give you a fifteen minute resting period before you blow again. If they don't, you can fight it later.

You can also pretend you're nauseous and have to puke, or, if you're a woman, feign cramps. A male cop will believe anything when it comes to menstrual cycles.

Or, if you're feeling ballsy, burp twice, then change your mind and ask for a blood test, then freak out at the hospital over the needle, and go back to the breath test. That's probably not the most realistic scenario—in fact, if you fuck around too much, the cop might write you up for refusing to take the test. But you get the idea: let that clock keep ticking as the booze in your bod dissipates, along with your drunk driving citation.

On the other hand, if your last drink was imbibed recently, don't play this game. Your BAC level is rising as the body absorbs that last tequila shot. So you want to get tested ASAP, when your BAC is at its lowest point.

Now, cops know about this alcohol rising/lowering deal. They use a mathematical formula to come up with estimates, based on the fact that alcohol leaves a normal human body at one drink per hour. Which is why they always ask you how long ago you had your last drink.

Say you don't know.

Here's why: If you just slammed down a brewski and you tell 'em that, they will assume your level is rising. Even if your test results put you just below the legal limit,

those anxious civil servants might note in their report that your BAC is rising and that it will surpass the limit shortly. Then you're busted. If you're a sobering drinker waiting for the evidence to dissipate, and you tell 'em that, they'll assume that at the time you were driving, your BAC was actually higher than the test result. Again, you're screwed.

Keep your mouth shut, and let your lawyer figure out how to make that number reflect the lowest possible amount at the time you were behind the wheel.

Finally, be ready for the field sobriety test—y'know, touching your hand to your nose, leaning back, reciting the alphabet, walking a line with arms extended. The cops are evaluating your divided attention skills—that's why they give you simultaneous tasks. The drunker you are, the more of a tendency you will have to focus on one thing, and that's what can give you away. They might not care as much about a few missed alphabet letters or the fact that your arms aren't extended straight as they will about your inability to do two things at once. That's what they're looking for, that's what you need to concentrate on. They might also ask you to close your eyes and estimate thirty seconds by counting to yourself. Alcohol slows the old internal clock, so you might try counting to 20.

Always carry gum or mints with you in the car, don't drive with empty bottles, cans or caps in the vehicle, be extra careful on holidays, and remember that a bartender will always call you a taxi. Cheers!

and nail your ass. Just take the matter to court. (If you can arrange a court date near a major holiday or at a time the cop isn't on duty, you have a chance of winning by default. No cop in court, no conviction. That's the rule.)

If things escalate and they ask you to step out of the car, don't ask why, just comply. If they're asking you to step out, they're either concerned about their safety or they're planning to drag your ass to jail. Either way, you're screwed. Resistance is futile.

THE DRUNKEN BRAWL

If you're in a brawl and see the boys in blue coming to break things up, go limp, fall to the ground and play the victim. Do not keep punching. Do not swing at the cops. That's just stupid. (See "Fighting" in Part IV)

THE BUSTED PARTY

So things got a little loud, some uptight neighbors complained, and you get that ominous knock. The host/owner of the pad should come to the door and do the talking. Make sure all illegalities—drugs, underage drinkers—are out of view from the entryway. If Johnny Law spots something suspicious in plain view, he doesn't need a warrant to nail your ass.

If the host is wasted, a sober (or at least less drunk) representative should handle things coolly and calmly, making the proper assurances that things will quiet down.

If everything is on the up and up and you have nothing to hide, feel free to ask the officers if they'd like to come in and have a drink. It's an empty invitation that they'll most surely decline, but it's a polite gesture that will be remembered when they come to bust up your next party.

"FREEZE!"

When a cop, any cop, utters this expression, stop and make like a statue. Cops are a stupid, paranoid lot licensed to carry firearms, and they have radios to call dozens of other stupid, paranoid cops licensed to carry firearms. If you don't comply, you run the risk of becoming a statistic. Likewise for the high-speed chase. You have no shot at escape, and your fifteen minutes of fame will only end in added fines or jail time. It will also serve as a major embarrassment for your entire family.

RADAR DETECTORS

If you have a radar detector, you'll probably avoid a lot of tickets. But etiquette dictates that you keep it out of sight. If you do get pulled over and it's in plain view, Joe Friday is going to grin and ticket you for as many infractions as possible.

METER MAIDS

In most big cities, meter maids (AKA parking enforcement) have no legal power beyond writing parking tickets. Feel free to cajole the maid until they start writing the ticket. Once they start writing, you're gonna get a ticket regardless, so get your money's worth. Be rude as hell. Question their manhood (even if it's a woman), call them every name in the book. Let the verbal abuse run rampant, but make sure not to threaten or touch them or they'll call in the real cops. And don't give that parking parasite an opportunity for revenge—keep clear of any nearby tow-away zones that might be on their patrol route.

URBAN LEGENDS

When purchasing the services of a prostitute or drug dealer, don't think that by simply asking them if they're a cop you relieve yourself of culpability. It's an urban legend. It's only considered "entrapment" if the police actually posit the criminal suggestion to someone who doesn't already appear to have plans to commit the crime—in other words, dangling an illegal carrot in front of a law-abiding citizen.

911

Don't ever dial 911 and then hang up. A dispatcher will call you back to find out what's up. By law, they have to check out all hang ups to make sure the caller hasn't been killed or abducted.

Imagine the news report: "Well, we did get a hang up from that address." If you call 911 by mistake, apologize and explain the error to the dispatcher.

If you're in immediate danger when the dispatcher calls back, wait for him/her to ask you if you're okay, and subtly try to alert them to your situation. They know what questions to ask, and they know the symptoms of a person in trouble.

BASIC BLUNDERS

Never tell a cop, "You can't do that." They can. You want to piss off the guy with the gun and ticket book? They'll just start looking for more shit they "can" do.

Never remind an officer that you're a taxpayer and that you pay their salary. This will win no points. The amount of hell they can raise with you is more than you can raise with them.

Don't ever give them a reason to remember stopping you. Be nice so that they don't have anything to write notes about.

Don't lie about your ID and give a phony name *unless you know* that name will come up without a warrant, and with your general description.

COOKED AND BOOKED

Once you've been cuffed and stuffed into the police car, you're on your way to jail. Do not pass "Go," do not collect $200; you've got a one-way ticket to palookaville. The best rule of etiquette we can suggest for this situation is to simply shut up, do what you're told, and wait to get your phone call. Now, we recognize that if it's gotten to this point, you're probably mad and/or drunk. Try to be cool, and adhere to these rules of etiquette as best as possible.

The Jailer

Once you're brought in, you'll be processed by a jailer. We've talked to several of them, and this is what they say: The jailer is not your friend, enemy, judge or jury. Don't cry your innocence or yell at the jailer for holding you. Specifically, their job is to process your arrest and be your host until you arrange bail or get arraigned in front of a judge.

BEING BLUNT

The Laws on Conspicuous Consumption

While we don't condone recreational smoking of the demon weed marijuana (our lawyers and publishers won't let us), what you put into your own body is up to you. But please be aware of the legal ramifications for others.

There's a common legal principle concerning possession of a controlled substance: actual and constructive. Actual possession means that the drug is in fact on your person (you're smoking it now); constructive means that you know the drug is in your presence (you'll smoke it later).

Most important for reasons of etiquette is how these concepts affect those around you. For example, you invite some *friends* over to your house. Someone takes out a blunt and starts smoking. If you know what's going on (whether you're smoking or not), you're liable and are subject to arrest. If that same friend lights up in the bathroom and blows smoke out the window, you're fine as long as you don't know about it.

This hairsplitting legal concept dictates situational etiquette. If you know that your friend doesn't care if you light up a fatty, puff away. On the other hand, if you're around people who don't like drugs, you can 1) refrain from toking around them or 2) find different friends. It is always uncool to put friends in compromising positions concerning illegal activity.

But there's a third option. If your friends don't really care whether or not you're stoned out of your head, but don't want to see it, do it outside their presence, then rejoin the party. No harm, no foul.

Don't kiss the jailer's ass, but do what you're told. If you need to address your jailer, refer to them as "Jailer" or "Jailer + their last name" (usually printed on their uniform). We suggest just Jailer because Jailer Smith sounds too brown-nosey. If the jail is actually run by a sheriff (or other law enforcement agent), call them by their proper title.

You will be asked for your name and information. At this point, best to tell the truth. But if you lie, be sure that the fake name you give them doesn't belong to someone with an outstanding arrest warrant.

Next you'll have your mug shot and fingerprints taken. The jailer has probably done this for years, and knows all the tricks. Save everyone a lot of time: don't smear your print or try to contort your face to obscure your identity. Since they're on the clock, they'll just sit and wait 'til you do it right.

In order to keep you safe in jail, it's best to give the jailer any pertinent information that would help them do their job. This information falls into two categories: gang affiliation and sexual orientation. Jailers know that Bloods and Crips don't get along, so they do their best to keep the gangs separate. If the jailer doesn't know, they could stick you in close quarters with a pack of sworn enemies. Furthermore, if your jailer knows your sexual orientation it will help them segregate you from folks who might want to make you their "bitch." Both these policies are used at all levels of incarceration.

Finally, don't resist. The worst place you can resist is inside a police station or city jail. What the hell are you thinking? There are like a billion cops milling around. You're a donut in a coffee store waiting to be dunked. Shut up and play nice.

Interrogation

Whether you've been arrested or merely brought in for questioning, you are under no obligation to answer questions. They can't make you say squat. Feel free to request an attorney at any time—as the saying goes, what you say can and will be used against you.

The Phone Call

Don't stress about getting a busy signal or someone's voice mail. Unlike in the movies, you can usually get several calls (heck, they may let you use your cell phone until you're actually put in the cell). The first few local ones are assisted by the jailer. The smartest move is to call the person most likely to bail you out or arrange a lawyer for you.

Once your first few calls are up, you may have to wait in line in the holding tank for the use of the pay phone. Cutting the line is considered bad form.

Going to Court

JUDGMENT DAY

A jury consists of twelve persons chosen to decide who has the best lawyer.

—Robert Frost

For certain people, after fifty, litigation takes the place of sex.

—Gore Vidal

So the wheels of justice are turning. THE MAN is pointing his ominous finger at you, and he wants to see you go down.

If you haven't pleaded down to *The People's Court*, odds are you'll have to hire an actual lawyer and face the music in front of judge and/or jury. And if O.J. taught us all one thing, it's hire the best goddamned lawyers money can buy and hope the person with the gavel is sympathetic to your plight.

Aside from that, we've outlined a few quickie tips to help you make the best of your day in court.

WHO'S YOUR BUDDY?

While at first it might seem counterintuitive to be nice to *any* lawyer, if you're in trouble with THE MAN, your lawyer is your best chance for freedom. Treat them with as much respect as you can muster for, well . . . a leech.

Hire the best lawyer you can afford. Otherwise, you will be appointed a public defender (PD). While we hold nothing against the Public Defender's office, our sources have suggested that judges tend to take paid employees more seriously than the freebies. PDs also tend to have more staggering workloads, and are able to devote less time to your case.

Picking a good lawyer is key. Generally we suggest getting a rec-
ommendation in lieu of letting your fingers do the walking. Your
cousin Tim got off for manslaughter? Find his lawyer. Feel free to interview him. Ask questions. How many cases like this have you won? And
more importantly, how much is this gonna cost? Do you finance? And
how much do you need to get started? These are all reasonable questions, and we suggest you ask them. Most lawyers will need a retainer
(that's money) to get started on your case. Don't take it personally—
you are, after all, in jail.

ATTORNEY/CLIENT PRIVILEGE

Now that you've hired a lawyer, a very important legal principle
takes effect: attorney/client privilege. Basically, this means that
your lawyer cannot divulge any information that you give them or they
will lose their license. The only exception is if you confess to a crime
that has yet to take place: "I'm gonna kill this guy on Tuesday." They'll
rat on you for that.

Many defense attorneys frown on the idea of putting their clients
on the spot by asking a mundane question like, "Did you do it?" Most
often, they don't care if you're guilty or not; rather, they'll ask for "your
side of the story" so that they can ascertain the best way to handle your
case. So help 'em out. Give them what they need. Proper etiquette
mandates that you be as forthright and honest with your lawyer as
possible. Guilty? Innocent? Plea bargain? Insanity? If you hold out on
certain facts, they might not be able to judge the veracity of the evidence against you. As in poker, your lawyer wants to know if you have a
winning hand before they decide how much to bet. You're paying them
to help you—it's stupid to hide your cards.

Sure, you hired your lawyer for their legal mind and wisdom, but
since it's your ass on the line, feel free to participate in your own
defense. You can tell your lawyer how you want to proceed and suggest
strategy. If you don't like your lawyer or how they're handling your
case, you can always fire them. They are in your employ and act at your
discretion. Do note that canning your lawyer can affect your case,
depending on how close you are to trial, and how much time your new
lawyer has to bone up on the facts.

HERE COMES DA JUDGE

If your case is not dismissed, plea-bargained or settled by Judge Judy, prepare for court. Your lawyer will prep you on how to go in front of the judge, but here are a few tips.

Attire

You don't have to wear a suit. It's far better to be neat and tidy than it is to wear a monkey suit and look like *My Cousin Vinnie*. If you look like a phony, the judge and jury will take note. Be who you are, but . . . be clean, shaven and non-odor-producing.

R-e-s-p-e-c-t

Address the judge as Your Honor. Nix any ideas about calling him Judge Wapner, Your Highness or "Yo." It's not funny, and it could get you a "contempt" charge on top of everything else.

Silence, Humility and Economy

Don't speak in court until spoken to. One guy actually got the judge so mad that she had him strapped and zapped with an electric restraining belt!

Do you know why they call those eight-and-a-half-by-fourteen-inch yellow pads "legal pads"? Well, that pad is the preferred form of in-court communication between you and your lawyer. If you need to say more, wait until the break. Anytime the judge chastises you in court for speaking is one more time you look bad in front of them and the jury.

Always look awake and interested, and never make mean or threatening faces. Rolling your eyes or showing disbelief is fine, just don't say anything.

If you're plea-bargaining, appear remorseful and apologize.

If you testify during a trial, either answer the question posed to you specifically, or plead the Fifth Amendment. Never try to explain or qualify an answer to a question unless it's posed by *your* attorney. If you don't know, say so. The default answer to most questions you feel uncomfortable with is, "I don't remember." Do not use profanity. Never yell on the witness stand. Just be as nice and direct as possible. If the court thinks that you're dishonest, mean or stinky, then you're going down.

If you win, feel free to celebrate. If you lose, don't start threatening the witnesses, telling them that you'll get them. It won't help your appeal.

Jail

THE REAL LOWDOWN ON LOCKDOWN

In prison, those things withheld from and denied to the prisoner become precisely what he wants most of all.

—Eldridge Cleaver

Hey, they've got the wrong kind of bars in those places.

—Charles Bukowski, *Barfly*

If you're reading this section, it may already suck to be you. Depending on where you end up (city, state or federal jail), your experience will range from bad to really fuckin' bad.

On the other hand, this information might just save your life.

The trick to jail is keeping to yourself while not looking weak. By avoiding any problems, it's less likely you will get sucked into prison politics, and possible that you will do your time as quickly and painlessly as possible. Appear weak, and you run the risk of becoming everyone's little whipping boy. Here's a lowdown on how to behave in lockdown.

THE BASICS BEHIND BARS

Jails and prisons vary from site to site. New York City jail is considered very bad, but other city jails are quite nice (hell, some people pay to get to serve their sentence in cushy Burbank!). Generally, state prisons are the worst, since murder and rape are usually state beefs. Federal prisons tend to have a lot of white-collar criminals and drug dealers, and are thus less violent (Club Fed). We cannot possibly go over all the specific rules behind bars, but here is some fundamental etiquette.

ATTITUDE

Much like being booked in city jail, doing time involves walking the line between compliance and not kissing up. If you don't do what the guard tells you, you will be disciplined (sent to the hole, privileges denied, additional time added to your sentence). On the other hand, butt-sucking won't win you big points with your fellow inmates. Do your time as quickly as possible with the least amount of bodily harm from guards and fellow inmates. The best prison etiquette tip is to mind your own business.

CELL ETIQUETTE

When you first meet your cellie, introduce yourself and take the bunk available (usually the bottom, as it's closer to harm's way than the top). Keep your stuff clean and neat and don't try to become fast friends. Usually, your cellie will prep you for the next five to ten years by telling you a bit about the prison and protocol. Or your new roommate might just quietly size you up. If they don't offer advice, feel free to ask what's up. If they don't want to talk with you they won't.

Since there's no privacy (a combo toilet-sink unit), don't stare when your cellie is taking a piss, shitting or masturbating. For your part, be discreet when you jerk, and give a heads-up if you take a really stinky dump.

RACE RELATIONS

As liberal as you may be, prison is not the right place to solve the race issue. This doesn't mean that you have to become a racist; rather, realize that prisons are racially polarized places complete with racially divided gangs (Aryan Brotherhood, Black Power, the Mexican Mob).

Generally, the first level of people who will look out for you are people of your own ethnicity. Right or wrong, that's the deal. If you're a white boy, the Aryan Brotherhood will be looking out for you. But if you hang out with blacks or Latinos, the deal's off and you may end up in no man's land.

Proper *life* etiquette is to not judge or hate anyone based upon their race or color; in prison, being a "race traitor" will hurt your chance for survival.

JAIL FOOD

Prison food can range from all right to downright terrible. If you're vegetarian or follow a special diet, legally your needs have to be met, but the result can be food that meets your dietary rather than your taste needs. Swapping food back and forth might be considered rude at a formal dinner party, but not behind bars. Don't like your stew? Trade it for some rice. The chef won't be insulted.

FIGHTING

Unless you want to be a victim of robbery or rape, you have to stand up for your rights. That means fighting, and there's no way out of it. Proper prison etiquette dictates that if you know you're in a compromising situation (you're being threatened, bullied, etc.), hit first and ask questions later. Make a preemptive strike against your opponent. Since prison fights are usually broken up quickly (unless the guard has money on one of you), the first few punches are the most important—make them yours, and make them count. The less people think of you as an easy mark, the better. You'll win a few confrontations, you'll lose a few, but most important, you'll establish the fact that no one can mess with you without a fight.

Never use the line "I'm a lover, not a fighter." In prison, better to be a fighter.

BEHAVIOR ON THE OUTSIDE THAT WILL MAKE YOU UNPOPULAR

There are three offenses that are considered the worst of form by most prison inmates, and may result in ostracism or bodily harm: child molestation, rape and snitching.

If you're in for child molestation, rightly expect to get your ass kicked on an hourly basis. Child molestation is considered the lowest of the lows, since kids can't fight back and the molester is usually a weakling who can't pick on someone his own size. You'll get what you deserve.

If you can pick on somebody your own size and do so in the form of rape, you've moved up a notch. But you are still considered scum by most prisoners, since your victims could just as well have been their mom or sister. You'll get what you deserve.

Snitches are vermin. It's the worst rep to have coming in. If you snitched on someone at trial, expect either retaliation or zero protection. Once you're in, never snitch on another prisoner, even if you've been victimized or think you can cut time off your sentence. Snitch on an inmate, and you'll become a marked man.

If you're being victimized repeatedly, the proper etiquette is to fight back, get in enough trouble to end up in solitary (away from your tormenters), or try to get transferred.

INFRACTIONS ON THE INSIDE THAT WILL MAKE YOU DEAD

Never steal anyone's drugs (that includes sneaking a hit or two). Don't fuck anyone's "girlfriend" or "wife." Don't cheat when you gamble, and always pay your debts on time (which might be on the spot). And never, ever tell the guards anything.

Remember: In prison, Emily Post carries a shank!

YOU SURE HAVE A PRETTY MOUTH

Rape in prison is somewhat of a fiction. Many ex-cons claim rape, lest they be thought of as homosexual either for having their needs met, or for falling prey to a sex-for-protection scenario. Many of the prisoners we talked with said there's usually enough consensual sex in prison to make prison rape relatively rare.

Consensual sex, however, is a loose term. Being drawn into a "wife" or "girlfriend" role in prison can be as easy as one inmate being nice to the new kid and protecting him against other inmates in return for sex. Such exchanges of services are not recommended, but are sometimes unavoidable. Say "no" or make your deal with the devil. Up to you.

In general, true cases of prison rape are more about retaliation and punishment than they are about sex.

PAROLE

*O*nce you serve your jail time, you will likely be required to serve parole. Parole means you are under constant supervision by a parole officer. Failure on your part to adhere to your P.O.'s rules will result in termination of parole and your return to jail.

Proper P.O. etiquette is simple: Do what they say. Don't leave the city without their permission. Get a job. Don't hang out with other cons. When they tell you that you can't drink while on parole, don't argue with them (they'll just be harder on you).

One of the new things P.O.'s are doing to make sure someone is drug- and alcohol-free is assigning them a number, and having them check in every night at 10:00 to a special phone service. The service randomly lists several numbers. If your number is called, you're required to go to a location and give a blood or urine sample. Pass and play. Don't pass or don't show up, and you risk going back to jail.

If that's the case, try to bring back some Prell, Skittles, smokes and Vaseline for all your old pals. It's nice to return bearing gifts.

Homeless Etiquette

SURVIVAL OF THE FITTEST

Life stinks.

—Mel Brooks

Home is where you hang your hat.

—some guy

Okay, so you've done a stint behind bars, and then spent the next few years in and out of rehab. Your spouse left you, no employer in their right mind wants to hire a substance abusing ex-con, and voilà—you're out on the street, without a roof over your head or a pot to pee in.

You never thought it could happen to you, but those dirty, stinky, lazy-ass eyesores you used to hate—the bag lady you kicked out of your alley, the window washer you told to get a real job, the teen sleeping in the store entryway whom you stepped on, the squatters you called the cops about—are now your new neighbors! You'll quickly discover an array of characters ranging from waste-case losers like yourself to very normal, morally decent families who just happen to be down on their luck.

And while it might not be a tight-knit gated community, this motley crew—like any other subculture—abides by certain conventions of conduct, both among themselves and with the public. These codes are not etched in stone—a man who hasn't eaten in several days might throw any rules out the window for a meal. But there is, nevertheless, a universally recognized etiquette.

Learn it, and you might survive. Ignore it, and you're toast!

A LITTLE BACKGROUND ON YOUR PLIGHT

Over twelve million Americans have experienced homelessness at one point in their lives, and in a given night, two million will be roaming the street. An increasing amount of anti-homeless ordinances do little to help the growing national homeless crisis—they just move it around, like using a garden hose to disperse a spillage of toxic waste, or a fan to disperse napalm.

So don't feel so bad. You're not alone.

MEET YOUR NEIGHBORS

No one *opts* for a homeless lifestyle by choice. It is not a conscious decision. Like an alley cat, all people want a warm place to sleep, but it's not always an option, so they learn to adapt. Recognizing this fact is paramount to understanding how to interact with folks living on the street.

Your new neighbors are a wide and varied bunch. You have the high-profile shopping cart people seen muttering to themselves around town. Others are invisible, living in encampments off the beaten path—freeway overpasses, abandoned buildings. And many are normal, socialized "blend-ins." Utilizing public showers, donning Goodwill-donated clothing, and taking advantage of public meal services, or "soup kitchens," blend-ins are clean and well-kept, doing their best to reintegrate into society.

If you find yourself on the street, we suggest you strive for "blend-in" status.

Some of these homeless folks may have been productive, wage-earning members of society. Down on their luck, they couldn't pay rent, and things just snowballed. Once you're on the street, you start to lose the connections we take for granted—friends, family, potential employers. It's hard to get a job without a phone number or an address. Others have substance abuse problems, which magnifies the isolation and diminishes the possibility for employment.

As you now know all too well, it's just not that easy to pick yourself up by your bootstraps—if you're lucky enough to own boots—and clean up your act.

Q&A WITH A REAL-LIVE HOMELESS GUY!

Chet resides in a tent on a plot of beachfront property in the upscale suburb of Santa Monica, California. He's not strung out; he's not a loon. A string of bad breaks and a few bad choices landed him on the street, where he's lived for three years.

EFO: What's the worst thing someone can do or say to you?

CHET: Nothing . . . to ignore me. That's an insult. I'm a flirtatious fella. The worst reaction I get is when a girl looks at me, and turns her head. I had one girl do that, and I said, "I'll tell you what: If your nose gets any higher, and it rains, you're gonna drown. Why don't you let me take you home and fuck you 'til your nose comes down to the ground." She was like, "Huh? Nobody's ever talked to me like that before!" And I said, "Well, you just don't ignore people like that," and I chewed her out right then and there. Her mouth opened wide, her eyes got all big. She said, "No man ever talked to me like that." And I said, "Then you ain't ever met a real man, because no man would take that crap from you."

EFO: Any homeless rules of etiquette that we might not be aware of?

CHET: There's no etiquette to it, but we try to keep each other clean. A lot of us don't like to smell someone else's funk . . . especially if they've been drinking or using, and all the stuff's coming out of their pores. Go take a shower, man. We've had to chase people to the [public] showers. We've got a guy around here called Ogre. He's honestly proud of the fact that he can pull the crud off of his body.

Still others are out of touch with reality, as in disturbed or completely wacko. Some social workers estimate that at least 50 percent of their homeless "clients" are mentally ill. You may opt not to socialize with this contingent during your stay on the streets.

Here's what you should take away from all this: Don't judge, and don't assume that a person on the street is dumb, weak or undisciplined. As one homeless woman told us: "If you're dumb, you're dead." In other words, you have to be sharp and durable to survive out there.

SURVIVAL FIRST

The first rule of the streets is, do what you gotta do to survive.

Homeless people, like any subculture, have their own rules and conventions. But as we noted earlier, it is an extremely fragmented subculture, and the rules are frequently bent for the sake of survival.

MY BENCH, MY TURF

Homeless people are territorial. Once they establish a spot, whether it's a gas station or a corner for panhandling, or a stairwell or storefront for sleeping, they protect it. Some people become "permanent fixtures" in a particular area. There's an implicit understanding among longer-term street residents that you're not supposed to infringe on another's turf, though the rule isn't always observed.

Sleep wherever it's safe. Everything is game: benches, Dumpsters, abandoned houses. Breaking into a car is generally taboo, as it's a good way to get caught and hassled by THE MAN.

Many homeless people clique up and form camps, or "squats," for purposes of safety, company or mutual substance abuse problems. In such camps, sharing and watching over each other's possessions is quite common. Not a bad idea for someone who's just learning the ropes.

Within the camp, guys watch out for the girls. Outside of a camp, homeless women frequently sleep in the open during the day for reasons of safety.

Don't go into a camp that isn't your own without first being invited. A camp is someone's castle, and you can bet they're going to defend it. Uninvited guests might be robbed. If the squat is home to drug users, you might be killed.

Don't waltz into an unattended camp. We heard a number of stories about booby traps set for intruders.

Don't shit or piss in your backyard, or someone else's. If you need to unload, make sure it's not where people sleep or eat.

You're not supposed to steal from someone else's camp. Of course, this happens all the time. It's not like the victim can file a police report. On the other hand, it's not like the perpetrator has a door he can lock at night, and payback can be a real bitch.

FAMILY LIFE

In addition to squats, many people on the street adopt a surrogate family that can become as tight-knit as blood relations. You can adopt someone as your wife or husband, your brother or your daughter. Theoretically, the basic hierarchy and rules of respect and discipline are quite similar to a normal family unit.

One difference: If you mess with someone's family on the street, you might not wake up.

SNITCHING

You don't snitch, no matter what you see on the streets. Any excuse for the cops to come down on one homeless person is an excuse for them to hassle all homeless people. The general rule is to handle street problems with street savvy and street justice.

In fact, any kind of behavior that might attract the attention of police or the city is frowned upon.

SOUP KITCHENS AND SHELTERS

Most cities have certain services and limited aid set up for the homeless. You can consult the phone book or police department for local programs, shelters and food services.

Never cut in line at a "soup kitchen." It is, however, okay to save a spot for someone in line. And don't yell at the servers. They are either underpaid or unpaid volunteers.

Shelters provide accommodations and other services, but the space is limited. Some shelters have a lottery system for a bed; you might only get a blanket and a mat on a floor, and it might only be for a night. With curfews, drug-free policies, and common sleeping rooms with as many as 100 people, some folks would rather stay on the street.

If a homeless person opts to stay in a shelter, he is expected to abide by the following: 1) respect the rules of the house, 2) respect staff members, and 3) respect staff property and the property of other guests. For many, the shelter is a sanctuary. Disrespecting the sanctity of the shelter or those helping you is rude and will be dealt with swiftly by the staff or more appreciative guests.

Despite these ideals, prudence (and distrust) is warranted: If you leave the shelter during the day you should take all valuables along with you. Nice things have a way of disappearing.

ROMANTIC RELATIONSHIPS BETWEEN HOMELESS PEOPLE AND CIVILIANS

Most rent- or mortgage-paying folks wouldn't think of going out with a street person, but the homeless community is a big advocate of such cross-cultural relationships. Why *wouldn't* a street person want to shack up with a home owner? More of a viable option for homeless females, hooking up with someone who has their own apartment or house is a great way to get off the street. Go for it without hesitation.

Just make sure the civilian is not underage or doesn't have rich parents who might freak out and call the fuzz, who in turn might harass everyone.

Suicide

SUICIDE AS SUCH

It is always consoling to think of suicide; in that way one gets through many a bad night.

—Friedrich Nietzsche

I drank what?

—Socrates

You have no say about entering the world, but you can make your exit on your own terms. Suicide is that option.

While checking out is a matter of personal choice, bear in mind that it will impact those you leave behind. That head-splattering bullet might end your life immediately, but the heartache of your friends and family will linger indefinitely. That's where etiquette comes in.

Our publisher wouldn't allow this section in our book unless we stated the following: If you're having suicidal thoughts, don't do it! Come down off that precarious ledge. You have so many things to live for. Call any suicide hotline and they'll enumerate those things for you. Things will work themselves out! There's always a better way!!!

FEELING SUICIDAL?

The Decision

If you can't come up with a better way, think harder. As this decision is irreversible, it's best not to kill yourself over something trivial that can be fixed. You can always find another job, girl, school, house, etc.

In order to make sure that there are no ways out, go to a counselor or other trained professional. No embarrassment necessary. It's certainly better than the alternative. Always, always, *always* talk to someone first and give them a crack at your problem. It's the least you can do.

Settling Your Affairs

Still not convinced that life's worth living? Well, okay then. If you're absolutely, positively 100 percent sure there's no way out . . . yadda yadda yadda . . . it's always best to tidy up your affairs before go. It means that your loved ones will have more time to grieve rather than fill out a mountain of annoying paperwork.

First, make sure you've written a will and placed it in an obvious place. Make a copy and stick it in your safe deposit box, or mail it back to yourself so it's dated and sealed.

If you know that your bills are worth more than your assets (which after you die will be liquidated to pay them), give away any possessions of value *before* you go, or everyone will be in probate hell.

Remember that funerals are expensive. Make sure you've socked something away to cover casket and service, so that their last memories of you aren't that you "stuck them with the bill." Nobody likes that.

And finally, if there are any last wishes about the funeral or wake, make sure that it's duly noted or written down somewhere. Who can forget the striking rendition of "You Can't Always Get What You Want" played at the funeral in *The Big Chill?!* Which reminds us: pick out some music—a swan song of sorts. That would be nice.

The Note

Always leave a note. A suicide without a note is like a book with its final pages torn out. "Why did she do it?" "Was it me?" "Was there something we could've done?" Everyone wants to know. Clue them in.

Since your emotions will be running high on the day of the event, jot it down a day before, when you're thinking more clearly. There's no shame in writing several drafts so you can get it right (also make sure to proof it for errors).

If your goal is to absolve others ("Don't blame yourselves"), make sure to put it in writing—letting other people blame themselves for your decision is inconsiderate, as it will haunt them for the rest of their days. Also be thorough, spelling out all the reasons why you're pulling the plug: health, money, love, whatever.

If you're killing yourself to *hurt* others—wife, boss, parent—your note can ensure that blame is directed at the right folks. However, killing yourself to get back at others is kind of like cutting off your nose to spite your face. Find a better reason, or reevaluate.

If, by the time you've finished writing, you don't feel like you've made a very convincing case for yourself, perhaps you were too hasty. Take a few days to reconsider.

The Deed

Still dead set on death? Fine. We're done trying to talk you out of it. Now all that remains is the method: Gun? Sleeping pills? Eating a dozen 7-Eleven hot dogs?

Or maybe you just want to jump off a building. As the old adage goes, look before you leap. You could hit some poor innocent bystander by mistake. Killing yourself is one thing, but killing someone else in the process is simply unacceptable. If you plan to take the plunge, we suggest a shout-out to make sure all is clear below. Other suicide no-no's include jumping into traffic during rush hour (gridlock is bad enough as it is, don't you think?), jumping in front of a bus (potential bus accident—way uncool), killing yourself with a friend's gun (the guilt), and blowing up a city block so you can die a hero (self-explanatory). Bad choices all.

In addition to your method or instrument of doom, you must carefully consider a) location, and b) who's going to find you.

If you have roommates, have some common courtesy and don't kill yourself at home. Don't make others move just because you can't cope! If you live alone, you're pretty much covered. Find a dark roomy closet, a tub, or the garage—nowhere where there's carpet or antique hardwood floors. If your method is messy, we suggest the shower. Make sure the drain isn't clogged.

Be mindful of the fact that whoever finds you is going to be traumatized big-time, and that's no fun for anyone. Calculate the odds about who might suffer least from discovering the body. Decent dying decorum dictates that such careful consideration should figure prominently into any decision about location and method.

GROUP SUICIDE

While we weren't big fans of the Jonestown suicides, as they were a product of mind control, drugs and stuff, we have no beef with the Heaven's Gate folks who went off to meet ET: More power to you! Indeed, Darwin has his ways of thinning out the species.

But overall, we're not big fans of the group thing. The decision to end it all is ultimately your decision, and your decision alone. If the final decision is made by someone else, it's called murder.

If you're going for a murder-suicide, civility suggests you reverse the order. Try the suicide thing first, just to see if you like it, before trying it out on your victim.

A CRY FOR HELP

You never know whether or not someone is telling you the truth about killing themselves (or just fucking with you). If a friend mentions in passing that he'd like to die, etiquette dictates that you take them seriously. Listen to what they say, and try to outline all the positive aspects of their life (including your friendship). Don't ask if you can have their car or their big-screen TV. Instead inquire about whether or not they've considered a method, and if they have the means to carry it out. Find out if they've ever tried killing themselves before. Since they're hitting you up with their problems (and putting you in a bad spot), you have the right to ask as many questions as you wish. Odds are that it's a cry for help—those truly bent on suicide will just do it. Your buddy is reaching out to you, and the more information you have, the better you'll be able to help them. Always suggest they see a counselor, or try to get them to call a suicide hotline.

Unless you're Jack Kevorkian, you must always try to help someone who's suicidal.

If they're under the influence, a 911 intervention call may be the ticket. Technically, a suicide is a crime, and the cops will get involved to prevent it. We know that tattling on a friend is generally bad form, but in this case, we'll make an exception.

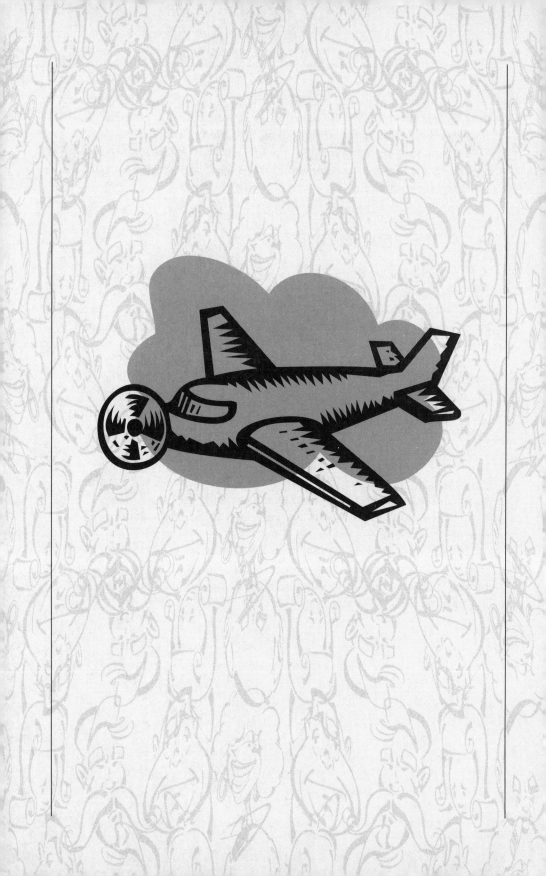

PART VII

Travel

Toto, I have a feeling we're not in Kansas anymore.
—Dorothy in *The Wizard of Oz*

Sinning Abroad

THE WORLD IS YOUR OYSTER

I have been a stranger in a strange land.
—Moses in Exodus, Old Testament

Hey, if it's not allowed here, go somewhere else!

The world is your oyster. Whatever your kink, you can probably find somewhere where it's either legal or tolerated. You like Cuban cigars? Try Cuba. Want to smoke hash, hire a prostitute and get publicly flogged? Amsterdam's the move. Most travel brochures won't go into the really fun, juicy stuff, so we've provided you with a basic guide to global sin.

The most important tip we can give you is that travel is a privilege, not a right. You can mess around in other countries, but always remember that you're their guest. Not only that, rampant international debauchery can sometimes make for a difficult homecoming.

TIJUANA

Welcome to TJ, where the streets are paved with mud, cheap margaritas flow like wine, and underage drinkers puke in the streets like Florentine fountains! It's sin on a budget!!! Park on the American side and walk across the border; your driver's license is the only Visa you'll need.

The Donkey Act

Shamefully, we must admit we've never seen the famed "TJ donkey act," but not for lack of trying. If you want to hunt it down, ask a friend who's seen it to tell you where, and never believe what the cab driver says. They'll dump your butt anywhere they can, and the only ass around will be you.

HOTEL ETIQUETTE

P. J. O'Rourke once referred to the rental car as "the ultimate off-road driving machine." In many ways, this same piece of advice lends itself to the hotel/motel. It ain't your house, your mom's house, or your friend's house, so let's party! Land of the one-night (if that long) stand, the hotel room can allow you to indulge in all kinds of messy behavior, with the magic wand of a cleaning staff ready to make it right again the next morning.

As corporate-run chains dot the nation's landscape, the rules of the hotel/motel industry have more or less standardized. These rules include needing a credit card and identification for room reservations. The odd hotel that doesn't require ID is probably rife with crackheads. Stay at your own risk. If you don't have a credit card, expect the management to check your room before you leave.

Beyond that, follow three simple rules and you'll do fine at almost any hotel.

1. **Tip the maids.** Hey, if anyone's got your back it's the underpaid cleaning staff. Drop 'em a few bucks, they'll give you extra soap, towels, and keep any minor problems with the room to themselves.

2. **Keep the decibel level reasonable.** Feel free to have the kinkiest sex of your life, just make sure the guy next door doesn't call the management or the cops. If the call is made, you'd better make sure your room is in order before you check out. Remember: They have your credit card number.

3. **If you must steal,** the rule of thumb is that you can get away with about a third of the room before you get billed or put into jail (this doesn't include the TV or any heavy stuff). In a land of few traditions, the obligatory theft of the hotel towels still ranks high on the list of things to do while on vacation. Hey, the hotels know that and have worked it into their budgets. While we hope you don't consider your room a gift shop, a towel never killed anyone. They will, however, charge you for the (super-expensive) bathrobe.

Less in line with tips of etiquette, we can't resist giving any hotel novices this fun bit of advice. If you're planning either a romantic night in a hotel or perhaps a good old fashioned orgy, make sure to get two queen-sized beds. Use one for fun, and the second for sleep. This way, you won't be fighting over who has to sleep in the wet spot—or spots, as the case may be.

Prostitution

Looking for south-of-the-border flavor? Ask the locals for suggestions. Interestingly enough, a few years ago some Mexican prostitutes started a union. Sure, it might help keep things clean, but if you can't drink the water, we can't recommend eating the fishes. If you must, a condom is de rigueur.

Drinking

If you're over eighteen, it's legal for you to consume alcohol in Mexico; if you're under eighteen, you can try a fake ID at your own risk. TJ is rife with bars and clubs, and the drinks are reasonably priced. Do consider the source of the ice in your margaritas, and stick to straight drinks and bottled beer. Getting stinking drunk in Mexico is not only a bad idea, but public intoxication is frowned upon, and could land you in jail. Likewise for public urination.

The Laws

Fortunately, the cops are not as corrupt as they used to be, because it was impacting tourism. Still, they don't like rude, cocky Americans shitting all over their country. Feel free not to start bar fights or be an asshole to the cops. If you get in trouble, their jail is not exactly fun. You also run the risk of getting hauled off to Mexico City by the Federales, and that ain't no fun either.

Fireworks

Fireworks are legal, but illegal to transfer over the border. Either have fun with them there, or leave 'em behind.

Guns

Whatever you do, do not bring a firearm into Mexico. Even if you've made a wrong turn on the way to a hunting trip, Mexican border patrol agents view any gun entering Mexico as arms trafficking and you will end up in jail. Avoid this at all costs.

Drugs

Just say "no." Don't bring 'em in, don't buy 'em. TJ authorities are hypersensitive about drugs. While they will permit underage drinkers, they clamp down hard on any drug use, especially by American tourists who think they own the country.

CUBA

While officially still a taboo for Americans to visit, you can hop on a plane from Mexico or Canada and visit this island semi-paradise. There is horrible poverty, but nice people and good beaches. American public relations would have you think that smoking cigars is the national pastime, but in truth, with nothing else to do, sex and partying are the norm of day-to-day life for most of Cuba's young. If you're a young outlaw with fun in mind, Cuba should rank high on your list of places to travel. But beware, it's a Communist country led by a dictator. If you get pinched, the State Department might not have your back.

Definite No-No's

It's a bad idea to bring the following items into Cuba: anti-Cuban literature, the music of expatriots (like Gloria Estefan), pornography, firearms and drugs.

Smoking

Guess what: Cuban cigars are totally legal in Cuba! However, unless you go to the cigar factories, you cannot be assured that what you're getting is the *good* stuff. There are plenty of tourists in Cuba who don't know better than to pay good money for crappy tobacco. Don't try to haggle with street merchants, just say "no thank you" and head over to the factories. Unlike in the States, it's perfectly cool to smoke your stogie anyplace you'd like, though if you're in a taxi or someone's house you might want to ask first.

Sex and Prostitution

Depending on Castro's mood, prostitution is sometimes officially condoned, sometimes not. You can gauge the climate by its availability on the street (you'll know).

But you don't need a pro to get laid. Since all the women are poor and see tourists as a meal ticket, it's really easy to pick up hotties. Feel free to buy them drinks and meals (you'll see), though many clubs, hotels and restaurants won't let locals in unless they're with a tourist. Since they're into sex, you stand a good chance at getting lucky. Just make sure to bring your own condoms—they might not be able to afford their own. If you're into the group or kink thing, make sure to bring a good translation book, and odds are you'll be talking the same language. Pros you tip, others you buy breakfast.

Drugs

Drugs (called "*contra*") are a big no-no in Cuba. If someone comes up to you and offers to sell you weed or cocaine, odds are they're secret police and you should say "no" firmly and go your separate way.

Feel free to drink all the *mojado* and *cerveza* you like. *Muy barato.*

AMSTERDAM

Some stuff's tolerated, some stuff's legal, and, well . . . other stuff you'll just have to see to believe. Hookers, live sex shows, and drugs are accessible and almost perfectly legal, and you can smoke Cubans, too! It's ironic that amid all this freedom, you might have to pay a few guilders to use the bathroom at a club. Go figure.

Drugs

While the possession of marijuana in Holland is technically illegal, it is tolerated (the official term is "*dogen*"—illegal but permitted). The coffeehouse is the epicenter for pot use. The drill is, you go inside and sit down. You're handed a menu with a list of what's available (hash, Thai stick, skunk weed, pot brownies). You choose. You can order by the gram or by the joint. If you prefer to use a pipe or bong, bring your own. We do not recommend that you bring one with you into (or out of) the country. Hopefully, the smoke will be up to snuff, but if it isn't there are no refunds, and you'll look like a tourist if you ask. Get stoned as much as you want. Like bar etiquette, getting too hammered to walk is considered bad form, although being fucked up is totally permitted. One other thing to watch out for is the spiral stair-cases—very dangerous stuff.

It's lawful to take some for the road, but don't go with any more than is tolerated (between 4 and 5 grams for personal use). Tipping is not necessary, and sharing with others is up to you. Check out the Kadinsky Coffeehouse while you're there, and expect to hear lots of reggae. It is never legal to buy drugs on the street, so we suggest that you don't.

Prostitution

If you can't stop it, regulate it. That's the battle call of legal prostitution in Amsterdam. Relegated to the "red light district," store fronts of scantily clad women beckon you for your guilders as you walk down the narrow streets and alleyways. You can window-shop, but don't take pictures or make faces (they're working girls; be proletariat).

If you choose to go inside, don't expect tender lovin', expect sex. These women are pros; they want to make you come and go as fast as they can. It's a volume business. Since most of the women speak English, you should have no problem making a deal. Generally, the cost is fifty guilders for straight "fuck or suck," with an additional fifty-guilder charge added to anything else you want. You can try to haggle, but it might not work, and it's a crummy seduction trick. There's no foreplay, unless you pay for it. You must wear a condom.

After they introduce themselves, it's proper to refer to them by name. *Baby, doll,* or whatever is fine, but the name works best. Always pay first and don't go over the agreed-upon game plan. If you venture into uncharted areas, expect them either to stop you or ask you for more dough.

If you use the bathroom, feel free to peek around, as many are equipped with peepholes or hidden video cameras for web transmission.

ORGASM AT 40,000 FEET

Joining the Mile-High Club

If you're not already a member of this not-so-exclusive club, you should consider it. Screwing on an airplane is something everyone should try it at least once. Besides, it's always more entertaining than the in-flight magazine.

If you're lucky enough to own your own plane, or are flying on private charter, you can pretty much do as you please, as long as you don't distract the pilot or cause too much turbulence.

For the majority of travelers, though, in-flight fucking generally takes place in the lavatory. A midweek flight, late at night when the lights are off, is the optimum time. Doing it on a crowded flight with long bathroom lines can be inconsiderate.

Here's how it's usually done: one person goes ahead, and the second follows shortly thereafter with a secret knock, sometimes accompanied by an excuse of some sort to any onlookers ("She's not feeling well. Honey, I have the Dramamine"). Here's a tip: While discretion is cool, ultimately no one really cares, particularly the flight attendants. They don't give a hoot, as long as you're back in your seats before landing. One flight attendant we talked to suggested taking in a blanket and a pillow, which can come in handy for padding.

Make sure the door is locked, and be efficient. If you've planned it ahead of time, wear clothes that are easy to get in and out of—a skirt rather than a catsuit, for example. Popular positions include girl sitting on sink counter, legs spread, back against the mirror, or girl standing, bent over sink.

Using a condom means the girl doesn't have to drip-dry. After you're done, wipe off the counter. And no after-sex cigarette! You are, after all, on an airplane!

Gambling

Gambling is legal in Amsterdam, but there's really only one casino: Holland Amsterdam Casino (by Leideseplein). It's like Vegas but with more baccarat! (See "Gambling" in Part I)

JAMAICA

Ganja. Reggae. Tropical sun. Irie, man!

Weed

The common perception is that those crazy, dreadlock-adorned Jamaicans smoke wonderful, pungent weed by the truckload. Which is true. But that doesn't mean you can buy it or spark up just anywhere.

Don't buy it right when you get off the plane, wait until you're out of the airport. Your cab driver or hotel staff can hook you up. People will approach you on the street. One dollar a joint is reasonable. Expect to pay higher prices in tourist hubs like Negril, Ocho Rios, or on the beach. If you can, try to make friends with the dealer. Buying him a beer could get you a better deal. Don't buy weed from one of the many crackheads walking the streets—they're more likely to rob you.

The key is not to buy in bulk. Purchase a spliff or two at a time, and try not to travel too far with it before you smoke it. There are undercover cops in Jamaica, and they can stop you and search you. A joint or two ain't no thing, but if you're carrying any kind of weight, they won't take kindly to it.

Don't even think about taking home any herbaceous souvenirs.

Sunsplash

Smoke away and enjoy the world's biggest reggae bash. Bring a pillow, because the party goes on all night. Watch your wallet, and don't flash a wad of bills.

Sex

There are plenty of pros in tourist spots, but as in Cuba, it's easy enough to "date." Girls grow up fast in Jamaica, and sixteen- and seventeen-year-old Jamaican girls are not the jailbait they are in the States. You have a good shot at scoring if you buy them dinner and presents. But beware: With each "date" they'll up the ante and expect a better gift.

B A N G K O K

Asia's Babylon offers any fantasy you want, no matter how depraved. But while the stories of mega-hookers and women shooting ping-pong balls from their cooch can be rather inviting, the country is rampant with HIV and is neither a safe nor sanitary place to go hog-wild. A good tip: If the city's been featured on *60 Minutes* more than Andy Rooney, it's best to avoid going there.

C L U B   M E D

Okay, so technically it's not a real location, just many "virtual" locations, but the same rules stand for the entire company.

Booze

The first thing to bear in mind is that since you didn't take the time to plan a real holiday, you're generally at the will of the club: about when to eat, drink, et cetera. At Club Med, the deal is this: You can eat and drink (cheap wine or beer) all you want during meals, but any subsequent food or booze will cost you what it would have cost you if you went to your local pub back home. Our suggestion is this: Bring your own booze. Sounds weird, but it beats shelling out $7 bucks for a watered-down drink.

Sex

Club Med is like a giant singles bar. The combination of lonely people, alcohol, beautiful locations, and forced mingling activities makes getting laid a no-brainer. Consider this vacation a chance to indulge yourself without entanglement, as you will meet and mingle with singles from around the world. With few exceptions, you'll never see or hear from these people after the trip. Don't try the long-term seduction bit, it's old. Be upfront, have a good time, go home happy, and hide any incriminating pictures from your sig-o.

TRAVEL GUIDE

	Legalized Prostitution	Decriminalized Prostitution	Great Bondage Scene	Lotsa Available Sex	Decriminalized Drugs	Cuban Cigars	Automatic Weapons
Nevada	✔			✔			✔
Tijuana		✔		✔		✔	
Amsterdam	✔		✔	✔	✔	✔	
Bangkok		✔	✔	✔		✔	
New York			✔	✔			
Cuba		✔		✔		✔	
Club Med				✔		✔	
Jamaica		✔		✔	✔	✔	

NEVADA

If you don't have the time or cash for international travel, you can find all the sin you need in your own backyard. With legal gambling, whorehouses within striking range, free drinks and gun ranges where you can shoot semi-automatic weapons, Nevada is truly the stateside mecca for outlaws.

The epicenter of the state is Las Vegas, AKA "Sin City." The biggest misconception about Vegas is that they allow prostitution. Though prostitution does exist on the Strip, especially if you're hanging out alone at one of the more seedy bars, you do have to go out of town to attend one of the state's legal whorehouses.

Rules of the House

Nevada whorehouses are regulated by a bunch of city, county and state laws regarding health and hygiene. Before a woman can work legally, she has to test negative for gonorrhea, chlamydia, syphillis, and the HIV virus. In some areas in the state, she must also test for herpes, hepatitis and TB. She must pass a local FBI check, cannot be an ex-felon and must be a legal resident or at least have a green card. Once tests and checks are completed, she receives the equivalent of an independent contractor's license. In addition, the women are supposed to be examined weekly by a physician. Blood tests are monthly. Condoms are mandatory for *every* type of sexual contact, and women are supposed to cleanse themselves with a douche and disinfectant before and after *every* encounter.

Bottom line: Next to monogamy or abstinence, sex in a Nevada brothel is some of the safest sex you can have. Sit back, relax and enjoy the ride!

There's thirty-plus brothels to choose from, ranging in size from one girl to seventy-five. Smaller ones might be cheaper, but might also be less stringent about health codes.

There is no dress code, but be clean and don't smell, or they might make you bathe.

The bigger brothels often introduce you to potential playmates via a lineup: five women stand ten to fifteen feet from you and introduce themselves. Please refrain from derogatory comments like "too ugly." It won't win you points with anyone. You can choose a woman right on the spot or you can lounge at the bar for a while, mingling with the ladies. Have some cocktails, but don't get drunk and rowdy or they'll kick you out.

If you're into kink, feel free to ask the "madame" or "floor maid" for a specialist. Likewise for a specific body type, size or hair color. Repeat customers can call ahead to reserve a favorite gal.

Once you see something you like, don't negotiate the type of party you want, the amount of time you want, or the cost in the public areas or in the bar. You pick a girl and retire with her to her private quarters, and that is where you begin the negotiations about what you want, how long and how much. Haggling is allowed. She'll set the rates, but the house has rules about minimums, so don't drive too hard a bargain, or you'll just look like a cheap bastard from Jersey. The house take is generally 50 percent, so keep that in mind. If she can't accommodate your price or your physical needs, she will probably take you back to the public area and introduce you to someone more acceptable for your tastes.

Don't show up if you've got an STD. Most women will examine your genitalia and anus prior to any action. If they find anything symptomatic of an STD, you're probably outta there, though they will give you a pamphlet (both in Spanish and English) with health care advice. Expect a refund, but feel free to tip the gal for her trouble.

What you can do to the women is basically up to them, but there are some basic house rules. Fuck and suck is pretty standard, but kissing is another matter. There is generally no kissing on the mouth, and don't even think about giving hickeys. Some girls will let you kiss them everywhere but on the lips. Ask first if you want to go down on her. She'll usually oblige. Just make sure that you don't have three days of beard growth. Anal sex is pretty much a thing of the past, due to AIDS. There are women who will do it, but butt *always* costs more. No putting your fingers inside.

Like we said, condoms are mandatory. By law, you're supposed to be sheathed for all sexual contact, including masturbation and tittyfucking. Don't whine about it. It won't help your case and will just piss off the girl.

The ultimate no-no is roughness. Not every brothel has bouncers, but even the smallest operation has someone to deal with problematic clients, be it the owner, the bartender or a good-sized madame. Many of the rooms are miked for sound, so a simple *yawp* is enough to get you ejected.

Don't worry about shooting your wad too quick. Sex in a brothel—or at least at the better ones—is not the volume business that street hooking is. Your session isn't automatically over once you bust a nut. A good whorehouse makes sure that the girl gives you your money's worth, even if you're a jackrabbit. At the very least, your date will have a drink with you or give you a value-added back rub. The aim is customer satisfaction and repeat business; they want you to leave with a smile on your face.

Always tip. Ten to twenty-five percent is an acceptable amount for a good time. Unfortunately, the women have to split the tip with the house as well. Tip bigger if you plan to go back. Lots of guys send letters and flowers. We think that's just gilding the lily. She'd probably prefer a bigger tip.

No need to inquire about anonymity. At any given time, the guy in the room next to yours may be a senator or governor, so rest assured, the house has your back.

Guns

Admittedly not as fun as fucking, but still pretty cool. Although you can't buy 'em, Nevada allows you to rent and shoot semi-automatic weapons at their firing ranges. The same rules in "Guns" in Part III apply to autos. At one point in time Las Vegas had a shooting range where you could shoot guns next to scantily clad women, but we guess that idea was before its time.

Shameless Plugs

The following are promotional mentions for the pros and experts who helped us in our research.

JACKIE MARTLING ("The Joke Man Drinketh"): The Joke Man is currently promoting his latest CD, *F. Jackie* (Oglio). Hear samples of all five of his CDs at his piss-in-your-pants-funny site, www.jokeland.com, or call (516) 922-WINE for filthy jokes, 24 hours a day. (Don't worry—it's not a pay service, just a regular call!)

PENN JILLETTE ("Wild Card"): Penn & Teller have been touring the country for the past 25 years with their twisted brand of magic. Don't miss 'em when they come to your town—their show truly kicks ass.

ICE-T ("Strip-Hop"): Rap's Original Gangsta continues to record albums and perform live, and can be seen weekly on TV's *Law & Order: Special Victims Unit*.

RON NEWT ("When a Strip Club Just Isn't Enough"): No longer in "the life," Ron is currently building his publishing company, Runaway Slave. His semi-autobiographical novel, *Bigger Than Big*, is on shelves now.

JAMES STONE ("Fashion Tips for Your First Fetish Ball"): James is best known for throwing large-scale, sinful soirees such as L.A.'s Fetish Ball. For info on his upcoming events, call (323) 644-1811 or visit www.fetish-ball.com.

DAMIAN HALL ("He Said/She Said"): Damian works strictly as an independent contractor, and he's always looking for new clients. Shoot him an e-mail at damianhall@aol.com.

SHAWNA KENNEY ("He Said/She Said"): Several years back, Shawna hung up her whip and picked up a pen, chronicling her S/M adventures in the hip and funny *I Was a Teenage Dominatrix* (Retro Systems). For more info, visit www.retrosystems.com.

GENITORTURERS ("C'mon Baby, Make It Hurt So Good"): Look for the band's latest CD of erotically charged industrial rock at your local record store or find out more about the band at www.genitortures.com.

PETER FONDA ("No Cages"): In addition to his upcoming role in the movie *Wooly Boys*, Peter has authored his autobiography *Don't Tell Dad* (Hyperion), a richly detailed memoir that includes everything from titillating, behind-the-scenes escapades with Brando and Nicholson to life-changing epiphanies. This guy's the ultimate free spirit, and his book is a fun ride.

MACK 10 ("Mack 10's Low-Rider Rules"): The Cali-based rapper is currently promoting his latest album, *The Paper Route* (Priority). In addition to making music, he runs his own Hoobangin' Records label, and his own production company. The flick *Thicker Than Water*, which he produced and stars in, and which features some badass rides, is available in video stores nationwide.

LORAY BARTELS ("Motorcycle Mama"): Loray is one of the coolest chicks we met while writing this book. She currently helps organize an annual 10,000-member Harley ride in Southern California for charity.

PAT BOONE ("The Butt of a Good Gag"): The legendary Pat Boone's latest album release was *In a Symphonic Mood*, pop songs performed with a full orchestra, in stores now. He's currently finishing up an R&B classics album. He also hosts the nationally syndicated radio show "Then & Now" on the "Music Of Your Life" network. He runs his own record label, The Gold Label, for 45+ artists who've sold a million records or more. For more info, visit www.patsgold.com.

ANNABELLA ("Dancefloor Decorum"): Annabella and Bow Wow Wow recently staged a comeback with their album, *Wild in the U.S.A.* In addition, she's just finished a solo disc, *A's Solo Tang.* Watch for a solo tour.

MR. MARCUS ("Luckiest Black Man Alive"): Mr. Marcus continues to act in adult films. He is also directing music videos, penning his autobiography and contributing articles to a myriad of mags. For the complete skinny, visit him at www.mrmarcus.com.

SUMMER KNIGHT ("Homemade Porn"): Summer's finest performances include *Blond Justice* (Vivid), *Fantasy & Reality* (Dreamland), *Contract for Service* (Twisted), and *Extreme Passion* (Wicked Pictures). For more on Summer, visit www.summerknight.com.

DAVE NAVARRO ("When They Want More Than Your Autograph"): Dave is currently finishing up a solo project under the name spread/Dave Navarro. He's co-authored a picture book, *Trust No One*, and contributes a monthly movie review column to *Raygun* magazine. Check out his ultracool site at www.6767.com.

SLICK ("Slick Style"): The SoCal graf legend now does graphic design and blazes his twisted street aesthetic on his own super-dope line of clothing, Shaolin Worldwide/ShaoBros Unltd. We'd tell you more, but the dude is MIA. You *might* be able to contact him at slick@digitalbombing.com

THEE PARLOR ("Tattoos"): Most of our tat photos and tat trend tips came from the folks at Thee Parlor, a badass ink spot located at 23 East 11th Street, Eugene, OR. Drop by if you're in town or visit them at www.theeparlor.com. Much thanks to Bill, Lucky, and the joint's other mighty inkslingers for their help.

ROB & DAVID See anything in here that really pisses you off? Harass the authors of this book at www.etiquetteforoutlaws.com.

Index

A

AA (Alcoholics Anonymous), 235-40
abortions, 196-97
accessories, 101-48
  boomerangs, 137
  brass knuckles, 137
  broken bottles, 137
  guns, 130-35
  knives, 136-37
  leather and fur, 144-48
  for martial arts, 137
  for motorcycle riders, 123-24
  piercing, 111-16
  tattoos, 103-10
  wheels, 117-29
  whips, 137
adult bookstores, 70, 73
adult entertainment, defined, 191
adult film industry, 191-200
adult websites, 79
aerosol art, 220-26
aftermath, 233-69
  in court, 251-54
  homelessness, 260-65
  in jail, 255-59
  police, 241-50
  rehab, 235-40
  suicide, 266-69
aggressors, armed, 152
airplanes:
  and guns, 135
  mile-high club, 279
alcohol, 3-12
  apologies, 12
  BAC testing, 244-45
  bar behavior, 3-9
  buying someone a drink, 7-8
  choosing your poison, 10-11
  and cigars, 23
  in Club Med, 281
  and fighting, 161

  hangovers, 12
  hard liquor before beer, 4
  at home, 11
  at live concerts, 175, 180, 182
  Martling on, 4
  at a party, 11-12
  and rehab, 235-40
  and vomiting, 4, 10
  see also drinking
Alcoholics Anonymous (AA), 235-40
alternative sex, 81-95
Amsterdam, 277-79
Annabella, on dancing, 183, 289
anus, damage to lining of, 95
apologies, 12
applause, at live concert, 174-75
art, graffiti, 220-26
ashes, 15, 24
attorney/client privilege, 252
attorney's disclaimer, v
authors, where to harass, 290

B

BAC (blood alcohol content) testing,
  244-45
baccarat, 38
bacchanalian flesh fests (orgies), 94
backstage passes, 176
backup, 162
Bangkok, 281
bar behavior, 3-9
  apologies, 12
  buying someone a drink, 7-8
  choosing your poison, 10-11
  getting cut off, 9
  getting loaded, 9
  getting noticed, 5-6
  giving 'em room, 7
  knowing what you want, 6
  money talk, 5, 6-7
  pool table etiquette, 6-7